Traditional OBC Artisans Castes in India

Traditional OBC Artisans Castes in India

K. Murali Manohar
Gopu Sudhakar

Avni Publications
New Delhi - 110046

Traditional OBC Artisans Castes in India

First Published in 2023

₹ 995

ISBN 978-93-82968-97-9

Published by : **Avni Publications**
RZ-45D, Street No. 2,
Main Sagarpur, New Delhi-110046
Tel. : 09891896481
E-Mail: avnipublications@gmail.com

Laser Typesetting : Ankita Graphics, Delhi

Printed at : Balaji Offset, Delhi

Printed in India

Preface & Acknowledgements

Caste and religious composition is an important indicator of the social value structure and political power equation, especially in a country like India. In India, the Hindu society is divided into various castes and sub-castes in and hierarchy manner and they were particularly divided in to do and not to do certain things'. The lower the level the caste, the greater the discrimination they are met with in their social life and they were condemned to perform the physically heavy, monotonously menial and even unclean tasks on half of the society. Basically, the caste is governed by the twin principles of division of work and division of people and based on hierarchy or categorization of communities into a gradation of high and low. The Backward Castes or also known as Other Backward Castes are mostly found at the intermediary level of the hierarchy, which include artisan castes, service castes and various semi-nomadic castes. Each of the caste or the community has distinct occupation to carry out and this is done for several generations, the children carrying out of the parents' occupation.

The description of some of caste based traditional occupations reveal that there are two types of backward castes, one 'commodity producers' and the other 'service providers'. The nature of production activity and services led to cultural differentiation among them and stratification in the social hierarchy. Despite many limitations today these traditional occupations still continue to play a significant role in the rural economy and provide them sustainable livelihood.

The present book is an integral part of major study on "Traditional OBC Occupational Communities in South India", present in this book twelve major caste-based traditional occupations as case studies. The study was undertaken in Telangana and Andhra Pradesh States and was sponsored by the Indian Council of Social Science Research (ICSSR), New Delhi. We express our deep sense of gratitude to the authorities of ICSSR, for their financial assistance in carrying out the study.

We are personally indebted to several distinguished scholars and agencies for extending their timely help and assistance at different levels of completion of the study. We are thankful to all of them. We would like to place it on record to highly appreciate the work of various communities, and their representatives, who volunteered themselves to spare their valuable time and share their experiences with us. We are thankful to Dr. D. Suresh, Chief Editor of Avni Publications and its management and staff for bringing out this publication in a record time.

--- K. Murali Manohar

--- Gopu Sudhakar

Content

List of Tables

1

Introduction

Social phenomena have never been static. It goes on transforming itself based on the 'happenings' in history. Catching these 'happening' and explaining the casual relations for the same has been the primary responsibility of a social scientist in his research. The present study is such an attempt undertaken on a moderate scale to study the issues relating to select OBC Artisans Groups in Telangana and Andhra Pradesh States.

During the course of analysis, it has been found in the whole range of studies on the socio-economic history and development, the dominant concern of Historians, Sociologists and Social Anthropologists and other Social Scientists has been with the study of agrarian social structure. They have focused particularly on the landlords, peasant-proprietors, tenants and money-lenders that were undergoing rearrangements and readjustments under the changing conditions. However, the artisans or the handicraftsmen who also constitute a major segment of population involved in production and distribution and were also much to do with these 'agrarian actors' in their day to day operations and occupational activity. These artisan groups specializing in their inherited skills and working in family groups or as individuals in villages and towns and cities forming almost half of the society have been the last to receive serious attention from historians and other social scientists.

In the traditional socio-economic set-up the artisans were an integral part of the village society. Their manufacturing activity and agricultural production were complimentary to each other. They manufactured agricultural implements, clothes, household utensils, furniture, housing material and various other Products used by the people in their daily life and provided services and in return received a certain share of crops under the arrangement synonymous to the traditional system 'jajmani' or some other kind of informal socio-economic arrangement of a dominant-dependent mode.

Both in the Pre-Independence and also during the Post-Independence Period for long, the manufacturing activity of the artisans was important for the sustenance of the both rural and urban economy as well. The artisans were identified by their castes corresponding to their inherited skills. In the changed socio-economic conditions under the complimentarily between the manufacturing activity in villages and processes of agricultural production was disrupted and new 'forces' have entered the system to displace the traditional 'artisans' who were later not much involved in production and distribution of services and goods. . This was followed by some sort of forced occupational mobility and changes in the social and economic conditions among the artisan castes which lead to the emergence of new pattern of social relations among the artisan castes themselves mostly not to their advantage.

Studies so far undertaken, especially on artisans were piece-meal in nature and cover micro level situation depicting dispersed phenomena. Regional variations are plenty and precisely due to this whatever information is available which may not be able to provide a national perspective. Gaps persist but on some count especially in the absence of studies, the available studies still constitute a rich source of information. These studies as found do not wholly analyze the impact of various developments that have taken place affecting different sections of the Indian society and noted the response of the people. Nor do these studies present an integrated picture of social and economic change being promoted under different regimes in the past and present. They are, however, useful in presenting an overview of the general social and economic conditions of the society and the changing pattern of socio-cultural life of various sections of society.

In the absence of studies undertaken by academics, the census reports however remain the most important source of our information on the artisan castes and professions. Village surveys conducted as part of Census Studies also throw some light on the physical and occupational mobility among the artisans. Further, by putting together the information provided in the gazetteers, it is possible to get a fair picture of the economic conditions of the artisans in the traditional set-up, especially in the case of Pre-Independence Period. Census studies in Post-Independent period however could not go deep as it was done earlier. There has been several methodological problems as well as non-comparability of the data, is a serious difficulty that we face while using the Census returns. 'Even where it is possible to reconcile all definitional differences between the 'Census' periods it is almost impossible to compare the data provided in one census report with that given in another. The discrepancies in figures and the lack of uniform criteria for classification notwithstanding, the variety of information provided by the Census and other official reports on the artisans is invaluable. On the basis of this information, supplemented by non-government sources, field work and oral evidence, it has been considered possible to identify the trends and arrive at some broad generalizations about the changing social relationships consequent upon the changes in the socio-economic condition of the artisans in the Southern India.

In the traditional socio-economic set up artisans were an integral part of the village society. They were all identified by their castes corresponding to their inherited skills. The majority of the artisans for centuries were concentrated in the countryside of the well cultivated and more populous areas including towns. The concentration of the artisans in the agriculturally well developed areas was obviously due to their usefulness and external support in all sorts of agriculture operations from sowing to reaping and selling of the crop. The artisans provided the services and furnished agricultural implements to the village society according to their specialized skills under some sort of social-contract arrangement and shared with the land owners mutual obligations for work and payment. Alongside they had fixed duties assigned by tradition.

The remuneration of artisans was determined by local customs and they were paid in kind by a fixed share of the produce from land. The blacksmiths, Carpenters and potters were paid at almost the same rates. They were also allowed to have the last pickings of agricultural product.

On social occasions, like marriages and births, the artisans made ritual accessories for their patrons for which they were entitled to a fixed fee. Clothes and ornaments were furnished by the weavers and goldsmiths. The artisans, barring the goldsmiths perhaps, were employed during the sowing and reaping seasons of the harvest as field labourers. They were paid separately for serving in their non-professional capacity for the weeding, reaping, threshing, sifting and stacking of the crop.

The artisans barely subsisted on the meager payments received for performing various professionals and non-professional services. They were the first victims of any failure in crops caused by famines. Floods, Droughts or Epidemics. Being the poorest and living a hand to mouth existence they did not have the means to tide over the difficult phases. The chances of an average artisan to supplement his income by working outside the village or by supplying goods to the neighboring towns and villages too were not many. The artisans, thus, depended upon the agriculturists who invariably belong to Upper Caste had an upper hand in the traditional economic and social relationships in the village.

The artisans, particularly in large villages and in towns and cities, were expected to live within their separate residential enclosures which were Known according to their castes, such as Chakaliwada, Mangaliwada, Kurmawada, Kummariwada etc., Even when the artisans understood their low economic level and corresponding social status was because of they occupy lower position in the caste hierarchy in relation to the Upper Castes and nature of their occupational dependency, they continued to work in the same capacities because the system guaranteed them a living. Perhaps because the landowning castes also would not easily allow them to move outside of their rule, there had been very few openings for the artisans outside the traditional relationships.

Considerable inroads into the traditional socio-economic set up were made within a few decades of British rule. With the extension of agriculture and its increasing commercialization—supported by the development of the means of communications—the villages were more effectively integrated with markets within and outside their place of work. Under new conditions, the agriculturists produced for sale in the market for cash. By the 1920s, market purposes dominated the nature of cultivation in all the well-developed agriculture regions. At the same time, greater interactions between the urban and rural areas facilitated the infiltration of factory made goods and mill-made cloth in to villages hitting directly the income of village artisans.

The unity and complimentarily between agricultural production and artisanal production in villages was thus disrupted and changes in social and professional relationships between the artisans and agriculturists became its natural corollary. The slackening of the age old economic relations, however, was slow. From regular exchange of services paid at each harvest it gradually moved towards the curtailment of their traditional support followed by its payment in cash and finally by the isolated exchange without any other obligation. With the decline in their regular income, the artisans were pushed out of their traditional socio-economic order to find 'new opportunities' outside. The new opportunities-- educational, economic and political --- which were supposed to be caste—free, at least in theory, helped to some extent some of the enterprising individuals and Kin-groups among the artisan's castes to pull out of their state of uncertainly and traditional bondage. But this has been confined to certain limited groups of people. Various developments like the colonization of land in areas under canal system, extension of cultivation, development of the means of communications, commercialization of agriculture, growth of industry and service sector and the spread of literacy etc., supposed to provide them with new avenues of employment. Those artisan castes of some of the better off families who could get their children educated and shift to other avenues like business and industry could reap the benefits of change in the early stages. By the turn of the 20th century, percentage of the 'actually working' artisans who had abandoned their traditional occupations became rather significant. And the situation during the later period continues to aggravate. There was not much change during the post-independence period as there was title support they could get from government agencies as they were left to their own fate of the hanging circumstances which led to further deterioration of their conditions. The policies evolved from time to time made a negative impact on their lives. During the LPG (1990s) era the situation is further worsened as multinational companies had entered every field of social life while destroying the traditional artisan production and service structures.

Change of occupations by the artisans in the early stages was thus largely towards agriculture and later on towards industry where they could employ their skills and energies more effectively and advantageously. These changes, however, did not appreciably help them to improve their social situation. They continued to be evaluated with reference to their caste, which remained the source of frustration and discontent. The increasing educational opportunities however provided a section of the artisans another avenue for change to the disoriented and discontented artisans.

Occupational mobility among the artisan's castes brought them face to face with new situations in their social relationships with other castes as well as within their own castes, the mobile artisans wanted to get out of the rut of social disabilities imposed on them for centuries. However their level of mobility is limited except in the case of Padmashalis who moved to Gujarat, Maharashtra and other places and joined cotton mills. Those who shifted totally from their occupation in search of new avenues went too far off places including Gulf Countries while depending on physical labour. Those who had improved their socio-economic position through regular income tried to achieve a higher social status for themselves by borrowing customs, manners and eating habits of the groups traditionally superior to themselves. In the process they tended to move out of the localities they earlier lived in and to even disassociate themselves from the parent exogamous or kin group. Their success, however, depended on the response of the higher evaluated caste groups. The attitudes of the upper castes particularly the landowning castes in villages, was generally repulsive. They discouraged the movement of the lower castes enter into their occupational sanctuary.

Those who changed their professions through education and other training a couple of them become land owners, teachers, lawyers, clerks and officers were however, unable to get recognition commensurate with their new occupations and improved economic conditions. This situation obliged the lower castes in general and the artisan castes in particular, to seek to transform the existing norms of social interaction through collective mobilization.

Some of these developments that have taken place are found out in 'case studies' specially collected for this purpose as part of the study. Case Studies presented herein are detailed perceptions of connected processes in individual as well as collective experiences of select kin-based groups of artisans chosen for the study.

They contain cases, instances of theoretical principles. Not every case need be typical, but 'ideal-typical' cases sometimes provide particularly 'apt illustrations'. They discuss particularities; including particular individuals rather than merely the abstracted roles of, for example, spouses. They carefully follow events such as those proceeding particular events, particular strikes or particular development schemes before generalizing about incompatible roles, causes of conflict or achievable policies, data transcend analysis, inviting alternative interpretation. They are frequently social problem oriented. Disputes are analyzed long before they come to court-if they ever do. Case studies unearth processes which lead to some activities being labeled as social problems but of little public interest. Case studies demonstrate the principle that issues alter as different groups adopt them.

The present volume focusses its attention on Case Studies and Profiles of select Artisan Communities and

Individuals. The objective of presenting Case Studies and Profiles is to narrate 'exclusive phenomena' of the environment of artisans where they live and make their living, the interpersonal relationship, the changes that are taking place effecting their lives and the actual problems they are met with and the suggestions offered by them for their readdressal.

Keeping in view of the several deficiencies that exist in the available data and with all limitations the present study makes an attempt to collect field level data on 12 artisan groups found in both in rural and urban areas. The main purpose was to analyze the socio-economic and work situation of the select artisans and present the 'status' of these groups based on field information. Table-1.1 indicates the select list of artisan groups chosen for the study. It include Medari-The Bamboo worker, Bestha-The Fisherman, Dudekula-The Cotton Cleaner, Padmashali-The Weavor, Meru-The Tailor, Mangali-The Barber, Kanchari-The Brassworker, Kammari-The Blacksmith, Vadrangi-The Carpenter, Chakali-The Washermen, Kamsali-The Goldsmith and Kummari-The Potter.

Table 1.1

Select OBC Artisan and Service Occupational Groups and their Economic Activity

Sl.No	Caste/Occupational Group	Major Economic Activity
01.	Medari, Gundla, Godaba	Basketing
02.	Bestha, Gangaputra, Agnikulakshatriya	Fishing
03.	Dudekula, Noorbasha, Luddaq	Cotton Carding
04.	Padmashali, Sali	Weaving
05.	Meru/Chippolu, Rangrej	Tailoring/Dyeing
06.	Mangali/Nayee Brahmin	Hair Dressing
07.	Kanchari	Brasssmith

08.	Kammari	Blacksmith
09.	Vadrangi	Carpenter
10.	Chakali/Rajaka	Washing of cloths/ laundry
11.	Kamsali, Vishwabrahmin	Gold Smith
12.	Kummara, Kumhar	Pottery

These artisan groups chosen for field studies were drawn from both rural and urban areas, covering a sample selected from six Mandals and two Districts of Telangana State and four Mandals and two Districts of Andhra Pradesh State. The sample includes both male and female respondents

Table 1.2
Sample of Respondents

Sl. No	Caste	Male	Female	Total
01.	Medari	120 (80.0) (6.80)	30 (20.0) (7.93)	**150 (100.0) (7.0)**
02.	Bestha	165 (83.34) (9.35)	33 (16.66) (8.73)	**198 (100.0 (9.24)**
03.	Dudekula	132 (84.62) (7.48)	24 (15.38) (6.40)	**156 (100.0) (7.28)**
04.	Padmashali	216 (67.29) (12.24)	105 (32.71) (27.78)	**321 (100.0) (14.99)**
05.	Mera	135 (75.0) (7.65)	45 (25.0) (11.90)	**180 (100.0) (8.40)**
06.	Mangali	216 (100.0) (12.24)	Nil	**216 (100.0) (10.09)**
07.	Kanchari	72 (100.0) (4.08)	Nil	**72 (100.0) (3.36)**
08.	Kammari	126 (97.67) (7.14)	03 (2.33) (0.79)	**129 (100.0) (6.02)**
09.	Vadrangi	135 (100.0) (7.65)	Nil	**135 (100.0) (6.30)**
10.	Chakali	189 (68.48) (10.71)	87 (31.52) (23.02)	**276 (100.0) (12.89)**
11.	Kamsali	108 (90.0) (6.12)	12 (10.0) (3.17)	**120 (100.0) (5.60)**
12.	Kummari	150 (79.37) (8.50)	39 (20.63) (10.32)	**189 (100.0) (8.82)**
Total		**1764 (82.35) (100.0)**	**378 (17.65) (100.0)**	**2142 (100.0) (100.0)**

chosen conveniently on random basis. Table 1.2 indicates the details relating to the sample respondents of the study. The overall sample include 2142 respondents (1764 male and 378 female) drawn from 12 select OBC Communities. The sample constitute 150 Medari (7%), 198 Bestha (9.24%), 156 Dudekula (7.28%), 321 Padmashali (14.99%), 180 Meru (8.40%), 216 Mangali (10.09%), 72 Kanchari (3.36%), 129 Kammari (6.02%), 135 Vadrangi (6.30%), 276 Chakali (12.89%), 120 Kamsali (5.60 %) and 189 Kummari (8.82%) respondents.

Thus in the proceeding chapters, a detailed discussion is made on each of the select Artisan Communities and presented the field situation in Telangana and Andhra Pradesh States.

2

Medari- *The Bamboo Worker*

The Medaris are a community of bamboo workers who have been marginalized by society. They are from the low Sudra caste (lowest class of servants and peasants), in the lowest tier of the four classes. The Medari continue in the traditional occupation of weaving baskets and other bamboo products like winnowing fans, mats, sieves, flutes and rattles which they sell at local markets and fairs. Some keep cattle and pigs, and are drum-beaters for the village. Some work as daily-wage casual labourer. A majority of the Medari are landless, while some have small plots of land which they farm.

Literacy levels are much lower than the state and national averages; especially for girls it is much lower. Although the status of the Medari women is secondary to that of men, significantly their opinions are taken into consideration in most of the family issues. In addition to housework, the women contribute to the family income by working but are forbidden from doing certain types of work like making roofs, ploughing, sowing, breaking coconuts and participating in worship in the village. The Medari are Hindu by faith and worship most Hindu deities and female deities at the clan level. The Medari villages have shrines dedicated to Kali and Durga.

Medari Community is a semi nomadic and semi settled community manufactures Bamboo items. But over the years, they were found settling down in villages and towns to carry on their profession. Medari Community, apart from producing Baskets, Chattas, Chibbies, Handfans, Gunnis, Tadkas etc., also undertake 'Pandiri making' in front of houses during marriages and other ceremonial functions seasonally. Both men and women in the families do the work and are involved in the production of Bamboo products. Generally Medari Community does the work seasonally during the non-agricultural season and goes for agricultural work during the rainy season. Now plastic products are replacing the bamboo products and except the products or articles which are used in ceremonial functions, the Medari Community started avoiding the production of others. During the recent years, they are also found not getting sufficient work in agriculture and due to this they stand nowhere now and displaced altogether. Due to this there may be found re-migration of these communities from one place to the other in search of livelihood, found even alienated from their Bamboo or basket making work.

Sample and Size of Family of Respondents

Table-2.1 provides details relating to the sample of respondents chosen, their rural-urban background, age-group and the number of family members. It indicates that out of 150 respondents chosen 60% (90) belong to rural areas and 40% (60) belong to urban areas. The age-group details indicate that 40% belong to 36-45 age group, while 26% belong to 26-35 age-group, 18% belong to 46-55 age group, while 10% were drawn from 56-65 age group. Respondents under 25 age group were 2%, while above 65% were 4%. There were a large majority of respondents who were youth and middle aged. It may be found that 38% of respondents had four members each in their respective families, while 30% were of three member group families. 16% of families had two members in the family, while 2% were of single member families. Significantly 14% were drawn from five-member families. Thus predominantly the sample constitute youth, early-middle-aged, mostly rural-based and drawn from families whose number is between 3 and 4.

Table 2.1

Sample and Size of Family of Respondents

Sl. No	Age	Place	Single	Two Members	Three Members	Four Members	Five Members	Total
01.	Up to 25	Urban	-	-	-	-	-	-
		Rural	-	-	3 (100) (6.67)	-	-	**3 (100) (2)**
02.	26-35	Urban	-	-	9 (50) (20)	6 (33.33) (0.52)	3 (16.67) (14.28)	**18 (100) (12)**
		Rural	-	6 (28.57) (25)	6 (28.57) (13.33)	6 (28.57) (10.52)	3 (14.29) (14.28)	**21 (100) (14)**
03.	36-45	Urban	-	9 (37.50) (20)	12 (50) (21)	3 (12.50) (14.28)	-	**24 (100) (16)**
		Rural	-	3 (8.33) (12.50)	6 (16.67) (13.33)	18 (50) (31.66)	9 (25) (42.88)	**36 (100) (24)**
04.	46-55	Urban	-	3 (25) (12.50)	3 (25) (6.67)	3 (25) (5.26)	3 (25) (14.28)	**12 (100) (8)**
		Rural	3 (20) (100)	3 (20) (12.50)	3 (20) (6.67)	6 (40) (10.52)	-	**15 (100) (10)**
05.	56-65	Urban	-	-	-	3 (100) (5.26)	-	**3 (100) (2)**
		Rural	-	3 (25) (12.50)	6 (50) (33.33)	3 (25) (5.26)	-	**12 (100) (8)**
06.	66 & Above	Urban	-	3 (100) (12.50)	-	-	-	**3 (100) (2)**
		Rural	-	3 (100) (12.50)	-	-	-	**3 (100) (2)**
Total			**3 (2) (100)**	**24 (16) (100)**	**45 (30) (100)**	**57 (38) (100)**	**21 (14) (100)**	**150 (100%) (100%)**

Education

Out of total 810 members in the families of 150 respondents chosen, a little over 39% were illiterates. 16.41% of members of the families had education between 1 to 5th class, 27.78% had studies between 6-10th class. 9.62% of family members of respondents had intermediate qualification, while 7.04% were graduates. As usual female members of the family were less educated, while youth are found to be relatively more educated. As far as the respondents are concerned 18% were illiterates, 18.67% had education between 1 to 5th class, 48% studied between 6th to 10th class, while 16% held intermediate qualification. In the overall sense Medari Community seems to have educationally less developed while the present generation seem to be showing more interest in education and their parents began to recognize the importance of education.

Table 2.2

Education of Family Members

Sl. No	Relationship with the Respondent	Illiterate	1-5 Classes	6-10 Classes	Inter	Degree	ITI/Other Technical Courses	Others	Total
01.	Respondent	27 (18) (8.41)	27 (18.67) (20.30)	72 (48.0) (30.79)	24 (16.0) (30.79)	-	-	-	**150 (100) (18.53)**
02.	Father	102 (85) (31.17)	12 (10) (9.02)	6 (5) (2.66)	-	-	-	-	**120 (100) (14.81)**
03.	Mother	117 (97.50) (36.44)	-	3 (2.50) (1.33)	-	-	-	-	**120 (100) (14.81)**
04.	Brother	27 (39.16) (8.41)	3 (4.34) (2.25)	18 (26.08) (8)	15 (21.73) (19.23)	6 (8.69) (10.52)	-	-	**69 (100) (8.51)**
05.	Wife	42 (31.11) (14)	27 (23.68) (20.30)	57 (42.22) (25.33)	9 (6.66) (11.53)	-	-	-	**135 (100) (16.70)**
06.	Son	-	24 (22) (18.05)	45 (42) (20.00)	12 (11) (15.38)	27 (25) (47.37)	-	-	**108 (100) (13.33)**
07.	Daughter	-	30 (30.30) (22.55)	24 (24.24) (10.66)	24 (24.24) (30.76)	21 (21.22) (36.84)	-	-	**99 (100) (12.2)**
08.	Other	6 (66.66) (1.57)	-	-	-	3 (33.34) (5.26)	-	-	**9 (100) (1.11)**
	Total	**321 (39.62) (100)**	**133 (16.41) (100)**	**225 (27.78) (100)**	**78 (9.62) (100)**	**57 (7.04) (100)**	-	-	**810 (100%) (100%)**

Occupation

It has been found in table-3 that all the four generations way back were to be totally found in their community-based traditional occupation without any exception. Only in the present generation of youth in the families of respondents began to shift from their traditional occupation and choose some other available. However it may be found that only 33.96% of the male children in the families of respondents respectively had found doing the same occupation, while 5.03% were significantly opting for some other traditional occupation, only 3.77% were found in modern occupations, while 1.89 % of were in Government jobs. The remaining 55.34% were in studies.

Table 2.3

Occupation

Sl. No		Same Occupation	Other Traditional Occupation	Modern Occupation	Government Job	Others/ Study	Total
01.	Respondent	150 (100) (23.70)	-	-	-	-	**150 (100) (23.36)**
02.	Respondent's Father	150 (100) (23.70)	-	-	-	-	**150 (100) (23.36)**
03.	Respondent's Grand Father	150 (100) (23.70)	-	-	-	-	**150 (100) (23.36)**
04.	Respondent's Grand Father's Father	150 (100) (23.70)	-	-	-	-	**150 (100) (23.36)**
05.	Respondent's Son	33 (78.57) (5.20)	-	6 (14.29) (100)	3 (7.14) (100)	-	**42 (100) (6.56)**
	Total	**633 (98.59) (100)**	**-**	**6 (0.93) (100)**	**3 (0.48) (100)**	**-**	**642 (100%) (100%)**

Further examination found that family members of the respondents irrespective of whether they adopt the traditional caste profession or not, they learn the skills of the trade in their early ages in the family. All the family members help each other in case there is heavy work order. Even old age is no bar for the members of the community to work. Irrespective of the educational quotations, there may be found work-culture in the families of Medari Community like any other OBC artisan community.

Migration and Educational dropouts

Over the years there may be found an increased migration of male members-sometimes along with the families to urban areas in search of work. In the recent years the practice is widespread due to lack of employment in rural areas.

There has been wide-spread dropout earlier from education in the families but only in the recent years especially of the present generation, the importance of education has been widely recognized and families began to educate their children. As a result of it there has been lesser dropout rate and higher percentage of educated people in the present generation of families.

Occupation of women in the families

It may be found that all the women in the families share the work of the occupation. Men and Women in the families are always found doing some or the work in the family. As over the years Medari Community is not getting sufficient work in the families they are found searching for other jobs such as agricultural work, construction work or other physical labour where ever they get. Seasonal variation may also be found as during the agricultural season more Medari men and women temporarily found shifting to agricultural work.

Assets

It may be observed that about 18% of Medari sample households living in rural areas own agricultural land to their credit, while they cultivate seasonally apart from doing their own traditional work. The remaining 82% do not own any land. 62% of sample households own a house of different kinds. Around 14% families own bullocks, birds and other. As far as amenities available at home, 88% had bathroom facility, 84% latrine facility, 94% had electric power facility at home, while 82% had cooking gas, 80% T.Vs, and 30% of families had Radios and 24% had Rice cookers. About 14% had sewing machines at home which the women folk use to supplement their income. In all, the positions indicate nearly quarter of households lack facilities like latrines and bathroom, though they own TVs and power connection. The fact that 38% of households do not own houses and live in rented houses indicate their 'poor background', creating additional burden on the families because they need separate accommodation to run their traditional occupational work at home or workshop.

The primary work relating to their occupation mainly revolves around the Bamboo work of various kinds. Both men and women were involved in the primary work and during the marriage seasons and functions they will have additional work of supplying Bamboo Tadakalu, Bamboo Articles and other decorative materials which they prepare by themselves offer them to consumers both on rental basis and outright purchase. Because of the controls and regulations it seems difficult for them to get raw bamboo. Most of the Bamboo available in the Forest region of the State is taken by paper mills on contract basis and in that process; it becomes difficult for the Medari families to get raw bamboo whenever needed. In that context, they need to pay 'higher rates' to procure raw material which may result in higher investment.

It has been found that 61% of respondents had their own sources of investment, while the remaining had to depend up on various sources such as money lender and chit fund companies which normally charge high interest rates. Banks and other Government Financial agencies seem to have hardly helped them and in this context they were completely deprived of Government help. Over the years many a Medari Families are found shifting to other occupations, because of growing costs in relation to investment needed, shortage of raw materials and others. Since most of the Medari families operate on a smaller scale, they will not be in a position to supply needed materials for marriages and functions on a large scale and hence they give way for 'event management companies', Tent companies or other firms. All this make them frustrated with the prospects of the Bamboo work.

Earlier for a longtime, Medari families have been in various ceremonial job associated with marriages and other auspicious celebrations in all Hindu families. But gradually it has lost its significance in urban areas and rural areas and now-a-days only some families seem to follow those traditions and engage them. As a result of it, most of the Medari families had lost social significance, work availability and consequent income earning capacity.

Government Schemes

It may be noticed that government has not recognized the need for initiating policy measures to help these communities to continue in the trade and modernize it so that it will be beneficial to them. So far no government has proposed any specific policy exclusively meant for them. A general policy seem to have adopted while treating the problems of all backward class groups of people as common problems of poor and proposed general anti-poverty or welfare measures to be made applicable to all poor people. Certain programme like Artisan credit cards, Adharana schemes are meant for certain occupational groups, but they did not reach the Medari Community. Pension schemes meant for old age persons also did not cover all. Bank loans are extended to only a limited number of people and others did not get it. No other schemes have any role to play to extend any sort of development support to these people. Simply they were left to their own fate.

Table 2.4
Government schemes

Sl. No	Government Scheme	Available	Not Available	Total
01.	Artisan Credit Card	-	150 (100)	**150 (100)**
02.	Aadarana Scheme	-	150 (100)	**150 (100)**
03.	Bank Loans	3 (20)	147 (98)	**150 (100)**
04.	Govt. Pensions	12 (8)	138 (100)	**150 (100)**
05.	Occupational Pensions	-	150 (100)	**150 (100)**
06	Others	-	150 (100)	**150 (100)**

Role of Associations

It is generally expected that Community Associations play a positive role in representing the problems of their respective Communities and get their things done at the governmental level. Although several Associations exist and operate at different levels, no Association could play worth the role to exert pressure on government and get recognized by it for consultation. They have also failed to get their demands approved.

General Occupational Problems and Demands

Table-2.5 indicates the general occupational problems faced by the Medari Community. Some of the problems identified are almost identical to both rural and urban Medari community people. The problems as said by the respondents include lack of supply of Bamboo and lack of its availability in the open market, privatization of Bamboo trade, lack of investment capital and family financial problems, lack of market for their products, lack of proper business and competition from private corporate companies etc., As a result of many such problems, there have developed a feeling among themselves that 'bamboo work' has became a liability for them. Over the years there may be find many a Medari families leaving the profession and migrating to urban areas for want of work.

Table 2.5
Main Occupational Problems

Sl. No	Response	Rural	Urban	Total
01.	Lack of Supply of Bamboo	90 (63.82) (16.30)	51 (36.18) (13.71)	**141 (100) (15.25)**
02.	Lack of Bank Loans and subsidies	87 (59.18) (15.76)	60 (40.82) (16.13)	**147 (100) (15.90)**
03.	Privatisation of Bamboo	90 (60) (16.30)	60 (40) (16.13)	**150 (100) (16.24)**
04.	Financial Problems and lack of investment capital	90 (60) (16.30)	60 (40) (16.13)	**150 (100) (16.24)**
05.	Lack of Markets	90 (60) (16.30)	60 (40) (16.13)	**150 (100) (16.24)**
06.	Lack of Proper Business	90 (60) (16.30)	60 (40) (16.13)	**150 (100) (16.24)**
07.	Market Competition	15 (41.66) (2.74)	21 (58.34) (5.64)	**36 (100) (3.89)**

Solution to the Problems

The respondents also suggested a number of solutions to get relief from their problems. Though most of the suggestions are general in nature and may not be able to directly meet their grievances, a majority of respondents said that a policy frame work consisting of these suggestions would save their profession. The suggestions include:

Provision for Personal Loans, Regular supply of Bamboo through Societies, Provision for supply of tools and implements, Provision for Housing and workshops, need for separate market yards and SEZs, Facilities for training and modernization of occupation, Free residential education to children, Provision for occupational pensions, imposition of ban on plastic items and reorganization of skills and provision for awards for workmanship. Urban respondents had inclined more towards supply of bamboo, tools and implements and provision of for housing and workshops, while rural respondents expressed their desire to have training facilities, supply of materials, provision for tools and equipment etc., both urban and rural respondents said that their basic problems need to be tackled by government with a definite policy framework. An analysis to the suggestions made by the respondents indicate that there has been skepticism among Medari Community that Government has been indifferent towards their problems and officials concerned hardly bother about them. Most of the respondents think that Government policies are not helping them and which are even found against their interests. In view of the deteriorating conditions and also government's failure to extend necessary assistance to them, they have started finding their own way and means to get their children somehow educated and look out for shift in their occupations.

Table 2.6

Solutions to Problems (Cumulative)

Sl. No	Response	Rural	Urban	Total
01.	Personal loans	90 (60)	60 (40)	**150 (100) (13.36)**
02.	Regular supply of Bamboo Through Societies	90 (60)	60 (40)	**150 (100) (13.36)**
03.	Provision for supply of Tools and Equipment	90 (60)	60 (40)	**150 (100) (13.36)**
04.	Provision for Housing and workshops	90 (60)	57 (38.78)	**147 (100) (13.10)**
05.	Separate Market yards and SEZs	45 (60)	30 (40)	**150 (100)**
06.	Modern Occupational Training	48 (44.44)	60 (55.56)	**108 (100)**
07.	Free Residential Education to Children	51 (53.12)	45 (46.88)	**96 (100)**
08.	Occupational Pensions	45 (48..38)	48 (51.62)	**93 (100)**
09.	Ban on Plastic Items	42 (56)	33 (44)	**75 (100)**
10.	Reorganization of skills and provision for awards	33 (42.30)	45 (57.70)	**78 (100)**

Table-7 indicates the opinion of the respondents on the future of their profession. 64% of the respondents said that the future is not hopeful. Among them 59.37% were drawn from rural areas and 40.63% were from urban areas. 18% of the respondents had said that feature is uncertain, while another 18% has said that future is hopeful. In all rural respondents had very much skeptical about their future than the urban respondents and thought that things may not improve even in future.

Table 2.7

Future Perspectives

Sl. No	Response	Rural	Urban	Total
01.	Hopeful	18 (66.66) (20.68)	9 (33.34) (14.28)	**27 (100) (18)**
02.	Not Hopeful	57 (59.37) (62.08)	39 (40.63) (66.66)	**96 (100) (64)**
03.	Uncertain	15 (55.55) (17.24)	12 (44.45) (19.06)	**27 (100) (18)**
Total		**90 (60) (100)**	**60 (40) (100)**	**150 (100%) (100%)**

Profiles of Select Artisans as narrated by Concerned

Chiliveru Rajender (Medari)

My name is Chiliveru Rajender studied upto 10th class aged 47 years. My village and Mandal is Venkatpoor of Warangal District. I learnt this Medari or Bamboo work from my father, grandfather and doing it for the last 30 years. I prepare articles useful in house construction work and household articles. My wife aged 37 years studied upto 10th class and assist in my work. We have two children. One son, aged 25 years completed M.C.A and one daughter, 22 years old completed degree. They also assist us in our work during their holidays and other free time.

We have one RCC building with minimum facilities like Toilet, Electricity, Cooking Gas and other. We have good neighbourhood belonging to other castes and they also treat us as friends. I have 30 Guntas of agricultural land and I cultivate it to produce rice required for us. We need bamboo raw material and tools like hammer, nails and some other materials which are useful in preparation of articles. We purchase them from outside market or from other private agencies. We prepare chairs, stools and some other useful material for building construction. We sell these articles and also we give them for rent, especially the construction material. We sell the material at home or sometimes in the market. The capital amount required for our trade is invested by me without any assistance or grant from government or any other agency.

We need Bamboo for preparation of materials and purchase it from Bamboo society and also in case needed more from private Bamboo contractors. We prepare the materials useful for household purposes and sell them in the market. Customers will approach us and ask for preparation of needed articles. When the customers approach us for bulk quantities, they need to pay some advance and collect the material after preparation.

We need the assistance from the government and other non-governmental organizations to prepare and sell the materials and also financial assistance from the bank on loan basis, but not much has been done from any side.

We feel that our Problems gets resolved in case

1. Financial assistance is needed from government and banks.
2. Provision to purchase the raw material on subsidized rates from the forest.
3. Need to establish a Bamboo society for purchase and sale of material produced by our workers. It will be better if some percentage of bamboo is spared for our purposes.
4. Free education and hostel facilities to our children.
5. Implementation of BC Sub Plan for artisan workers.
6. Self Employment schemes are to be introduced.
7. Pension schemes to senior citizen.
8. Free medical checkup and medicine to our caste workers.
9. Government should support marketing of our products and arrange to organize product exhibitions and meals.

Pandilla Ramesh (Medari)

My name is Pandilla Ramesh aged 40 years. I studied upto intermediate and discontinued due to poverty. My native place is Kistapur village, Jainoor Mandal, Adilabad District. I learnt the work of Medari Profession (Bamboo work) from my parents and I am doing this work since 18 years.

We are four members in our family. My wife aged 36 years, illiterate. We have two children, one daughter 17 years old studying intermediate and one son 21 years age studying degree. Apart from bamboo work, I also go for agriculture work during the season. I feel that my children should get good job either in Government sector or private sector and hence they need good education. I do not want to see them doing my ancestral profession. With this objective, I have admitted them in to schools and then colleges. My forefathers are all illiterates and were in this occupation because there was no other alternative for them. I have one acre of agriculture land. All our family members work in this field and get crop which will be useful to our family.

We do not have our own house. We are living in a rented house. We get the drinking water from outside from a public tap. We do not have such facility at home. I am living in Kistapur since 40 years. Our neighbors are friendly and helpful each other. I get the required tools and bamboo needed from the market. We live near by the forest where the bamboo is easily available. We prepare the bamboo articles at my house itself and my father and my wife sell them in the streets in the village.

I get some income from agriculture land and save the amount for my children's education. But whatever we earn it is hard to live with that amount. We have financial problems and we do not get any help from the Government or any other agency.

We have a number of problems which we cannot resolve on our own. We have not receive any financial assistance from Government; neither any loans from Banks; No agency is helping or striving for the development of our community; No co-operative society or caste societies are in a position to extend any help as most of them are ornamental or nominal in nature.

Our Suggestions Include

Government should assist us financially; provide subsidy to purchase the raw material; Individual loans are to be sanctioned; Free education, scholarships to the children should be provided; Market facility should be provided to sell the material produced; Technical skill orientation is required to prepare modern materials like flower wases, photo frames etc.

Mulaguni Rajamouli (Medari)

My name is Mulaguni Rajamouli aged 52 years and doing Bamboo work since 35 years. I learnt it from my parents and did not go to school. My wife aged 45 years illiterate as she came from a poor family. I am having one son and one daughter. My son aged 22 years studied upto 7th class and discontinued and working as lorry cleaner. My daughter aged 21 years studied upto intermediate. We are having a small house without minimum facilities like electricity and other needs like bathroom, toilet. We shifted our family to Jammikunta near Railway station selling the material prepared with Bamboo sticks. My wife prepares Gampalu, Chatalu with Bamboo cane.

My father and grandfather did the same work as I do the Bamboo work. We need Bamboo and cane to prepare the material which was once easily available. But now it is difficult to get the same. We have to purchase it now by paying high cost or get from forest which is not easily accessible. We sometimes purchase the Bamboo sticks from Bamboo society whenever it is available. It is very difficult to run the family with this profession as not much returns are expected. Now-a-days due to development of Technology different verities of plastic material has come into market which is easy to purchase at low-cost and looks good. Hence public are going for such articles and ignoring bamboo products.

We did not receive any support from our community associations or caste societies, or government facilitating us to get required work. As a result of it a large number of our community members started migrating to other areas and resorting to physical labour or joining whatever work is available. We have not been received any loans from Banks, Neither any assistance from any non-governmental organizations.

In our bamboo work myself, my wife and sometimes my daughter also works. I don't have any capital amount to invest and to setup a big workshop. Since we did not get any loan from any bank or any other finance agency, we could not realize our dreams. We cannot afford to go to a money lender and barrow loans and pay exorbitant rates of interest. When my family members and myself do not have sufficient bamboo work, I go for labour work in the morning at 8:00 am and work beyond 5:00 pm or sometimes later in the evening and for that and I would get Rs. 200/- per day, which is insufficient.

I shifted my family to Jammikunta where some minimum work is available to lead our livelihood but we did not witness any progress in our life style. When we sell the material prepared on seasonal and festival days, we will be happy but when we do not sell them it will be painful. My health is not cooperating even then I have to work to lead our life. Sometimes we are getting it difficult to purchase the raw material (bamboo) and then we look out for assistance which is not available and no one comes to our rescue. We have submitted memorandums and applications for sanction of regular raw materials, but there was no help from any corner. In the overall sense, our traditional occupation, which once upon a time supported our families for generations; now forcing us to forget about it and go for alternate work. Since we have neither education nor any training, we cannot think of modern employment and hence we have to depend up on our physical labour that has also now become scarce and highly competitive. Our future is bleak.

Following are my Suggestions which can improve our life to some extent and government should come forward liberally to assist:

1. Government should provide financial assistance to meet our investment needs.
2. Banks should help us in extending loans.
3. Government should provide free education to our children and hostel facilities.
4. Government should provide Subsidy to purchase materials.
5. Government should also extend Pension to the senior citizens in the medari families.
6. Government should also provide Medical assistance and free medicines.
7. Government should also provide Market facility to purchase articles which we produce.
8. Medari community should also get the benefit of free house allotment.
9. Community cooperatives should be strengthened and role of middlemen should be reduced.

Thallakuntla Shankar (Medari)

My name is Thallakuntla Shanker. I am 40 years old. I studied only upto 2nd class. Due to financial problems I could not study further. Our native place is Muthyapeta village. For livelihood we came here 5 years ago. I learned this profession from my parents. Now I do my Medari work as well as work as Agricultural labour. My father's and forefathers were in the same their traditional occupation. I am had no other alternative except to continue in this profession.

My wife is 35 years old. She has studied upto 5th class. She also due to financial problems could not study further. She does household work as well and take part in our traditional occupational work. She learnt our profession from her parents. We have 3 children, two male and one female. My eldest son has completed 10th class study and youngest son, 14 years old studying 6th class. My daughter 11 years old is in 5th class. They are studying in Government School. We are not able to send our children to convent schools. Our children help us in our work during the school vacations. We live in a thatched house. It is in the place allotted to us by the government for house site under weaker sections housing scheme. We cook food with firewood or bamboo wastage. We bring water from outside for our purposes. We don't have electric power in our house nor the facility like Latrine and others. We built Bathrooms with bamboo net. There are some houses in the neighbourhood nearby. There is open place around our hut. We have been living since 5 years. We have good relations with our neighbours and they extend help.

I have been doing my profession for the last 22 years. I have work instruments like Knife, Ammu, Mottu, Asif black, Hammer, Nails etc. we purchase bamboo from private persons nearby. The middlemen bring bamboo from forest and sell. When I was learning the profession by doing work along with my parents, my father used to sell 'Chatas' keeping on his head wondering from one place to other place. I also used to go with my father.

We are not getting bamboo over the years, though forest is around us. As a result of it there is a lot of scarcity of it. This is the basic raw material we require and in the absence of it there will be no work to us, resulting in loss of income and livelihood. We are not able to purchase bamboo privately as sometimes they charge heavily. We are not getting satisfaction from our profession. We are not allowed to go into the forest and cut the Bamboo but government allows contractors to move freely in the forest and cut Bamboo illegally. They bribe police and forest officials and get their things done. But whenever we insist our entry into the forest police and forest officials harass us. Gradually the situation has changed as the bamboo production from the nearby forest has decreased due to over use by the contractors for various purposes. Due to scarcity of bamboo we were to reduce the level of our production and confine ourselves to home and sell various items like tubs, chatas, etc., and not going outside. Due to this, we lost our work and occupational importance. Our income also decreased to a considerable extent. Lack of availability of Bamboo had a negative impact on our lives.

We have arranged our own capital from our own savings for the purchase of raw material. If it is not sufficient, we adjust with that because no one gives us any loan. We purchase raw material especially bamboo from wherever it is available and prepare articles. No one helps us in procuring raw material. We make our livelihood by selling articles and also go for outside labour. Whenever we don't have sufficient work at home, we have no other source of income except to depend upon our labour. We could not lead normal livelihood because of various problems and children's education has become a burden.

I have so many family problems, mainly financial problems. I cannot meet family needs. Housing situation is worse. We have been doing our profession since 22 years, but now it has become casual and secondary. We are not getting enough work and income from our profession. Further my family also faces severe health problems as we are suffering from joint pains and neuro problems. It is a paradox that we are able to get relatively more income when we go for physical labour than the income which we get out of work from our traditional occupation.

My Suggestions to the Government include

1. Government should provide sufficient bamboo for the Community to carry on our professions.
2. If the bamboo is available in the nearby forest, Government should permit us to cut bamboo for our professional use.
3. There should not be harassment by police and forest officials.
4. Strict vigilance of police should be provided not to cut bamboo by forest thieves and contractors.
5. BC Corporation must give personal loans without insisting on any guarantee.
6. Government should give training to our Community members to produce designer bamboo products.
7. Eligible professionals must be given house sites and extend Government social welfare benefits.
8. Professionals must be given modern tools and equipment after necessary training.
9. Cooperatives must be strengthened to avoid middlemen in procuring raw material and marketing of our products.

3

Bestha - *The Fisherman*

The Besthas are a community mainly inhabiting in the coastal regions of Andhra Pradesh and Tamil Nadu and some parts of Karnataka. They are also spread over almost all the districts where tanks, water ponds exist nearby the villages. As per the Madras Census reports (1891), the Besthas are a Telugu people, their hereditary occupation being hunting and fishing. They have now largely taken to agriculture or the occupations such as bearers and cooks. The 1901 census reports stated that the fisherman caste in the Deccan districts are called Besthas and Kabberas. In Andhra Pradesh, of the total population of 97,556 (B.C Commission, 1970). Only 12% of the Besthas are literates. They are found predominantly in Chitoor, Nellore, Prakasham, East and West Godavari districts. Due to modernization, many Bestha people have migrated to neighbouring districts. In Telangana, they are found in almost all districts.

Most of the Besthas maintain extended families. But due to social mobility, the number of nuclear families is also increasing. Though the Bestha women have low social status and are not allowed to take part in decision making, they actively participate in the economic activities. By tradition, the Besthas are fishermen. But the ecological conditions, modernisation and the available resources have made them shift to agriculture. At present, most of them engage in agricultural activities and only occasionally they go for fishing in rafts, wooden Boats, with floats made of cane or cork wood supporting their fishing nets and fish-baskets. The traditional Bestha fishermen use small fishing nets.

The Besthas with agriculture as their extended occupation cultivate both wet and dry lands. But due to poor irrigation facilities they depend on monsoons, and tank water. Pesticides, fertilizers and organic manure are used. Their main products are paddy and groundnut, which are sold in the weekly markets or to middlemen or money lenders who have advanced loans to them.

The Besthas literacy rate is slowly increasing. Some are migrating to the towns for skilled or semi-skilled jobs in the industries. Though they are not fully aware about the welfare programmes of the government, they utilize them to a reasonable extent. There has been thus a lot of changes in their occupational pattern and life styles. The field work undertaken for the purpose of the present study highlights the detailed activity of the occupation.

Sample and Size of Family of Respondents

Table-1 provides the information about the sample of respondents chosen, their rural-urban background, age-group and the details relating to the number of family members. It clearly indicates that out of 198 respondents. The respondents are equally divided between rural, urban and urban areas. The 33.33% each (66) belong to urban areas, rural areas and rurban areas respectively. The age-group details indicate that 36.36% belong to 36-45 age groups, while 27.27% belong to 26-35 age group 15.15% belongs to 66 and above age group, 9.09% belong to 56-65 and 46-55 age groups respectively, while only 3.03% belong to the age group 'upto 25 years'. The data shows that the majority of the respondents belong to middle aged. It may be found that 39.40% of respondents had four members each in their family, while 18.18% each had two members, four members and five members respectively and 6.06% of families had 'six and above members' category respectively. Thus, predominantly the sample constitutes middle aged, and equal proportion them drawn from rural and urban areas.

Education particulars of the family members of the respondents

Out of the total 702 members in the sample families (276 respondents) 39.31% were illiterates, 18.80% of members of the families had education between 1 to 5th class, 29.08% had studied between 6th to 10th standard, 5.98% of family members of respondents had intermediate qualification, while 5.98% were graduates and 0.85% had other qualifications. Among the illiterates, in 42.42% cases both wife and husbands were illiterates while 47.05% had education between 1 to 5th class. It may be observed that in most cases the children of the respondents were found educated or persuing education. Interestingly, it may be found that the respondents are found encouraging the girl's education equally along with their male children.

Table 3.1
Size of the Family

Sl. No	Age	Place	Single	Two Members	Three Members	Four Members	Five members	Six Members & Above	Total
01.	Up to 25	Urban	-	-	-	6 (100) (7.70)	-	-	6 (100) (3.03)
		Urban	-	-	-	-	-	-	-
		Rural	-	-	-	-	-	-	-
02.	26-35	Urban	-	-	-	24 (100) (30.76)	-	-	24 (100) (12.13)
		Rurban	-	12 (66.67) (33.32)	6 (33.33) (16.67)	-	-	-	18 (100) (9.09)
		Rural	-	-	6 (50) (16.67)	6 (50) (7.70)	-	-	12 (100) (6.06)

03.	36-45	Urban	-	-	-	-	12 (100) (33.33)	-	12 (100) (6.06)
		Rurban	-	-	12 (40) (33.32)	18 (60) (23.07)	-	-	30 (100) (15.15)
		Rural	-	-	-	18 (60) (23.07)	6 (20) (16.67)	6 (20) (50)	30 (100) (15.15)
04.	46-55	Urban	-	-	-	-	12 (100) (33.33)	-	12 (100) (6.06)
		Rurban	-	-	-	-	-	-	-
		Rural	-	-	-	-	-	6 (100) (50)	6 (100) (3.03)
05.	56-65	Urban	-	6 (50) (16.67)	-	-	6 (50) (16.67)	-	12 (100) (6.06)
		Rurban	-	6 (100) (16.67)	-	-	-	-	6 (100) (3.03)
		Rural	-	-	-	-	-	-	-
06.	66 & above	Urban	-	-	-	-	-	-	-
		Rurban	-	6 (50) (16.67)	6 (50) (16.67)	-	-	-	12 (100) (6.06)
		Rural	-	6 (33.34) (16.67)	6 (33.33) (16.67)	6 (33.33) (7.70)	-	-	18 (100) (9.09)
Total				**36 (18.18) (100)**	**36 (18.18) (100)**	**78 (39.40) (100)**	**36 (18.18) (100)**	**12 (6.06) (100)**	**198 (100%) (100%)**

Table 3.2
Education of Family Members

Sl. No	Relationship with the Respondent	Illiterate	0-5 Classes	6-10 Classes	Inter	Degree	Others	Total
01.	Father	78 (86.66) (28.26)		12 (13.34) (5.88)				**90 (100) (12.82)**
02.	Mother	78 (100) (28.26)						**78 (100) (11.14)**
03.	Brother	30 (41.66) (10.86)	6 (8.35) (4.54)	24 (33.33) (11.76)	6 (8.33) (14.28)		6 (8.33) (100)	**72 (100) (10.25)**
04.	Wife/Husband	84 (42.42) (30.43)	24 (12.12) (18.18)	78 (39.39) (38.23)		12 (6.07) (28.57)		**198 (100) (28.20)**

05.	Son		48 (30.76) (36.36)	72 (46.15) (35.29)	12 (7.69) (28.57)	24 (15.40) (57.14)		**156 (100) (22.22)**
06.	Daughter	6 (5.88) (2.19	48 (47.05) (36.36)	18 (17.64) (8.84)	24 (23.55) (57.15)	6 (5.88) (14.29)		**102 (100) (14.52)**
07.	Other		6 (100) (4.56)					**6 (100) (0.85)**
Total		**276 (39.31) (100)**	**132 (18.80) (100)**	**204 (29.08) (100)**	**42 (5.98) (100)**	**42 (5.98) (100)**	**6 (0.85) (100)**	**702 (100%) (100%)**

Occupation of the Family Members

The Table 3.2 focused on the occupational background of 5 generations way back and it indicates that all of them in their community continue to be in their traditional occupation without any exception. Only there is a little exception as in the case of present (respondents son) generation 83.33% are following the community based traditional occupations and 16.67% have had shifted their occupations from their traditional occupation to choose a modern occupation ever available to them.

Further examination found that all the family members of the respondents irrespective of whether they adopted the (16.67%) traditional profession or not, they learnt the skills of the trade in their early ages in the family.

Table 3.3

Occupation of the Family Members

Sl. No	Occupation of Family	Same Occupation	Other Traditional Occupation	Modern Occupation	Government Job	Others/ Study	Total
01.	Respondent	198 (100) (24.08)	-	-	-	-	198 (100) (23.91)
02.	Respondent's Father	198 (100) (24.08)	-	-	-	-	198 (100) (23.91)
03.	Respondent's Grand Father	198 (100) (24.08)	-	-	-	-	198 (100) (23.91)
04.	Respondent's Grand Father's Father	198 (100) (24.08)	-	-	-	-	198 (100) (23.91)
05.	Respondent's Son	30 (83.198) (3.68)	-	6 (16.67) (100)	-	-	36 (100) (4.36)
Total		**822 (99.27) (100)**	**-**	**6 (0.73) (100)**	**-**	**-**	**828 (100%) (100%)**

Education and Length of Occupation

Out of the total 198 respondents, a large number (21.23%) were found to be illiterates. Around 57.57% of respondents with an occupational background between 26 and above years had studied between 6th to 10th classes. About 9% of respondents with considerable length of occupational service had intermediate qualifications. Thus the data shows that education is not a criterion to determine the type of occupation they undertake. The things are developed in such a way that whether they are educated or not they must depend on their traditional-based occupation for their livelihood.

Stated Occupation of respondents children

It can be observed from the table-4 that 45.45% of respondents were drawn from rural areas are found to be 'continuing' in the same traditional occupation and 54.55% were pursuing their education, while in urban area 79.92% were pursuing their education and 9.09% are found in modern occupations. Regarding the rurban areas 38.46% are found persuing studies.

Table 3.4

Stated Occupation of Children

Sl. No	Place		Same Occupation	Student	Modern Occupation	Total
01.	Rural	Migrant				
		Local/Non Migrant	30 (45.45) (100)	36 (54.55) (23.08)		**66 (100) (34.37)**
02.	Urban	Migrant				
		Local/Non-Migrant		60 (76.92) (38.46)	6 (9.09) (100)	**66 (100) (34.37)**
03.	Rurban	Migrant				
		Local/Non -Migrant		60 (100) (38.46)		**60 (100) (31.26)**
Total			**30 (15.62) (100)**	**156 (81.25) (100)**	**6 (3.13) (100)**	**192 (100%) (100%)**

Education dropout of children of the respondents

There has been wide-spread dropout earlier from education in the families but in the recent years especially of the parent's generation, the importance of education has been recognized and families began to educate their children. As a result of it 18.18% has been found as dropouts. 78.78% of children are found to have continued their education without dropping out.

Occupation of women in the Family of the respondents

It may be found that all the women found always working in some or the other job while 69.69% sharing the work of the traditional occupation of their male partners. As per the data, out of the total percentage regard to sharing the work 26.08% belong to young and middle aged and 21.73% belong to 56-65 age group, 13.4% youth, 8.69% above middle aged and 4.38% belong to '66 and above aged' respectively. Out of the total respondents, 24.25% of women found as unmarried or housewife and they were found working along with their family members in their traditional occupation, apart from their household duties.

Occupation Training

It may be observed that every member in the family received occupational training (informal) from the elders in the family. It may be interesting to find out that 57.57% of respondent's children had learnt the skills while they were pursuing studies between 6th to 10th class. The data clearly indicates that even when they were pursuing education they could find time to learn the skills of their trade.

Assets Position

Table 4.5 indicates the 'Asset Position' of the respondents, it may be observed that 78.78% of respondents had their own houses and shockingly, 90% of the houses all were thatched houses, in other words huts. However 9.10% of families had chicks or other fowls. 72% own two wheelers vehicles of different sorts and among them 80% own only bicycles. Only 42.43% of the houses had drinking water facility, which would mean that 57% of household depend upon outside sources and carry drinking water from longer distances. Only 30% had bathroom facility while only 60% had latrine facility at home, interestingly 96% had electricity connection at home, 66% had gas connection, 57% had cable TV connection, 72% own Radios, 15% had sewing machines and 42% households Rice cookers. Only 3% read News papers. As far as major Asset such as agricultural land is concerned, only 18% had some agricultural land, which they cultivate or lease out as per their convenience as they adopt no single policy. But during the agriculture season, if it does not clash with the availability of 'fishing work' they invariably prefer to go to agriculture work than any other alternative work. In all, the table indicates the conditions in which these Besthas live and survive are not in any manner comfortable.

Table 3.5

Assets or Facilities

Sl. No	Particulars	Yes	No	Total
01.	House	156 (78.78)	42 (21.22)	198 (100)
02.	Cows/Animals	-	198 (100.0)	198 (100)
03.	Fowls	18 (9.10)	180 (90.90)	198 (100)
04.	Vehicle	144 (72.72)	54 (27.28)	198 (100)
05.	Drinking Water	84 (42.43)	114 (57.57)	198 (100)
06.	Bathroom	60 (30.30)	138 (67.70)	198 (100)
07.	Latrine	120 (60.60)	78 (39.40)	198 (100)
08.	Electricity	192 (96.96)	6 (3.04)	198 (100)
09.	Gas	132 (66.66)	66 (33.34)	198 (100)
10.	T.V	114 (57.57)	84 (42.43)	198 (100)
11.	Radio	144 (72.72)	54 (27.28)	198 (100)
12.	Sewing Machine	30 (15.15)	168 (84.85)	198 (100)
13.	Rice Cookers	84 (42.43)	114 (57.57)	198 (100)
14.	News Papers	6 (3.03)	192 (96.97)	198 (100)
15.	Agricultural Land	36 (18.18)	162 (81.82)	198 (100.0)

Occupational Priorities

The primary work relating to their occupation mainly revolves around the fishing and followed by sale of fishing in the open market. Whenever they do not get full time fishing work about 13.80% respondents prefer to go for agricultural work alone. The remaining go for either agriculture work or other available work.

Source of Employment

Out of the total respondents, 78.95% are found depending on self employment and remaining 21.05% are on wage employment. Regarding the self employment 83.33% are depending on fishing and 16.67% of them on net making. Refer to fishing; the data reveals that the majority of the respondents are depending for their livelihood on fishing and sale of fish, while partially on other activity.

Unseasonal Activity

During the rainy season, Bestha households do not go for fishing and during those times they go for agricultural work or other allied works. Around 20% of respondents work in market or go for petty business such as sale of vegetables and fruits. A Small percentage goes for construction and other labour work.

Source of Investment

It has been found that 75.75% of respondents had their own sources of investment, while the remaining 24.25% had to depend up on various sources such as chit fund companies or money lender who normally of high interest rates. Refer to urban areas majority of the respondents (73.73%) are depending on other available (mostly for interest) sources and remaining 27.27% had their own investment, while in rural areas 33.33% depend up on their own sources while the remaining an other sources. It may be observed that either in rural or in urban areas majority of the respondents found investing by their won sources while the remaining are on private sources such as money lenders. Banks and other government financial agencies seem to have hardly helped them and in this context they are completely deprived of government help.

Investment Details

Regarding the investment on the objects by the respondents, out of the total respondents 43.10% each of the families invested on nets, equipment and other tools respectively. While the remaining 13.80% had used it for construction of shed/hut/shop. Regarding the investment amount, 86.20% of the respondents had invested about the amount ranging from Rs. 1000 to 10,000 and mostly they spent it on tools and fishing sticks nets.

Government Schemes

The available data indicates that except 9% of respondents, who benefitted by government schemes, all others did not benefit in any way at all. The Artisan credit card scheme, Aadharana Scheme, Bank Loan Facility or Occupational Pensions etc., did not reach them. Whatever Government policy 'exists' on fisheries, which is helpful only to big companies or contractors which are generally owned by other communities.

It may be noticed that government has not recognized the need for initiating any policy measures to help these communities so as to help them continue in the trade and modernize it so that it will be beneficial to them. So far no government has proposed any specific policy and the general policy that exist do not reach them. All other general anti-poverty or welfare measures also could not extend any help to this community. Aadharana schemes did not reach the Bestha Community, old age pensions did not cover all, bank loans are extended to only a couple of people and others did not get it. No other schemes have any role to play to extend any sort of development support to these people.

Table 3.6
Government schemes

Sl. No	Government Schemes	Available	Not Available	Total
01.	Artisan Credit Card	-	198 (100) (20.37)	**198 (100) (20)**
02.	Aadarana Scheme	-	198 (100) (20.37)	**198 (100) (20)**
03.	Bank Loans	-	198 (100) (20.37)	**198 (100) (20)**
04.	Govt. Pensions	18 (9.10) (100)	180 (90.90) (18.52)	**198 (100) (20)**
05.	Occupational Pensions	-	198 (100) (20.37)	**198 (100) (20)**

Impact of Government Schemes

In the absence of any specific scheme or programme concerning the Bestha Community, there was very much discontentment in these families. The impact of general welfare or development programme has been either marginal or negative.

Role of Community Associations

Out of the total respondents, 51.52% of the respondents although felt that community Associations exists, they are either ineffective or sometimes indifferent towards resolving their problems. The remaining 48.48% felt that they are even negative. Both rural and urban respondents felt it that way and there was no difference of opinion.

It is generally expected that Community Associations play a positive role in representing the problems of their respective communities and get their things done at the governmental level. But it may be observed that the Bestha

Community Associations are not playing their expected role as to initiate various steps at various levels to exert pressure on the government and get their things done.

Sale of Fish

Normally it may be found that men go for fishing and women in the family go for selling the fish. Women are found selling the fish by the side of the lake or tank or sea, where the fish has been caught, or the market or street corners or supply to wholesalers or contractors. Some also undertake street vending while moving from one street to the other. Especially fish contractors collect the fish from the 'lake sides'. Some Bestha people sell particularly only to their 'assigned contractors as they provide money in advance or extend loans whenever necessary. In most cases however the choice of sales is very much limited and they have hardly had any independent option.

General Occupational Problems

It reflects the occupational problems of the respondents in rural and urban areas. Out of the total percentage, 33.34% of the respondents are found facing problems such as non availability of Boats and equipments or other instruments. 33.33% each of respondents suffering from non availability of capital and market competition respectively. This has been the major problem both in rural and urban areas.

The data indicates the general occupational problems faced by the Bestha Community. Some of the problems identified are almost identical to both rural and urban Bestha community people. The problems as said by the respondents include non availability of fishing instruments, lack of availability of modern technology, lack of investment capital, lack of market, lack of proper business and competition from private shops and family financial problems etc. Over the years it may be found that many a Bestha families leaving the profession and migrating to urban areas for want of work and livelihood.

Solution to Problems

In the course of the study, the respondents also offered some suggestions to find out solutions to their problems include; Extension of Personal loans every year without surety, supply of material, tools, boats; provision for a separate market, provision for separate occupational training programmes, housing facility, provision for separate occupational budget and occupational pensions. Both urban and rural respondents said that their basic problems need to be tackled by government with a definite policy frame work. An analysis of the suggestions made by the respondents indicates that there has been indifference towards their problems by the officials concerned as they hardly bother about their problems. Most of the respondents said that government policies are helping only vested interests. In view of the deterioration of the conditions and also government failure to extend necessary assistance to them, they demanded a definite policy framework exclusively meant to resolve their problems.

Future Perspective

It indicates the opinion of the respondents about their future perspective. Out of the total percentage, 60.61% said that their future is not hopeful, 33.33% had expressed that they have some hope on their future and remaining 6.07% expressed that they have no idea and did not answer the question. Among the 'hopeful category' 45.45% were drawn from rural areas while 54.55% were drawn from urban. Refer to 'no hopeful category' of which 30% were from rural, 45% from urban areas and 25% from rurban areas respectively. Refer to rural area 45.45% of respondents felt that they were having lot of hopes on their future and remaining 54.55% are not. Regard to the urban areas 81.81% had felt that they are not having any hopes on their future and remaining 18.19% said that they have no idea about their future.

Profiles of Certain Respondents

G. Appala Raju (Sea Fisherman)

My name is Appala Raju aged 22 years. We are four members in my family. My wife, my son and a daughter. I discontinued my studies after 9th class due to poverty. I learnt fishing through my father. My fore-fathers also did the same profession. I am doing this work for the last 10 years. I am living near Vodarevu from my childhood in a temporary shelter.

My wife aged 20 years studied 10th class and discontinued. My son 11 years and my daughter 3 years of age. My wife is working at home looking after my son and daughter.

We live nearby the seashore in a hut and most of our caste families live together. Any cyclone may damage whole of our dwelling place. Many times it has happened and now we have accustomed to it. On such occasions, we leave the place in case advance caution is given otherwise sudden cyclones create havoc in our lives resulting in human and material loss. We do not have minimum facilities in our house. We lead our life depending on the fish we get from the sea.

Nearly 15 members of our Community go in a boat for fishing together in the sea as a group. We take with us the material required for fishing in the sea. We go for 10 to 15 days for fishing. We take with us the food materials required for the period we stay on the sea. We share 80% to the owner of the boat and retain 20% to be shared amongst the members of the group. On an average for 10 days of work we get around Rs 2000 to 3000/- each. We take rest for a week later and again go for fishing after the week. During the leisure time in between we prepare or repair the fishing nets which we use it for fishing. We also undertake repairs for the Boats we use. In 90% of cases the Boats are owned by outsiders, who do not belong to our caste.

We are not getting any assistance from the government. We are not getting any material on subsidy. We do not have any life insurance to cover as social security scheme. Government should pay us individual loans to purchase the material required, especially the Boats and fishing nets. It should establish separate 'Community groups' like DWAKRA groups and extend necessary help. Government should help us during cyclone days and should come to our rescue; it should provide free education to our children. It should provide old age pension to senior citizens. It should provide housing facility and rehabilitation centers. Separate fish markets to be setup. Government should also impose restrictions on outside contractors. Unless Government initiates such policies meant for our welfare we have no better future.

Damera Raju (Tank Fisherman)

My name is Damera Raju, aged 43 years. I studied upto VII class and discontinued due to poverty. I belong to Nagaram village, Mandal Hasanparthy, Warangal District. I am a fisherman and my occupation is fishing. My father and forefathers also did the same occupation. My wife 40 years old studied upto X class and discontinued due to some domestic problems in the house. We have two children one son and one daughter. My son aged 21 years studying B.Tech and my daughter 16 years old and studied upto intermediate.

We have our own RCC building. I have got one bicycle and facilities at home such as drinking water, bathroom, latrine etc. I have a Television, Radio, and I read news papers outside. My neibours are very friendly and we used to help each other. I am also working as Honorary President of Gangaputra Co-operative society.

I am doing this work since 20 years. We have been trained in fishing occupation by Gangaputra Society. We were also trained by Fishermen Development Office (FDO). We have been trained for 20 days in fishing and we have been paid Rs.40=00 per day during the training period. After completion of the training a certificate to that effect has also been issued to us. Due to this modern training we became experts in fishing.

On behalf of the society, 8 to 10 members belonging to the Community go for fishing in nearby tanks in the morning 5 am, and work for 6 hours till 12 noon. We distribute the fishes we caught equally and we sell it in the village. Sometimes we all together go to big market in the city and sell the fish and distribute the amount equally. Generally we get Rs.100 to 200 on ordinary days and in the month of April and May we get more fish and also more income.

I have got a net and other material required for fishing which I secured them personally. Each member of the society contributed Rs.6000=00 as the capital amount towards the expenditure towards collective fishing in the village tank and we go for fishing collectively and sell the fishes collectively.

I purchased 20 Guntas of land for agriculture and I earn some amount through agriculture which is sufficient to meet our house hold expenditure. Previously I worked along with my father for fishing. We used to get plenty of fishes to our entire satisfaction but for the last 5 years the production of fishes has been reduced. We do not have a separate fishing market for sale. There is no transport facility to carry and sell the fishes in the city. The Government has given a loan to our society to the tune of Rs. 50,000/ but no individual loans have been sanctioned. We do not have any vehicle to the society. Sometime due to heavy rains travelling to the city has become difficult but no security measures have been taken nor are any insurance facility provided by the Government in this regard.

I have many problems related to my occupation and I suggest resolving some of these problems. Government should come forward to help our community members by providing material required for fishing; market facility is to be arranged for sale of fishes; Accident benefits are to be sanctioned by Government; free education, hostel facility, scholarships are to be given to our children. Loans and Subsidies are to be arranged. Cold storages have to be setup for preserving fishes and no outside contractors should be allowed to operate in fishing business.

M. Raju (Sea Fisherman)

My name is M. Raju aged 33 years, studied upto 7th class. Our native place is Vodarevu, Chirala of Prakasham District. I am living in Vodarevu since my birth and my profession is fishing which is my ancestor's profession.

My wife aged 26 years studied up to 10th class and discontinued. She works as a tailor which is actually not our profession. Neighbors give work to her. We are four members in our family. Myself, my wife and one son aged 11 years studying 6th class and one daughter aged 9 years, studying 4th class. My wife is also a DWAKRA group member.

In vodarevu we are living in a small hut, nearby the sea. We don't have any pet animals and we don't have minimum facilities at home. No Latrine, Bathroom facility but having current, T.V, Cooking Gas, Radio and a Rice Cooker. All our neighbours are also fishermen. There are various problems in my neighbourhood. There is no drinking water. We have to purchase water for drinking. There is every possibility of cyclones coming at any time. I am living at Vodarevu since 20 years. Sometimes due to Toofan and Cyclone we are unable to live at that place. We go out of that place for safety and again comeback there. We go for fishing in a boat as a group of 10 to 12 members. We take the Boat on rent and use it for fishing.

We go for fishing in the sea and sell the fish in the market nearby. We go for fishing for 9 to 10 months in a year and other days we do preparing fishing nets. We purchase the material required for fishing. We go for fishing in the morning. We take with us the food material required and sometimes we stay in the boat for 3-5 days, cook the food in the boat and sleep and stay in it only. We listen to the radio about the weather conditions and accordingly we carry on our fishing. We sell the fish in the market and sometimes when we fail to sell the fish we preserve them. We also dry some fish and sell it in the market.

We do not have enough money to purchase the fishing material and the boat etc., required. We take loan from money lenders 3% to 4% interest and repay them in equal installments. It is very difficult to repay the amount and interest. If bank loan facility is available it would be better for us. The amount which we get by fishing is very meager and not sufficient to meet the needs of our children's education and our other expenses. We do not have any other alternate employment to supplement our income. There is every fear that we may face some trouble due to Toofan and loose our lives. Always our families live with fear of danger and accidents. There is no security to our lives. When we get more fish we will be happy otherwise we 'feel' bad and have to starve ourselves.

I Suggest that

1. Government should provide one boat for a group of 4 members to go for fishing in the ocean.
2. Government should provide fishing materials like net and others on subsidy price.
3. Permanent Residential houses are to be constructed by the Government, nearby the sea.
4. Free education, hostel facility should be provided to our children.
5. Immediate help and rehabilitatory measures needed whenever cyclone or Toofans occur.

6. Pension scheme for senior citizens should be implemented.
7. Separate fishing markets are to be setup.
8. Cold storage and drying facilities are to be setup.
9. Government should avoid 'contractors' entering in to the field and monopolising the fish trade.

Gunti Sammaiah (Tank Fisherman)

My name is Gunti Sammaiah, 70 years old illiterate. My parents are also illiterates. My native place is Gatlakanaparthi Mandal Shyampet Warangal District. Fishing is my occupation, traditionally practiced. I learnt it from my father and all my ancestors did the same work. My wife aged 65 years an illiterate. My children live at another place separately. For the last 55 years I am doing the fishing work.

I have a small tiled house in my village without modern facilities. We cook on fire wood carry water from outside. I did not have any agriculture land. In my childhood days I used to go for fishing along with my father. There were good rains and we used to get more fishes from the tanks and there was a sufficient return to take care of my family. Now I am old unable to work and moreover there are no rains, no water in tanks and no fish is available and it has become difficult to lead our life.

We used to go for fishing to the nearby water tank in our village. It is known as Medaram tank. It spread over about 120 acres area. Some of our Caste members together go for fishing. We spent on amount of Rs. 80,000 towards the expenditure of growing fish in the tank and we collectively do the fishing on seasonal days and sell the fish on wholesale basis in the market and we take equal share amount of the profit. Sometimes on unseasonal days we go for other labour work.

Now-a-days no pond or water tanks are existing and there were no rains as previously we used to get. As a result we began to lose our livelihood. There is a need that government should develop water ponds and provide us necessary loans to purchase fish seed on subsidised rates. The ponds must be given to Fishermen to manage, while they should have a facility to sell the fish and make their livelihood.

From the age of 60 years I am getting old age pension and I am leading with that pension only. When I did fishing I lived very well earlier during the past, but now the situation is bad and I am surviving only because of the old age pension.

Pindi Nagaraju (Tank Fisherman)

My name is Pindi Nagaraju aged 28 years. I have studied upto SSC and discontinued due to poverty. I have learnt 'fishing' from my father. My grandfather and fore fathers did the same profession. I am doing this profession since 10 years and I want to continue in this profession only as I have no other alternative.

My wife aged 22 years studied upto 7th class and discontinued. She works in a house as domestic servant and also sells fishes and also goes for agriculture work seasonally and on other days as a labour. We have two daughters, one five years old and the other 3 years, both of them are going to school.

My native Village is Laknepally, Mandal Narsampet of Warangal District. I live here since my birth and do my profession of fishing. Laknepally is a village where we have small tiled house. We have Tap, Bathroom, Cooker, Gas, Television, Radio, Sewing machine and a Scooter.

I have 20 Guntas of agriculture land and we get the crop from it is useful to my family. My wife and I both work in agriculture land. My neighbours are good and we are friendly with each other and live together in the locality.

In our village there is a tank spreading over 30 Acres

of land and we have a fishing society. The members of the society spend the required amount on preparing the tank for the growth of fishes. It costs about Rs. one lakh per year. We share it equally and we get the tools and net for fishing from the society. Generally 8 to 10 members of the society go for fishing in the morning and return in the evening. Normally in the month of May and June we will be busy fishing and during the other months there will no fishing works as fish is not available. We share equally the fishes we get from fishing and we sell them in the village. We will go to neighbouring city to sell the large amount of fish sometimes we get by taking a vehicle. We share the returns equally.

When there is season we get good amount on fishes. Then we preserve them and sell them later. Sometimes we do not get good amount of fish then we face difficulties. Festival days we happily live together with family and celebrate in case the season gets good fishing.

Our Problems Include: Sufficient income is not available through profession; Middlemen and others interfere at various levels which affected our trade. No training facilities to the persons of this occupation to adopt new technologies and materials.

My Suggestions Include: Government should provide Bank loan, fishing material required on subsidy rates; Fish market should be opened in villages and towns. Fishery seeds should be provided; Health cards are to be supplied; Pension to the senior citizens should be arranged; free education and scholarship to our children needed. Fisher Cooperatives need to be strengthened. We should have complete monopoly on the village tanks and outside communities or contractors should not be allowed to carry on the fishing as well as fish trade.

4

Dudekula- *The Cotton Cleaner/ Band Player*

Dudekula are numerically a small community. They are known by synonyms such as 'Pinjari', 'Bhai', 'Panjakuttai; and 'Panjari'. The other synonyms recorded by Thurston (1909) are 'Ladaf' and 'Nurbash'. In Telugu the state language of Telangana and Andhra Pradesh, 'Dudi' means cotton and 'ekuta' means cleaning. Hence they are locally called the Dudekula, the cotton cleaners and mattress makers. They are mentioned as "a Mohammadan caste of cotton-cleaners, rope and tape makers". Telugu is their mother tongue and it is used for communication at home and with outsiders. They also use the Telugu script. The personal name giving pattern of Dudekula is similar to the Hindus but the names given are mahmadan.

Dudekula are Muslims because they worship Allah, go to mosque and fast during the month of Ramzan. The Dudekula are said to be Hindu converts to Islam (Francis as quoted by Thurston: 1909). Hindu society has its "own institutionalized inequality" or "hierarchical gradation" and created a caste society. Within a caste society each group is ranked in relation to the other [Sinha 1967]. The Indian Muslims also have caste-like groups. At the lowest level come the Dudekula the cotton cleaners, barbers (hazam), and mendicants (Fakir-budbudki) are located.

Customarily, the Dudekula women wear vermilion (kumkum) on the forehead. With this they are found just like Hindu women. The Dudekula women do not cover their face with cloth (purdah), which is symbol of Muslims belonging to upper strata. They go out to undertake agricultural activities such as paddy seedling transplantation, weeding and harvesting. Such outdoor jobs are not attended to by upper class Muslim women, but in contrast Dudekula women invariable go for it.

The traditional occupation of the Dudekula community is cotton cleaning (dudi ekuta). In view of the changes which have come in the matters of dress and consumer pattern, the younger generations of the community are not coming forward to learn it. Apart from the low income, the stigma attached to the profession has made them shy away from it. So, they have become petty traders or work as small time contractors in seasonal fruits and vegetables such as tamarind ('chinta pundu chetlu'), mango ('mamidi thoopu'), and tomato so on. A few have taken up trading in artificial pearls ('mutyalu') and diamonds ('vajralu'). Others have purchased irrigated land and cultivated it. As a whole the Dudekula when compared to past, dealing in cash have become mobile and move from one weekly market to another ('Santhalu') and easy quick means of transport has come to their help. There are persons who are businessmen and clergy among the Dudekula. A few are also teachers and hold other white-collar jobs. However there is nobody in politics either at village or state level. In Andhra Pradesh the Dudekulas are listed under economically and educationally backward list of castes. Hence, they get all educational facilities provided by the government such as free books, fee concession and free hostel facilities.

It is found that the Dudekula are favourable towards the family planning programmes and their women have undergone sterilization. Both Dudekula men and women have accepted modern education and have occupied jobs in different fields. All these have helped the Dudekula elevate their status in the society. The field work undertaken for the purpose of the study provides detailed account of all the activities of the occupation.

Sample and Size of the Family

Table-1 indicates the details relating to sample of Dudekula Community taken for the purpose of study. The sample indicates 11.53% of the families were drawn from urban areas and 88.47% from rural areas. The sample also indicates that 15.38% belong to 26-35 age group, 30.78% each belong to 36-45 and 46-55 groups, 11.53% belong to 56-65 age group and the remaining 11.53 belong to 66 and above age group. No one was found in the sample under 26 years of age. It is significant to observe that size of the family as it contradicts the general feelings of society. Dudekula community is part of Muslim religion and it has been generally felt that Muslim families will have large number of children. However, the sample of Dudekula families indicates that 50% of families were found to be four member families, while 30.77% of families had five members. Only 7.69% of Dudekula families had six members and above 3.85% of families had three members, while 7.69% had only two members in the family. Dudekula families are found to have scattered and there has been 'non-traditionalisation' of socio-economic life of these people over the years.

Table 4.1
Size of the Family

Sl. No	Age	Place	Single	Two Members	Three Members	Four Members	Five members	Six Members & Above	Total
01.	Up to 25	Urban	-	--	-	-	-	-	-
		Rural	-	-	-	-	-	-	-
02.	26-35	Urban	-	-	-	6 (100) (7.69)	-	-	6 (100) (3.85)
		Rural	-	-	-	12 (66.67) (15.39)	-	6 (33.33) (50)	18 (100) (11.53)
03.	36-45	Urban	-	-	-	6 (100) (7.69)	-	-	6 (100) (3.85)
		Rural	-	-	6 (14.29) (100)	24 (57.14) (30.77)	12 (28.57) (25)	-	42 (100) (26.93)
04.	46-55	Urban	-	-	-	6 (100) (7.69)	-	-	6 (100) (26.93)
		Rural	-	-	-	12 (28.57) (15.39)	24 (57.14) (50)	6 (14.29) (50)	42 (100) (26.93)
05.	56-65	Urban	-	-	-	-	-	-	-
		Rural	-	-	-	6 (33.33) (7.69)	12 (66.67) (25)	-	18 (100) (11.53)
06.	66 & Above	Urban	-	-	-	-	-	-	-
		Rural	-	12 (66.67) (100)	-	6 (33.33) (7.69)	-	-	18 (100) (11.53)
Total				12 (7.69) (100)	6 (3.85) (100)	78 (50) (100)	48 (30.77) (100)	12 (7.69) (100)	156 (100%) (100%)

Education of Family Members

Out of 156 families chosen for the sample of the study, the total number of members in their families comes to 666 who include the respondent's parents, spouse and children. Very significantly, out witting the general saying (being Muslim families) 98% of families are nucleus families and both boys and girls in the family are given equal preference in education. No children have been found as illiterates. However in the overall sense 12.61% were illiterates. 17.12% studied upto fifth class, 36.94% studied upto 10th class, and 10.81% had intermediate level education, while 10.81% had Inter/ITI qualification of their credit. 11.71% graduates are found in the sample, which include 46.16% sons and 20.84% daughters in the families. As far as the respondents are concerned, the table shows that 15.38% are illiterates, 69.33% had education between 1 to 10th class, 7.69% with inter or

ITI qualification, 3.85% graduates while another 3.85% had Certificates/Diplomas in other courses.

Table 4.2
Education of Family Members

Sl. No	Relationship with the Respondent	Illiterate	0-5 Classes	6-10 Classes	Inter	Degree	ITI/Other Technical Courses	Others	Total
01.	Respondent	24(15.38) (28.57)	12 (7.69) (10.53)	96 (61.54) (39.02)	12 (7.69) (16.67)	6 (3.85) (7.69)	-	6 (3.85) (8.33)	**156 (100) (23.42)**
02.	Father	6 (100) (7.14)	-	-	-	-	-	-	**6 (100) (0.90)**
03.	Mother	6 (100) (7.14)	-	-	-	-	-	-	**6 (100) (0.90)**
04.	Wife	48 (32) (57.15)	54 (36) (49.79)	48 (32) (19.51)	-	-	-	-	**150 (100) (22.52)**
05.	Son	-	24 (11.76) (21.05)	48 (23.53) (19.51)	48 (23.53) (66.66)	36 (17.65) (46.16)	-	48 (23.53) (66.67)	**204 (100) (30.63)**
06.	Daughter	-	30 (20.83) (26.32)	54 (37.5) (21.96)	12 (8.33) (16.67)	30 (20.84) (38.46)	-	18 (12.5) (25)	**144 (100) (21.63)**
Total		**84(12.61) (100)**	**114 (17.12) (100)**	**246 (36.94) (100)**	**72 (10.81) (100)**	**78 (11.71) (100)**	-	**72(10.81) (100)**	**666 (100%) (100%)**

Occupation of Family Members

The occupational details as seen in Table-3 indicates that for the last 4 generations including the Respondent's generation indicates that all of them were found in the same hereditary occupation without any change or shift. As far as their adult children are concerned (Prospective), only 19.23% has preferred to join the 'hereditary occupation land' the remaining either found in the studies or in other occupations other than traditional occupation of their parents.

Table 4.3
Occupation of Family Members

Sl. No		same Occupation	Modern Occupation	Government Job	Others/ Student/ No Children	Total
01.	Respondent	156 (100) (23.85)	-	-	-	**156 (100) (20)**
02.	Respondent's Father	156 (100) (23.85)	-	-	-	**156 (100) (20)**
03.	Respondent's Grand Father	156 (100) (23.85)	-	-	-	**156 (100) (20)**
04.	Respondent's Grand Father's Father	156 (100) (23.85)	-	-	-	**156 (100) (20)**
05.	Respondent's Son	30 (19.23) (4.60)	-	-	126 (80.77) (100)	**156 (100) (20)**
Total		**654 (83.85) (100)**	-	-	**126 (16.15) (100)**	**780 (100) (100)**

Education and Length of Occupation

Table-4.4 indicates that only 3.85% of the respondents incidentally who were Degree holders found to be in the profession ranging from a service background of couple of months to five years. Another 3.85% with certificate courses were found in the profession between 6 to 10 years. 42.31% of respondents with a qualification under 10th class found in the profession ranging between 11 to 20 years. 30.17% of the respondents between 21 and 30 years of experience in the profession had upto a maximum of intermediate education. 'drop-out' from education has been a normal affair has since most of the respondents had studied upto school education and dropped somewhere in between. These figures indicate that age-wise and education-wise both youngsters and elders in the family were away from the profession for their own reasons. Those who had higher education but found in the occupation had entered the profession recently as a stop gap arrangement, while others continued in the profession for want of other employment. Education has no value as far as this profession is concerned.

Table 4.4
Education and Length of Occupation

Sl. No	Education	1-5 years	6-10	11-20	21-30	31-40	41-50	51 & above	Total
01.	Illiterate	-	-	-	12 (50) (25)	12 (50) (33.335)	-	-	**24 (100) (15.38)**
02.	1-5 Classes	-	-	6 (50) (9.09)	6 (50) (12.5)	-	-	-	**12 (100) (7.69)**
03.	6-10 Classes	-	-	60 (12.5) (90.91)	24 (25) (50)	12 (12.5) (33.335)	-	-	**96 (100) (61.54)**
04.	Inter	-	-	-	6 (50) (12.5)	6 (50) (16.665)	-	-	**12 (100) (7.69)**
05.	Degree	6 (100) (100)	-	-	-	-	-	-	**6 (100) (3.85)**
06.	Others	-	6 (100) (100)	-	-	-	-	-	**6 (100) (3.85)**
Total		**6 (3.85) (100.0)**	**6 (3.85) (100)**	**66 (42.31) (100)**	**48 (30.17) (100)**	**30 (19.23) (100)**	**-**	**-**	**156 (100%) (100%)**

Table 4.5 indicate that only in 19.39% of the families, the male children found to be in the same traditional

hereditary occupation, while 40% of them were incidentally migrants from switching over from urban to rural and rural to urban areas with a limited stay in each place. 7.69% of the children were found as labourers in construction industry, while others were in studies or other jobs of lower level. No one was found in government service or in other modern occupations. The fate of children in the studies is yet to be realized. However, a large majority of the respondents had categorically said that they do not want to see their children to enter in to their profession and wanted them to join government services.

Table 4.5

Stated Occupation of Children

Sl. No	Place		Same Occupation	Modern Occupation	Labour	Others/ Study	Total
01.	Rural	Migrant	6 (11.11) (20.0)	-	-	48 (88.89) (40)	**54 (100) (34.62)**
		Local/Non Migrant	18 (20) (60.0)	-	12 (13.33) (100)	60 (66.67) (50)	**90 (100) (57.70)**
02.	Urban	Migrant	6 (100) (20.0)	-	-	-	**6 (100) (3.84)**
		Local/Non-Migrant	-	-	-	-	-
Total			**30 (19.39) (100)**	-	**12 (7.69) (100)**	**114 (73.08) (100)**	**156(100%) (100%)**

Occupation of women in the Family

Normally women in Dudekula Muslim families generally do not go out for outside occupation but the data indicates that 'due to hard circumstances' they too are found working 'both in and out' of the house. It has been found that age was no bar for them to carry the work. Almost half of the respondents go to undertake the 'paid work' available to them. This is more a trend in urban areas than rural areas. In rural areas most women are found in agricultural work. 23.08% of women in the families are found in family enterprise work, helping their men-folk. 26.02% of female members in the family were either in studies or stayed back at home. Over the years there has been a shift in the attitude of family members including 'males' to 'cross' cultural taboos allowing women to go for work supplementing the family income. The deteriorating work situation or lack of required quantity of orders for their products made them to change their attitude and life styles. It may be found that all members in the family including children-male or female learn the work from the early age. As a result of it they don't need any special training to learn the skills and techniques of work. Parental guidance makes them perfect in the trade. Parents generally in all artisan families think that children should be helpful to them in their work and learn it so that it will be some day useful to them.

Table 4.6

Occupation of Women in the Family

Sl. No	Age	Involved in Occupation	Doing other work	Idle/unmarried/ Housewife/Studies	Total
01.	Up to 25	-	-	6 (100) (14.28)	**6 (100) (3.85)**
02.	26-35	6(12.5) (16.665)	30 (62.5) (38.47)	12 (25) (28.58)	**48 (100) (30.77)**
03.	36-45	12 (20) (33.34)	36 (60) (46.16)	12 (20) (28.58)	**60 (10) (38.46)**
04.	46-55	6 (50) (16.665)	6 (50) (7.69)	-	**12 (100) (7.69)**
05.	56-65	6 (33.333) (16.665)	6 (33.333) (7.69)	6 (33.333) (14.28)	**18 (100) (11.54)**
06.	66 and above	6 (50) (16.665)	-	6 (50) (14.28)	**12 (100) (7.69)**
Total		**36 (23.08) (100)**	**78 (50) (100)**	**42 (26.02) (100)**	**156 (100%) (100%)**

Family Assets

Dudekula community living in the villages is found in many of places gradually shifting towards agriculture due to non-availability of work in their traditional occupation. Normally it has been expected that all families in the villages own some land and they can work on it seasonally for producing food grains or others. But gradually most of the artisans living on the villages had sold out the land for 'consumption' purposes or lack of availability of sufficient work in their traditional occupation. In the case of Dudekula family a 'new trend' could be found to carry out the agricultural work as was found it necessary to produce food grains. Consequent to these changes or some other local reasons, the 26.92% of sample Dudekula families could own some land to be used for agricultural purposes. 73.08% of sample households, however could not own any land. Among them it has been found that some had lost the land over the years. All the Dudekula sample households had their own home or the other kind of residential houses in both rural and urban areas. Around 12 % are found to be owning cows/bullocks, plough and other agricultural implements. Every family has a bathroom but around 20% of families did not own any latrines of their own. A large number of families had Electricity (82%), Gas (66%), TVs (62%), Radios (30.77%), Sewing Machine (11.54%), and Rice Cookers (7.69%). No family has been found owning a Refrigerator etc., No one gets News Papers. Around 30% of families own some vehicle Bicycle/Motor Cycle/Scooter. In the overall sense those who own agricultural land and also able to find their traditional occupational work, could be found owning more number of assets for their use.

Occupational Priority

As has been discussed Dudekula Community's primary occupation has been for long include 'Cotton Cleaning' and 'Bed works and that of Musical Band work to be performed' at the time of marriage and other functions. Out of the total sample, 26% of Dudekula families drawn from different villages and towns undertake to 'Band and musical' work found migrating to towns and cities to join 'other bands' maintained by their relatives or friends for livelihood. Over the years majority of Dudekula male members actually prefer to undertake the 'cotton cleaning' works but which is not available to them. It may be observed that most of the people prefer readymade beds of different sorts and some of them are 'cheaper' than cotton beds. Hence more and more people prefer other kind of beds and as a result Dudekula families have lost the 'cotton cleaning' work. The Research team has observed in much houses 'cotton cleaning' equipment hanging on walls unused at the homes. Other machines found outside in the open area available to them. Their works are available only seasonally and during the same season they also find some agricultural work. They have to choose either of it. In view of this they choose either of it based on the convenience or 'income range' that benefits them.

Despite the fact of shifting from 'cotton cleaning' to agriculture to 'band work or vice versa, all of them are found to be 'self-employed'. Women in these families prefer to go for wage employment whatever available to them outside.

Production Plan

It has been found that normally the sample households are found working from their own home as part of the house is converted in to 'their work place'. For Cotton Cleaning and Bed works, they plan production on the basis of orders they get. Whenever they get orders they purchase the raw materials needed for it from the local market. Apart from required quantities of cotton, they need threads, sewing machine, needles, scissors, cloth along with the equipment needed for the work. Sometime they make extra products and keep it on display for those who visit their houses and buy the articles. They also produce the articles on 'orders'. Sometimes hostel people and others place bulk orders for purchase of beds but it happens rarely.

Those who depend on 'musical band work' need Band, Key Board Player, Thasha, dresses and caps and they get these things from big cities. Those who do both need to invest more on the equipment or instruments required for this purpose.

Sources of Investment

It has been found that around 46% of respondents use their own savings to invest on various items required for their family enterprises. It has been found that, of those who invest the amount on their own, 83.33% were drawn from rural and the urban areas. Rural Dudekula households are found to be reluctant to depend upon sources other than their own. A large number of Dudekula respondents rely on their friends, relatives and other known people to borrow money for using the same towards investment needed. 8.33% were found to be depending upon the 'money lenders' to take short term loans whenever needed for undertaking the Bed works. In most cases, the customers do not pay any advances except in certain minor cases. Banks again do not come to their rescue. Cooperatives exist only in limited places and the present sample villages and towns no such cooperative society exists.

Government Schemes

Dudekula community also find it difficult to think about any government facility and schemes such as Artisan credit card, Aadharana scheme, Loans, Subsidies, Margin Money, Occupation Pensions etc., which were not extended to them. It may be found that 15.38% of aged people within the Community get old age pensions. No other government scheme is available to them. The government thinks that 'general welfare and developments' programmes meant for the poor will be able to help these communities and resolve their problems. But there is hardly any activities initiated by government.

Role of Associations

Dudekula community has its own Associations but these are however not active to represent the community in it's broaden perspective. The leadership has been found generally indifferent to fight with the government and get things done.

Main Occupational Problems

Dudekula community has certain peculiar problems as they belong to Muslim religion but considered as 'non-OBC communities' unlike other OBC Artisans. In fact in most of the states they were part of OBC lists recognized by government. They are being discriminated by both the religion as Muslims treat them as 'lower community' and Hindus consider them as aliens. Since it is a 'minority community' in relation to numbers and low level occupation, all others treat them as distinct and socially and culturally low. Further there has been steep fall in their incomes in both the cases of 'Band and Bed works' over the years which affected them economically. Lack of accessibility to Bank loans and government margin money, subsidies, indifference of bankers in extending loans, non-issue of identification cards and police harassment as these people walk or travel distances after attending to Band work at marriages and functions seems vulnerable to police petrol parties. Both Rural and Urban respondents had an additional problem of police harassment.

Table 4.7

Main Occupational Problems

Sl. No	Response	Rural	Urban	Total
01.	No Proper Benefits/Falling Incomes	144 (92.31) (34.29)	12 (7.69) (22.222)	**256 (100) (32.91)**
02.	Lack of Bank loans and margin money	102 (89.47) (24.29)	12 (10.53) (22.222)	**114 (100) (24.05)**
03.	Police Harassment	78 (86.67) (18.57)	12 (13.33) (22.222)	**90 (100) (18.99)**
04.	Caste Discrimination	24 (80) (5.71)	6 (20) (11.112)	**30 (100) (6.33)**
05.	Non Issue of health cards/ID Cards	72 (85.71) (17.14)	12 (14.29) (22.222)	**84 (100) (17.72)**
Total		**420 (88.61) (100)**	**54 (11.39) (100)**	**474 (100%) (100%)**

Solutions to Problems

There has been 'limited perception levels' and 'demand articulation' on the part of the Dudekula community, which hardly know what it wants and what is the reason for their growing problems and their emerging socio-economic and development issues. The opinions have been almost uniform in nature irrespective of the respondent's background. All rural, urban and rurban respondents had said that they have represented their issues to government to seek equipment and machinery required for modernization of their occupation, provision for bank loans and subsidies, provision for exclusive government orders, provision for true residential education, free housing, issue of ID cards, provision of pensions and other incentives. Most of the respondents had felt that there is no better hope for the future as they denied and discriminated in all respect of human development. It may be noted from the above analysis that government may need to evolve a separate policy framework for the welfare and development of Dudekula Community.

Table 4.8

Solutions to Problems (Cumulative)

Sl. No	Response	Rural	R urban	Urban	Total
01.	Supply of Modern Equipment & Machinery	48 (32) (17.39)	48 (32) (17.39)	12 (8) (15.38)	**150 (100) (15.92)**
02.	Provision for Bank loan & Subsidies	96 (61.54) (16.33)	48 (30.77) (17.39)	12 (7.69) (15.383)	**156 (100) (16.56)**
03.	Provision for Government work orders	78 (56.52) (13.270	48 (34.78) (17.39)	12 (8.70) (15.383)	**138 (100) (14.65)**
04.	Provision for Fee Residential Education	96 (69.56) (16.33)	30 (21.74) (10.87)	12 (8.70) (15.383)	**138 (100) (14.65)**
05.	Provision for Housing	60 (62.5) (10.20)	30 (31.25) (10.87)	6 (6.25) (7.70)	**96 (100) (10.19)**
06.	Issue of Identity Cards	96 (61.53) (16.33)	48 (30.77) (17.39)	12 (7.70) (15.383)	**156 (100) (16.56)**
07.	Provision for Pension Facilities	72 (66.67) (12.24)	24 (22.22) (8.70)	12 (11.11) (15.383)	**108 (100) (11.47)**
Total		**588 (62.42) (100)**	**276 (29.30) (100)**	**78 (8.28) (100)**	**942 (100%) (100%)**

Profiles of Select Respondents

Shaik Yakub (Dudekula)

My name is Shek Yakub. I am 55 years old. I have completed Intermediate. My native place is Laknepally Mandal: Narsampet District: Warangal. After completion of my Intermediate studies I tried for a Government job but I could not get it. I learned 'band work' from my father and doing that work now. I have been doing this work for the last 40 years. First along with my father even while persuing my studies and later independently. Our actual native place was Bithalapally near Ambala-but for the purpose of Band work which provided me livelihood, we came here. We came here when I was a boy. I came here with my parents. Now I have one son and two daughters. My wife studied upto 3rd class and stopped studies due to their financial problems. My son, 25 years now completed degree, daughter 22 years now in P.G and youngest daughter 18 studying Inter, I am educating my children to get them good private or government jobs.

We have our own House. We fetch drinking water from outside as we do not have any tap at home. We don't have bathroom, latrine, current, facilities at home.

My wife knows 'Nawar' netting work. She learned it from her parents. Now she does this work at home. I also help her in doing the Nawar work. Nawar raw material costs 1200/- rupees and machinery equipment costs extra, we have used our own savings to purchase the same. Nawar works does not give good benefits. We have to work for 2 to 3 days to prepare the Nawar used for one cot. We get less profit from it. Even though we could not get much income out of the work, we do it without stopping because we only know this work besides 'Band Baza' and also paradoxically 'Band Baza' also do not provide full employment all the time.

I go for Band work during the marriage season and I get 400/- to 500/- rupees as daily labour. In agriculture season I also do agriculture work. Whenever I get time I go to daily wage band work. In unseason I face financial problems and livelihood becomes very hard. We are working hard for educating our children. We would like to give good position to them in the society. I am the head man of our caste. I solve some of my caste people's problems. I am satisfied with my headmanship.

I go to Warangal to bring Nawar material for my wife. I also go to band work on scheduled days. I have to work there till the completion of programmes. We don't have any other Income source except these Nawar nettings work of my wife, I do other work to earn money for my children education for our livelihood. I did the band work and went to school and college and study simultaneously in the beginning. Then I had to focus only on my traditional occupation. Only during the seasons we find work. There are many changes taking place in our profession and some outside people are investing huge capital and becoming owners of D.J. Band material to rub our work. Now everyone prefers DJ Bands and we are hardly involved and only in villages we have some demand and there too there was lot of competition amongst us. Due to this we had to reduce the charges and we have to work for more hours to do for less now. Day by day our profession is changing due to technology and we are not able to cope up with the changes ourselves and as a result we had to stay back and become outdated.

Some of the Issues include:

1. We have work availability only in 'season' for some days.
2. Regarding health, we get joint pains, neurotic pains and eyes problems due to the drudgery work.
3. Family problems: We are facing financial problems to meet, Children's, education and daughter's marriage expenditure.

4. Caste Problems: We are discriminated because of our low caste. I am trying to unite our people as there is a division among the people.
5. We are not getting any loan facility from our society/ federations.
6. Band artists are harassed by police on the pretext lack of permission to do work at nights.

Mohd Hajmeera (Dudekula)

My name is Mohd Hajmeera, aged 62 did not go to school due to financial problems. My father and forefathers also were not educated and they were doing the band mela activity. Since 40 years I am playing the Band instruments in festivals and marriages.

My wife 52 years old uneducated and working as agriculture labour. We have three male children, one aged 28 years working in a tent house and other 27 years working with us and another 24 years studying degree.

I have small tiled house. I have bath room, toilet, cooking gas, facility at home. I have a Radio, Sewing Machine, one bicycle. We live with our neighbors in friendly manner and they are very co-operative with all of us.

We have the required tools for instrument keys and Band playing. We have purchased the instruments required from the city. We have a small shop in my house itself. We have started it with little budget. I have employed a couple of people we work as and as a team and daily wages are paid to them. Generally we have full work during marriage season and festival days. Whenever we have a programme we have to work in day and night as required by the families who hire us.

We are not getting any help from the Government or any loan from any other agency. Caste societies also helpless. In the night the police personal ask us to stop playing the band as it causes disturbance to the public. Sometimes they harass us while returning back from a function to go back to home and even demand money. Sometimes they are 'mistaken identities' which play havoc with our lives.

Our Community people are generally poor. We are a simple community. Our children do not have good education. We suffer from various physical problems such as knee pain and low vision etc., due to the occupational hazard of standing and walking for hours together while playing band. No one cares about these things when we were asked to do it continuously without break during the processions.

Our Problems Include

Lack of sufficient work; Due to availability of new sound technology, i.e., DJ sound system no one is offering work to us; Government no given subsidy for the purchase of the band instruments; No Bank loans; No work availability for doing cotton bed and pillows; No pension scheme to old age people.

My Suggestions Include

Government should assist us by giving employment to our caste members in temples and the Jataras; Free education to our children, and hostel facility and free books supply; old age pension to the workers; free medical checkup and treatment etc., Government should also extend financial assistance to purchase required band material and also equipment.

MD. Chand (Dudekula)

My name is Mohammed Chand. I am 42 years old. I have studied upto 10th class. Due to financial problems of my parents and also other family problems, I could not continue my education. My native place is Nagaram, village of Hasanparthy Mandal of Warangal district. At present I live in Nagaram village. My grandfather used to prepare cotton beds and pillows. My father also used to prepare cotton beds as well as worked as a Band Master. I learned both these works from my father. I have been doing these two works for 30 years. My wife is 37 years old. She studied up to 7th class. She is working in a Kiranam shop nearby my house. She gets 1000/- rupees wage per month. She goes to Kiranam work from 08:00 am to 6:00 pm and sometimes even after. She also does the household work at home and during the remaining time if any she helps me in bed preparation work. I have three children, one son and two daughters. My son is studying CA I year, daughter 19 in inter and youngest daughter is in 9th class. Children help my wife in domestic work. They do not do any other work relating to traditional occupation and we also do not allow them so that their education will not get side tracked. My wife is a member of Mahila group. We have our own RCC house, tap, bathroom, latrine facilities and also current, gas, radio, sewing machine, cooker etc., we have 20 guntas of agricultural land. We cultivate it and produce rice and the rice is useful for our family for sometime in the year. Our neighborhood is good and friendly.

My main occupation has been preparing cotton beds and especially during the marriage season I go for band work as a secondary occupation. I collect the required (cotton) raw material from Warangal town. During the college, school and admission time and in marriages seasons and other auspicious days, people come to our shop and purchase the cotton beds. During the peak season I employ extra person to do the work. I used to pay daily wage to him. I have paid 200/- rupees to him per day. People come to our home and purchase our cots and pillows. 10 years ago, there was much demand for our products, but now not many people prefer our material and the stock is piling up with us. We have all the raw material to prepare the pillows and cotton beds, brought from the market but the demand has been decreased heavily because of the availability of Jutes coir and Dunlop beds produced by big companies. Due to less demand to our pillows and Beds I was forced to mainly depend upon the 'Band Work' and other 'labour work'. As part of my work I trained a large number of our community people surrounding villages from in playing band instruments and they became Band artists now. I get Rs. 300/-to 400/- daily wage for this work. As per the programme we do the work during the day and sometimes during the nights. For night duties we get more but we face other problems too. Several of our Community men do not have their own band group and the material required for it. But to have separate band group of our own most people don't have enough capital. Government must provide personal loans to set up our own shop and Band group. Only then it would be beneficial to them. Otherwise they remain as workers throughout their life.

To prepare beds and pillows, in our own work shop we need an investment of Rs 50,000 rupees. I used my own savings of Rs. 30 thousand and borrowed Rs 20 thousand. I borrowed it from private money lender for interest. I paid the loan on easy installments. In preparation of beds and pillows, we have to work from morning to evening and sometimes we work for more hours, there would be no regular timings. We sell our products from our home and visit surrounding villages for sale. At present our sales are decreasing. We are not getting any government aid. My father is getting 200 rupees old age pension sanctioned by government in 2013.

In the absence of both Bed works and Band works, I used to go as daily wage worker. They give me daily wage and I feed my family with this money. Due to decreased professional work I am facing financial problems and I was forced to go for loans. We only expect that Government should come to our rescue and resolve the problems of our community.

Mohammad Sarwar (Dudekula)

My name is Mohammad Sarwar, native of Medipally village Jammikunta Mandal in Karimnagar District. I am 45 years old and studied upto 7th class and discontinued my studies due to financial problems. I am surviving now because of my traditional occupation. My wife 32 years old illiterate and she work in agricultural fields as a labour. We have two children, one son and one daughter. My son aged 21 years studied upto 8th class and discontinued and he is now working in a cotton mill in other village. My daughter aged 18 years completed 10th class but could not go for higher studies because of economic problems. My grandfather and my father also worked as a band Master and also worked in the agriculture field. We got a house under Indiramma Housing Scheme and having minimum facilities like electricity, water facility, bathroom, latrine, Radio and a Bicycle. My neighbours are friendly with us and we have one acre of agricultural land and all family members assist me in agriculture work. I work in a bed making workshop we prepare cotton beds and pillows and sell them in the market. I have learnt preparing cotton beds from my father. I also prepare other kinds of shaped material used for decoration as well as comfort with cotton materials. Our shop owner sells these cotton beds to the hostels on contract basis. I prepare 2 beds in a day and four pillows and I get upto 80 rupees for a bed and upto 30 rupees for two pillows. Whenever there is demand for beds we work for more number of hours and get more income.

We are facing many family problems due to poverty. Only in season we get some good amount of money and other days are very bad days for us and it is difficult to carry on our livelihoods. Our work is seasonal. Sometimes we get good work and sometimes no work. Unless we get some outside labour work we cannot pull on. Our community association is not in a position to help our members neither able to guide them to improve their occupational opportunities nor able to exert pressure on government to get welfare packages for their community. Since most of the Dudekula families are financially weak and poor they have no assets. They sincerely depend upon their traditional skill and labour.

I sum up that

1. Financially we are poor and need assistance from government and from other agencies.
2. To open a shop we need Bank Loans.
3. Government should supply cotton on subsidy basis.
4. We should be provided Health Cards and free medical checkup and medicines. We face problems affecting our lungs and also eyes, due to our occupational hazard.
5. Government should help us under the schemes like Balika Samarakshan and Kalyana Laxmi and other programmes.
6. Pension scheme to senior Dudekula professionals should be extended.
7. We don't have appropriate or helpful professional organizations or Cooperatives as such Government should encourage community cooperatives.
8. Government should provide us facilities to develop professionally, sanction training programme to establish own enterprises and extend necessary support.
9. Free and compulsory residential education need to be provided to our children.

MD. Abbas (Dudekula)

My name is MD. Abbas, age 66 years studied upto VI class. Due to financial problems I had discontinued my studies. My native place is Madipally Village in Jammikunta Mandal of Karimnagar District. I came to Kothapally from Madipally 50 years back. My father and forefathers worked as makers of cotton beds and pillows and also work in band melam on festival and marriage days. I am doing the same traditional occupation since 40 years.

We are three in my family. Myself and my wife aged 61 years and one daughter live together. My wife is illiterate. She helps me in my Bed preparation work. My daughter 36 years old studied upto inter and got married. She is working as Anganwadi worker. We are living in a rented tiled hose. I have one Bicycle and Cooking Gas, T.V and other minimum facilities. I have no pet animals in my house. As I live on the side of the main road, there has been lot of noise in the surroundings. We need cloth, cotton, stretching thread etc, to prepare the Beds and Pillows. We have opened one shop 15 years ago and in the beginning for five to six years there used to be plenty of work. But after that there has been gradual decrease of work and as a result, there was steep fall in our income. Presently our family is facing financial crisis. We have no capital amount, no modern technology and tools and as a result there has been no positive change in our family life.

I learnt to play Band and bed making from my father. Whenever is required I turn myself as Band master during marriages and festival days and maintain a band. I have started selling Beds and pillows from my house for some time and it was good in the beginning. But now-a-days on one is purchasing our products. Most of the people prefer factory made products and other material available outside and they are attractive and more useful. Some of the new bed making units come up recently is now doing the work with machines and due to this we are not able to get work. We have not received any assistance from Government nor any subsidy on material we use for the production of the beds.

We were neither trained in the use of new machines nor have any skills to adopt recent trends. Government is not assisting to us at all to promote our occupation. B.C Corporation is also not giving us any loan. Other caste members generally look down our community and our work. We also face a number of health problems.

Government should help our children and give free education with hostel facility, scholarships etc. Old age pensions, Health check up and medical aid to be given. Government should also provide loans, subsidy and margin money and help us to establish our own units. It should also provide needed material support, appropriate training and marketing facility. Otherwise there will be no hope for survival.

5

Padmashali- *The Handloom Weavers*

Padmashali (also spelt as Pamasali) is a Telugu Speaking Hindu artisan caste predominantly residing in the Indian states of Telangana, Andhra Pradesh, Karnataka and Tamil Nadu and were associated with the Satavahana Empire in olden days. The caste is traditionally recognized as an art and skill in weaving and textile businesses and is identified by different names in various regions throughout India. Some believe it is derived from the Sanskrit word 'Shali' meaning "silk cloth". In Tulu, Saalye or Taalye means "spider". Also, saaleedu means spider in Telugu. Probably symbolizing the weaving activity with the Spider's web, this word was coined for weavers.

The Padmashalis eventually specialized in weaving clothes of all varieties. They also made cloth from cotton and animate yarn (silk). Unlike other wool-based caste communities the Padmashalis developed exclusively cloth weaving skills. They produced cloth as a marketable commodity, without having any organic link or skills in the seeding and crop-cutting skills. Thus their skills structure, over a period of time, became one-dimensional. By the time the British arrived, the Padmashalis were producing huge quantities of cloth and controlled a leading cottage industry in India.

The introduction of the railways in 1853 by the colonial British government helped penetrate the self-sufficient rural economy. With the forced introduction of machine manufactured goods, especially finished cotton goods from the factories in Britain (making use of advances from the Industrial Revolution), the domestic textile industry suffered losses. Being an important node in the rural economy, the Padmashalis community also naturally felt the impact. Many Padmashalis as a result settled in the urban and semi-urban areas for better and those who can afford 'weaving occupation' and joining business activity.

The mother tongue of most members in the community is Telugu, even in areas where they have migrated generations ago to such places as Maharashtra, Karnataka and Tamil Nadu, except in the Dakshina Kannada district of Coastal Karnataka, where they speak Tulu. They have a visible tendency towards urbanization since the occupation of weaving and marketing cloth is easy from urban and semi-urban centers. Some urban Padmashalis who could persue higher education have abandoned their ancestral profession and have diversified into secular professions such as engineering, medicine, law, academia, administration, politics and business to name a few. A few of them have also migrated to foreign countries like the USA, UK and Australia. Though the community was always a socially advanced one, the majority of its members at the lower rungs are economically and educationally backward, as a result of which in the present day, Padmashalis are categorized as an Other Backward Class (OBC) by the Government of India despite its sanskritised practices. The Padmashali caste is highly Sanskritised, with all the men wearing the sacred thread like Brahmins and do Purohit work in the marriages of their community.

The Handloom Weavers

The Cotton textile industry in India consists of spinning and composite mills, power looms, and handloom industry is a significant one particularly in labour abundant countries like India because of its labour absorption capacity. Next to agriculture, handlooms provide more employment. The Indian handlooms have occupied an important position in respect to its exports to foreign countries.

The Indian handloom fabrics were popular in the world since Vedic period. Europe was a customer of Indian manufactures during 17th and 18th centuries up to the end of 17th century; the handloom industry in India was in a flourishing state. But its status was reversed during pre-independence era due to the colonial policies of the British Government on the one hand and the effect of industrial revolution on the other.

Tremendous expansion of productive capacity of manufactures resulted in increased demand of raw materials for British industry and the need to capture foreign markets. As a result, India was made sub-servant to the industries of Great Britain and was encouraged to produce raw materials for British factories. Consequently, Indian handloom industries as well as the life of the weavers were ruined. The establishment of textile mills in India and their capacity to produce even traditional varieties of cloth has further deteriorated the status of weaver. Handloom Cloth production came down during First World War period. The Civil Disobedience Movement helped the growth of international market for Indian cloth, by that to some extent the handloom industry progressed.

Till the middle of the 19th century, textile industry in India produced 100% handloom cloth and put it in circulation in the country besides a flourishing export market. But after the First World War, textile industry in India meant 75% mill cloth production and only 25% handloom cloth.

The Second World War however gave considerable stimulus for handloom cloth production for war requirements and enjoyed temporary prosperity.

The British Government of India gave importance to handloom industry in the middle of the 2015 century by appointing the Fact Finding Committee in 1941 to avoid the difficulties faced by handloom industry. This committee submitted its report on the size and scope of the handloom industry. As a result of its recommendation, First All India Handloom Board has come into existence.

After Independence, the Government of India has identified the significant role of handloom sector in the emergence of national economy. Consequently, several measures have been taken and priority has been given during Five Year Plan periods to preserve, protect and promote the sector.

Broadly we may find three categories of occupational workers drawn from the Padmashalis who were in the weaving profession:

1. Those who have their Own Family Enterprise.
2. Those who work under Master Weavers.
3. Those who are members of cooperative societies.

The following are the major works undertaken by Weavers as part of their activity

The handloom weaver weaves with the help of his whole family members. His female family members (especially wife) help him. Female workers helps him in bleaching, dyeing, winding, warping, street seizing etc. the whole family works at about 8 to 10 hours per day.

Bleaching

This work usually will be done women members of the family. Yarn should be bleached for whiteness in order to produce white cloth.

Dyeing

The women members of the weavers family dyes the yarn in different colours for weaving cloth in different colors and designs especially to produce silk sarees tyeing and dyeing work will be done by only women. They work 8 to 10 hour daily for dyeing and dyeing street sizing etc.

Winding

The women members of the weavers' family wind the yarn with the help of Charkha. Yarn is supplied to handloom generally in the shape of hanks. Ten hanks make one knot and 10 lakhs of such kinds are made into bundle and 40 bundles make one bale of yarn. These yarn hanks are taken to hand stand and wound on tin or wooden bobbins with the help of a charkha or winding machine by women.

Warping

About 40 or 44 bobbins at a time are taken to a horizontal warping machine and warps are prepared in required lengths ranging from 20 to 36 yards, one person with the help of another person can prepare 120 to 160 knots into warps per day. Prior to introduction of this horizontal warping machine, peg warping machine was in usage, with which about 4 to 5 knots only could be converted into wraps. This work is also done by women.

Street Sizing

To strengthen the warp threads of yarn, starch is applied and combed with brushed. This process is called street sizing. At a time 10 to 15 knots are taken for sizing and persons can do it in about 4 man hours, the women assist the weaver in street sizing.

Weaving

Weaving work will be generally done by only male weaver whereas other pre-weaving activities are done by female member of the family. The income derived by male waver in weaving is actually not of his own. Male weaver cannot weave without the help of his family members. It is the collective work of weavers' family. Therefore the remuneration should be called family remuneration and it is nor the income of the weaver alone. In some cases women also take part in weaving work and operate handloom (maggams) and it is found mostly in towns known for specialized weaving towns such as Siricilla, Pochampally, Chirala, Emmiganoor and other places we may find women weavers on a large scale.

The weaver has to exercise all his limbs, concentrate rate his eyes on work and be alert in mind at every stage sitting on the edge of a small pit, usually in a cottage the weaver operates the heralds with his legs and throws the shuttle from one side to the other either of his hands. At this stage the handloom is known as throw shuttle pit loom.

With the adoption of an improved device to swing the shuttle from one side to the other by pulling the strings tried to the shuttle driving cocks on either side, the handloom gets the name of a fly shuttle loom. Most of the weavers are weaving with the help of pit looms in their houses and only some weavers are weaving with the help of frame-looms as the societies are having less number of frame looms in their plants. Thus, most weavers depending upon pit looms, which gives less production. Handloom weaving, which has been done by the efforts of whole family makes female role high in the activity. The field work undertaken for the purpose of study highlights the detailed activity.

Size of Family in relation to Age & Place of Work

Table-5.1 indicates that around 35% of the respondents had three member families and a large majority of them belong to rural areas. Around 18% of the families had 5 and above members in their families. It is significant to observe that out of 321 members, 210 members were found to be in the age group of 56 and above. Further analysis indicates that only 36 respondents out of 321 were drawn from 'under 45 age group'.

It may be observed significantly that the younger generation amongst the Padmashalis was found leaving the profession in search of alternate employment. It has been found that those who could get education had the advantage of shifting towards modern occupations and those who could not join educational institutions had no other option except to continue in the hereditary occupation. The older generations with no education continue to uphold the occupation despite the unavailability of work and non-remunerative work situation.

Table 5.1

Size of Family in relation to age and place of work

Sl. No	Age	Place	Single	Two Members	Three Members	Four Members	Five members	Six Members & Above	Total
01.	Up to 25	Rurban	-	-	-	-	-	-	-
		Urban	-	-	-	-	-	-	-
		Rural	-	-	-	-	-	-	-
02.	26-35	Urban	-	-	-	-	-	-	-
		Rurban	-	-	3 (100) (4.76)	-	-	-	**3 (100%) (0.94)**
		Rural	-	6 (33.33) (5.40)	9 (50) (14.29)	3 (16.67) (5.88)	-	-	**18 (100%) (5.60)**
03.	36-45	Urban	-	3 (100) (2.70)	-	-	-	-	**3 (100%) (0.94)**
		Rurban	-	-	-	3 (100) (5.88)	-	-	**3 (100%) (0.94)**
		Rural	3 (33.33) (7.69)	-	3 (33.33) (4.76)	-	3 (33.33) (8.33)	-	**9 (100%) (2.80)**
04.	46-55	Urban				3 (50) (5.88)	3 (50) (8.33)		**6 (100%) (1.87)**
		Rurban	-	3 (33.33) (2.70)	-	6 (66.67) (11.76)	-	-	**9 (100%) (2.80)**
		Rural	3 (50) (7.69)	12 (20) (10.81)	6 (10) (9.52)	27 (45) (52.95)	3 (5) (8.33)	9 (15) (42.86)	**60 (100%) (18.69)**
05.	56-65	Urban	-	-	-	-	3 (100) (8.33)	-	**3 (100%) (0.94)**
		Rurban	-	3 (50) (2.70)	3 (50) (4.76)	-	-	-	**6 (100%) (1.87)**
		Rural	9 (9.09) (23.08)	36 (36.37) (32.44)	21 (21.21) (33.34)	9 (9.09) (17.65)	15 (15.15) (41.68)	9 (9.09) (42.86)	**99 (100%) (30.84)**
06.	66 & above	Rurban	-	-	-	-	-	-	**-**
		Urban	6 (25) (15.38)	12 (50) (10.81)	6 (25) (9.52)	-	-	-	**24 (100%) (7.47)**
		Rural	18 (23.08) (46.16)	36 (46.15) (32.44)	12 (15.38) (19.05)	-	9 (11.54) (25)	3 (3.85) (14.28)	**78 (100%) (24.30)**
Total			**39 (12.15) (100%)**	**111 (34.58) (100%)**	**63 (19.63) (100%)**	**51(15.89) (100%)**	**36 (11.21) (100%)**	**21 (6.54) (100%)**	**321 (100%) (100%)**

Education of Family Members

Table 5.2 indicate that amongst the Padmashalis persuing weaving occupation, 66.36% were illiterates, another 31% had education under 10th class and only under one percent had found to have been completed graduation. As far as the children and youngsters in the families of the respondents are concerned most of them in the current generation are found in the classrooms. There are a large number of families amongst the artisans whose first generation is just entered the portals of education. The fact that just around 6% completed graduation in the families indicates how they were continued to be neglected and 'excluded' from education. It has been found that women in the families are the major victims of 'educational exclusion' as they were found totally excluded or consciously neglected.

Generational Changes in the Occupational Pattern

Table 5.3 indicates the generational changes in the occupational pattern of the respondents and their parents and grandparents. The table significantly indicates that for four generations Padmashalis out of the five standards continue to stick on to their traditional hereditary occupation. It has been found that generations together 'weavers' continue to stick on to their age-old occupation. Some of those shifted from their occupations to other interestingly choose to join other traditional occupations. The table also significantly indicates that the present generation i.e., the sons of the respondents had changed the age-old occupational track to shift themselves towards other occupations or focused on their studies and education. It has been found that only 12.5% found opting to their father's occupation, while 4.16% shifted to other traditional occupations. While 41.67% had shifted to modern occupations and the remaining preferred 'education' to be the alternative. This shows that for various reasons there has been a change in the attitude of the present generation among the weavers to opt for other occupations.

Table 5.2

Education of Family Members (Cumulative Response)

Sl. No	Relationship with the Respondent	Illiterate	0-5 Classes	6-10 Classes	Inter	Degree	ITI/Other Technical Courses	Others	Total
01.	Respondent	213 (66.36) (41.52)	57 (17.76) (55.88)	48 (14.95) (26.67)	-	3 (0.93) (6.25)	-	-	**321 (100%) (34.85)**
02.	Father	12 (80) (2.34)	3 (20) (2.94)	-	-	-	-	-	**15 (100) (1.63)**
03.	Mother	18 (100) (3.50)	-	-	-	-	-	-	**18 (100) (1.95)**
04.	Wife/Husband	198 (84.61) (38.60)	12 (5.13) (11.77)	18 (7.69) (10)	-	6 (2.57) (12.50)	-	-	**234 (100) (25.41)**
05.	Son	51 (27.42) (9.94)	9 (4.84) (8.82)	66 (35.48) (36.67)	18 (9.68) (31.58)	27 (14.52) (56.25)	3 (1.61) (100)	12 (6.45) (66.67)	**186 (100) (20.20)**
06.	Daughter/ Daughter-in law	18 (14.63) (3.51)	15 (12.19) (14.71)	42 (34.15) (23.33)	36 (29.27) (63.16)	-	-	6 (4.88) (33.33)	**123 (100) (13.35)**
07.	Brothers/Sisters & Others	3 (12.5) (0.59)	6 (25) (5.88)	6 (25) (3.33)	3 (12.5) (5.26)	6 (25) (12.50)	-	-	**24 (100) (2.61)**
	Total	**513 (55.70) (100)**	**102 (11.07) (100)**	**180 (19.55) (100)**	**57 (6.19) 6(100)**	**48 (5.21) (100)**	**3 (0.33) (100)**	**18 (1.95) (100)**	**921 (100%) (100%)**

Table 5.3

Occupation (Cumulative)

Sl. No	Sample	Same Occupation	Other Traditional Occupation	Others	Study	Total
01.	Respondent	309 (96.26) (24)	12 (3.74) (57.14)	-	-	321 (100%) (22.48)
02.	Respondent's Father	318 (99.06) (24.71)	3 (0.94) (14.28)	-	-	321 (100%) (22.48)
03.	Respondent's Grand Father	321 (100) (24.95)	-	-	-	321 (100%) (22.48)
04.	Respondent's Grand Father's Father	321 (107) (24.95)	-	-	-	321 (100%) (22.48)
05.	Respondent's Son	18 (12.5) (1.39)	6 (4.16) (28.58)	60 (41.67) (100)	60 (41.67) (100)	144 (100%) (10.08)
	Total	**1287 (90.13) (100%)**	**21 (1.47) (100%)**	**60 (4.20) (100%)**	**60 (4.20) (100%)**	**1428 (100%) (100%)**

Education and Lengths of Occupation

Table 5.4 indicates the correlation between the education and the length of their occupation. The table indicates that only three graduates available out of 321 respondents who had entered into their parent's occupation (especially during the recent years) as they could not get any other job to their credit. The remaining 318 respondents had their education till tenth class joined their hereditary occupation at various stages of dropping out of their school education. As the primary purpose of the respondents was not to persue education, but only to pass time to make way to enter into their parent's occupation in their early age by dropping out. Thus for long education is no means of their choice.

Table 5.4

Education and Length of Occupation

Sl. No	Education	0-5 years	6-10	11-20	21-30	31-40	41-50	51 & above	Total
01.	Illiterate	-	3 (1.47) (20)	36 (17.65) (66.67)	66 (32.35) (70.97)	63 (30.88) (63.64)	33 (16.18) (78.57)	3 (1.47) (33.33)	**204 (100) (63.55)**
02.	0-5 Classes	-	3 (4.54) (20)	6 (9.09) (11.11)	15 (22.73) (16.13)	30 (45.46) (30.30)	6 (9.09) (14.29)	6 (9.09) (66.67)	**66 (100) (20.56)**
03.	6-10 Classes	6 (12.5) (66.67)	9 (18.75) (60)	12 (25) (22.23)	12 (25) (12.90)	6 (12.5) (6.06)	3 (6.25) (7.14)	-	**48 (100) (14.95)**
04.	Inter	-	-	-	-	-	-	-	-
05.	Degree	3 (100) (33.33)	-	-	-	-	-	-	-
	Total	**9 (2.81) (100)**	**15 (4.67) (100)**	**54 (16.82) (100)**	**93 (28.97) (100)**	**66 (30.84) (100)**	**42 (13.08) (100)**	**9 (2.81) (100)**	**321 (100%) (100%)**

Occupation of Children

It has been attempted in the study to analyze respondent's children's choice of occupation in relation to their migration. It may be observed that people migrate to other places in search of some or the other 'paid occupation', but the present study indicate that in the case of 'weavers', there was little choice. But significantly the present generation has by every means expressed their desire to 'shift' their choices of occupation.

Educational Dropout

It may be observed from the data collected that 50.47% of the respondents were illiterates as their parents did not send them to school due to various reasons. Significantly, the respondents did not think the away their parents, as they have started by themselves sending their children to schools. The remaining 49.53% of respondents had entered schools, but dropped out in the middle. They too now considered to send their children schools. Further analysis indicate that of those whose children were sent to schools, however only 27.10% of children continued their studies and the remaining 72.90% of children were dropped out and started either assisting their parents or doing some or the other odd job to support their parents families. It indicates that education still remained as a 'dream' for generations together and a major part of the families still unable to send their children to schools and those who attempted did not carry it forward.

Education and Training

Education status of respondents has no relation to their joining their traditional occupation and it also equally true in case of formal training. It has been found that 97.20% of respondents did not receive any formal training to carry on their jobs. The institution of family itself was their training institution and their parents themselves are their trainers. Children are drawn into the profession in their early age and since they assist their parents and observe the work of their parents and learn. The parents tutor them and help their children acquire skills needed. A few of the families send their children to their 'relatives' who found to have carried the profession successfully for training. Only 2.80% of respondents had the benefit of getting some sort of short term government sponsored training in an institution to learn new skills in weaving and designing. In the overall sense, the table indicates that the traditional weavers learn the techniques or acquire the skills needed by observing the work or assisting the parents in doing the work. It has continued generations together.

Family Assets and Facilities available in their Dwelling Places

It may be observed that only around one percent of families own some agricultural land which they cultivate seasonally or lease out to others. It is significant to observe that 99% of the sample families (318 out of 321) own residential accommodation with facilities such as bathroom and electricity at home. Only 45.79% families had toilet facilities and 46.73% of families had gas connection. They depend on various sources for drinking water. Around 43.93% own TV sets and 7.48% of families had sewing machines in their home, which their use for supplementing their incomes. In almost all the houses there was absence of pet animals. Other amenities such as Refrigerator, Rice-Cookers and Radios etc., are also not found in the houses, only under 19% of families own vehicles ranging from bicycles to motor cycles. In the overall sense except (under 10%) few most of the respondents are either found to be lower middle class or poor families which fall below the poverty line.

Occupation of Women in the Family

It has been observed that women in 81.31% families of respondents do some or the other work in the family enterprises. In most of the families women does almost all works including weaving various kinds of cloth. Early marriages are common in these families and women carry the occupation in their in-laws house. Age is no bar for women to carry on the job as women 'above the age sixty' also found in the occupation. Like men, women in these Padmashalis families work to support the families. It has been found that however those women in 18.69% of families of respondents shifted to other occupations such as petty trading agriculture work and other due to either of collapse family enterprise or non-availability of sufficient work in the families.

Occupational Priority

It has been said that modern economy provides plenty of choices to people for shifting their occupations, but it is hardly come true in the case of 'padmashali families'. 97.19% of respondents said that they had no choice except to stick on to their traditional occupation. Although some of them also does some other secondary jobs during some days, but it hardly influence their preference to shift their occupation. Amongst the sample respondents only 3% of respondents (9 out of 321 sample respondents) had shifted to some other jobs such as tailoring and other menial works. It shows that despite the 'weak economic support' the traditional occupation gives them, they had no other choice of occupation to look out for better survival.

Source of Employment

Table-5 indicates that only 14.95% had their own family enterprise or self-employment source as the remaining does the same job but outside their family enterprise. 75.51% of respondents does the job as 'price-rate weavers' in cooperative societies and the remaining 6.54% in wage employment under master weavers or working as piece rate workers in private societies who once upon a time had their own family enterprises to carry on their occupation independently. Most of them had their 'Maggams' (Handlooms) lying idle in their respective homes as scrap material. Thus the phenomena indicates forced shift from 'choice based self employment' towards a wage worker or piece rate work with lot of uncertainties.

Table 5.5

Sources of Employment

Sl. No	Respondent's Occupation	Self Employment	Society (Public/Private)	Wage Employment	Total
01.	Weaving	48 (14.95) (100)	252 (78.51) (100)	21 (6.54) (100)	**321 (100)** **(100)**
Total		**48 (14.95)** **(100)**	**252 (78.51)** **(100)**	**21 (6.54)** **(100)**	**321 (100%)** **(100%)**

Details of Production in relation to their Nativity

Table-5.6 indicates that the details of products produced by the sample respondents. It has been found that the sample respondents are found generally producing limited products such as Towels, Dress materials, Sarees, Lungis or Bed Sheets. It varies from rural to urban areas. It is significant to find that there is product variation in rural areas in comparison to urban areas. In rural areas 37.39% of respondents produce dress materials, 31.77% produce towels, 10.28% produce sarees, and around one percent produce lungis and bed sheets. In urban and semi-urban areas it has been found that a large number of them either producing Dress materials or to some extent lungis and bed sheets. Although everyone is proficient in producing all kinds of products, based on the demand or work assigned to them, they produce different kinds of products. Once up on a time in the families of several of the respondents (they narrate stories about the past glory when asked) used to produce fine cotton sarees, but now shifted to other products due to various reasons. Since the handloom industry 'both at the family level and also at the other production level' gradually found collapsing and the range of choice of products have become limited and getting reduced.

Table 5.6

Details of Production in relation to nativity

Sl. No	Name of the Product		Main Products	Total
01.	Urban	1. Towels	-	-
		2. Dress Materials	12 (100) (3.74)	12 (100) (3.74)
		3. Sarees	-	-
		4. Lungis/Bedsheets	-	-
02.	Rural	1. Towels	102 (100) (31.77)	102 (100) (31.77)
		2. Dress Materials	120 (100) (37.39)	120 (100) (37.39)
		3. Sarees	33 (100) (10.28)	33 (100) (10.28)
		4. Lungis/Bedsheets	3 (100) (0.94)	3 (100) (0.94)

Investment Details

It has been found that the maximum investment made by those who own family enterprises are of small or micro in nature even the cost of all assets put together. The maximum investment made towards construction of shop floor/shed, tools, raw materials and other was only Rs. 50,000/-. Out of 69 respondents who own family enterprises of their own, 86.96% (60 respondents) made a paltry investment upto Rs. 10,000/- most of it for purchasing tools and raw materials, while 13.04% (9 respondents) invested up to Rs. 50,000/- spending towards construction of shop floor/shed. It shows that the family enterprises owned are 'tiny' in nature and the investment made are not high.

The sources of investment made towards the enterprise have been mainly drawn from their savings, while the other had to rely on the 'money lender'. The Nationalized or regional banks had extended no support at all to these artisan communities. Despite the fact of lot of promises made by the Government officials or Political spokes persons or Bankers, they are of no use to these people. The organized sector can get financial assistance through banks or government departments in the form of loan or subsidy respectively without any difficult unlike these Own Account Enterprises. Despite the fact that these artisan groups need low cost technology, improved investments and raw materials they can invest money on their own and they do not get funds from public or private sources at reasonable rates of interest. Lack of proper guidance, lack of formal education and lack of sufficient economic background come in their way to procure public investment. As there was no other way, most of the artisans depend on money lenders who invariably try to exploit them by charging exorbitant rates of interest or purchasing their products at abnormally low price in return. Thus the role of institutional finance in extending financial assistance is very limited. All this makes their conditions highly deplorable.

Production Plan

The normal practice found in majority of cases was that they produce their products based on the market demand or orders received by them. In majority of cases other than the own account or family enterprises, their production plan depends upon the orders placed by the society or others. For the purpose of analysis the respondents could be classified into three types such as those working for society (both public and private) as its members, those who work under master weavers and those under family enterprises. Those who work as members of a weavers cooperative society draw their production plan as the society demands, while those work under master weavers (societies entirely owned by master weavers) do what their masters demand since they are only wage workers. Those belong to own account or family enterprise had some freedom to produce. Their customers vary from shop owners to individual salesmen to individual buyers to lenders and based on the general demand and demand from the regular customers, they work out their production plans.

Raw Materials

The normal practice has been that in the case of societies and master weavers, the supply of raw material is done by the managements and the individual artisan workers are nothing to do with it. While in the case of Family Enterprises procurement of raw materials is really a problem. The non-availability of quality raw materials in the open market, high price of quality raw material and travelling long distances to procure raw materials has been a major problem for them. Those who take loans from the money lenders, sometimes had to purchase the raw materials from their own stores with higher prices also cause much concern.

Sale of Product

Weavers belonging to Family or own account enterprises face a number of problems with regard to the sale of their products. Since the society members and those who work under master weavers, marketing was done by their employing agencies. But in the case of individual enterprises the following channels are found:

1. The Weaver Family themselves

The producers open an informal shop in their own house and sell their products or move around the places or villages selling their products or selling to their regular customers.

2. **Orders placed by shop keepers or money lenders (those who provide loans to the concerned) or other middle men.**

3. **The local market conditions and nature of customers.**

In all the above three categories, however the producers had little say in fixing the prices finding appropriate profit margin and in most of the cases the producer always stands at the receiving end.

Government Schemes

As far as the Padmashalis are concerned, the Government schemes hardly reach them as they were never been the target group for a government scheme. The policy statements of governments mainly bother about the Mills or big cotton industry societies and even master weavers but not individual family entrepreneurs. The general schemes such as Aadharana scheme, Artisan Credit card, Bank Loans etc., did not reach them at all. Some of the above 70 age group artisan gets government or occupational pension due to old age and it is too meager to resolve their economic problems. As a result of it not even a single respondent had developed any positive feelings towards the Governments attitude.

Around 30% of respondents felt that the government has been ignoring their interests and seem to be negatively disposed towards their problems. The rural producers face not only a large number of problems but they had also more or less formed a negative idea about government coming forward and helping them.

Role of Associations

Almost all respondents are found to be either members of their community Associations or their own artisan group associations. Female members are found to be the members of DWAKRA groups, it has been said by most of the respondents that although they were members of these groups/associations, they do not take much interest either in leading them resolve their problems or representing their grievances to government for readdressal. The respondents from rural areas feel much 'hurt' due to 'inaction' on the part of these Associations. As these sections are 'unorganized' and their Associations do only a little, they feel 'isolated' and deprived.

When probed further, the respondents had cited the following problems faced by them.

1. Non-availability of raw materials
2. Non-availability of investment capital
3. Growing market considerations/competitions from factory products
4. Quality problem
5. Pricing problem
6. Penetration of international market and monopoly branded items.

The individual weavers employed outside or self employed had to face all the above problems with variations in intensity and suffer from it.

The respondents also felt that the successive Governments have not shown any enthusiasm to express any concern towards their growing problems. They felt that there was no clear cut policy on the part of the government to tackle their problems. It has also been felt wherever there are certain policy directions aiming at resolution of the problems, they were hardly implemented by the concerning agencies or officials meant for it.

Due to some of these problems, the members of this community feel themselves let down by the society in general and the government in particular. A large majority of respondents feel 'degraded' and loss of 'self esteem' as the attitude of the general public towards them also seem to be generally 'indifferent'. Due to this there has been shift in the occupational pattern or to large scale migration to other areas in search of livelihood even to carry their own occupation there. It has been found that in almost every family there was 'out migration' ever to outside states and countries atleast by one member from the families during the last two generations. Due to this, there were many tensions in the families and large scale suicides have been committed during the recent years.

Select Profiles/Case Studies of Weavers

Chandanala Rajendar (Padmashali)

My name is Chandanala Rajendar. I am 52 years old native of Ellandu village, district Khammam. As the weaving work is not available in our village, I came to Hanamkonda 7 years back and settled here. I learnt our professional work from my father. We had been living on this profession since long back. I know how to weave on Maggam (Handloom). At the same time I learnt Tailoring from my uncle's son. Now I am stitching clothes also.

We are five members in our family. My wife, three children and myself. I stopped my education in 5th class and started weaving work. My wife is an illiterate she is doing household work. My son (24), is studying M.B.B.S, my daughter (23), is in B.Tech. My youngest daughter is in B.Sc (M.P.C) Degree Course. As I wanted that there should be a 'full stop' to the generational hereditary work our fore fathers are doing, somehow even with many difficulties I encouraged my children to only concentrate on education.

We used to own a house in our village, but we sold it and now living in a rented house with two rooms in Warangal. We do not have any agricultural land. I have a bicycle. We have electricity, water tap, bathroom, latrine facility in our house. We have a Television and L.P.G Gas connection.

Originally my primary occupation has been weaving cotton cloth. But at the same time I also do tailoring as my secondary work. We had our own handloom workshop in village. After the production of sarees, dress materials towels etc., we have to sell our products by ourselves. As the occupation is not able to earn the required income, I had decided to shift my place of work and also occupation. So we decided to go some other place from there. After my marriage I stayed there till my children's primary education. Later, came back to Warangal city to keep in my mind children's higher education. While coming to this place we sold all our properties in my village. In city I thought of making Tailoring as my primary occupation. In the beginning nobody gave me work in Warangal. I wondered a lot in different places and different employers for many days. My family faced a lot of trouble in the beginning later I could find some work somehow here. In the beginning I joined in a Tailor shop on piece rate work basis. The shop owner is known to me earlier. Every day I go to shop at 8:00am. If there is work I do work. If not I wait for the customers to come on the arrival of the customers, the owner handover to me the clothes to be stitched. I stitch clothes and give them back to my owner. Then the owner would decide my stitching charges. The shirt will have one rate and trousers will have another rate. The income would depend on the quantity of my daily work. I normally get 70/- rupees per shirt and I take 2 hours to stitch it and for trouser Rs. 100/- but I take 3 and half hours to stitch it. I can stitch at least two dresses per day. Whenever there is more work I do it at home overnight and handover the stitched dresses in the next day morning. After my initial years of work in a shop I started my own tailoring shop and the experience which I gained there in the shop where I worked, I developed many contacts which were later became helpful to run my shop successfully. Now I am able to establish myself as a successful tailor and started earning respectable income.

I didn't get any help from Government till today. I did not earn any property, with this work but I am somehow able to gain my normal livelihood and look after the education of my children.

I have been facing certain financial problems especially to meet the education fee of my children. I tried to overcome my problems. As I had little education, I thought good education to my children despite financial problem. For the last two decades no one in my family had joined in any good job. Hence I made up my mind to help my children get good education. I am successful in my attempts and my children had also worked hard to get free seats in their professional education.

Like other artisan professionals, this profession is also facing stiff competition from corporate and readymade dressmakers. We go further, it may be difficult to get sufficient work and assured income may be a remote possibility. In future we are afraid that we may have to either join a dress making factory or leave the profession and look out some other. As I have no education and other skills, choosing non-professional work will be the only alternative. In these circumstances the future of my profession seems to be uncertain and bleak and we are left to the mercy of our own fate.

Mulka Thirupathaiah (Padmashali)

My name is Mulka Thirupathaiah. I am 65 years old; my native place is Gangadevipally village, Geesugonda Mandal of Warangal District. I am living in my village since my birth and doing my traditional work since I attained the age of 20 years. I am doing handloom work for the last 45 years. I studied upto 3rd class and discontinued. My wife 56 years old, illiterate, my son 24 years old doing degree course. I am the only person working now in my family. My father, grandfather and all did the same profession.

I have got my own house. It is a tiled house; I have drinking water tap, bathroom, latrine, current and also cooking gas facility in my house. I do not have any agriculture land. My primary work is handloom work. I produce sarees, dhotis, towels, lungis, bed sheets and these will be sold by visiting villages going on Bicycle. My wife also participates in production as well as in sales by visiting houses. The amount which we get out of the work is not sufficient to lead a good life.

I have my own Maggam (loom), Nade (Jota), Vankelu, Sae Tadu, Ratnam, Tikkedi, Pakdlu, Chekkdu, Achu Karralu, Kalu, Kanche etc., (all the traditional instruments of production) in my workshop-cum-home. In the beginning I used to spend my own capital amount to get the raw material and produce on my own and sell it in the open market. But I was not successful and I incurred losses. Now I started collecting the raw material from 'master weavers or Asami' and give the product to him for which he pays me. There is no loss to me now but I get only insufficient price for my labour as there is a middleman who earns more.

Myself and my wife work in the house. We do not have any specified time to work. As and when we feel we work and finish the product. We know the time specified by the "Asami" is crucial as we have to handover the product on time to get continuous work from him. When I did the work on my own I used to sell the product as and when I get time and money is required. Now the raw material is given by the middleman. I have to give him back the product and the responsibility for its sale lies on his shoulders. But because of his market connection, it will be a smooth sail for him. Though it is our traditional occupation and since birth we learn and do it in the family, we have no control over either production or distribution. Although we are doing this work on full time or over time basis there is no good income out of this work. It is very difficult to lead a comfortable life. Even though we both work hard we do not get good returns. My son now studying degree course, but we find it difficult to provide him good facilities. We have most painful experiences in our life, which are hard to forget.

If the Government provides us Bank loan and subsidy on raw materials, it would ease our difficulties to some extent. Due to poverty and failure to pay the loans which we have taken from money lenders, we are in depression and one of our family members in my villages had committed suicide. Our health conditions are deteriorating because of bad production environment and lack of facilities. Unless Government do something and rescue us there will be lot of uncertainty in our future.

Devana Veera Nageshwar Rao (Padmashali)

My name is D.V. Nageshwar Rao. I am 48 years old, Native of Ramnagar village in Amodagiri town, in the district Prakasham district of present Andhra Pradesh State. My grandfather and father also were engaged in the same traditional ancestral occupation. I haven't taken any training for this profession as I had learnt it from my father while working and developed the necessary techniques.

We are four in the family, with my wife and two children's. I studied upto 9th class. My wife stopped her studies after 3rd class. She does only house work. My elder son (28) persuing M.Sc., course and later joined in private service. Second one (22) now in degree. My entire family has been completely dependent on this profession as we have no other alternative income generating employment.

I have my own house. I built it with my own hands. It has a tiled roof. I don't have facilities like drinking water at home. Due to this we have arranged a special borewell. We don't have any agricultural land. We have the amenities like Gas, current, Bathroom and Latrine Facility at home.

I have friends not only in my caste but in other castes. My wife is a DWAKRA Group member. We have good environment around us. We are very happy with our neighborhood. We all live together irrespective of caste, creed and religion.

I weave Maggam (loom) at home. I have been doing this work relating to my caste profession since 35 years. I don't have any separate shop. In my house I have spared a part of the house where I weave clothes. I do the work alone and my wife cooperates and assists me. We produce more cloth in winter and summer and during the rainy season we produce less material. Children do not participate in our work. The owner (shahucar or master weavers) gives us raw material and other necessary material to us. We prepare the finished material and handover to him. He pays labour charges on piece rate basis to us. We produce only those materials as asked and on the demand of the 'middlemen' or shaukar. We don't decide the price of the material. The Sahukar decides and sells the material. Sometimes we have to forego our labour charges in case of defective weaving. He won't bear any loss. My wife and myself both prepare materials required. My wife prepares (Kandelu) Cotton rolls and I weave on Maggam machine. We used to prepare material with our own capital 10 years back but gradually we found marketing of the material is difficult. We are paid less rate for the materials we produce but we have no option. We prepare the material as per their demand and in this context we get atleast our cooli (labour) charges. Moreover we don't have the risk of selling. It is the risk of the owner. Last year I have produced 50 to 60 saries and apart from that I also weaved lungies and ordinary cloth as per the orders.

Whatever we earn it meets only our subsistence expenditure. We don't have any other option except to do the work because we don't know any other work. Government has not evolved any policy to extend necessary facility. There is lot of competition in our profession, as other caste person also does the work. For the last two generations our people are not getting good work. Our caste people are not at good in education. That is why they cannot as pire modern jobs. There are so many ups and downs in our profession. Now a day's modern women do not prefer our saries as handloom cloths are expensive and they go for other mill made cloths. Cotton rate is increasing; and finally the product rate also increased coupled to the labour charges and profit margins. Government is not giving any subsidy on cotton. I have all the machinery equipment with me but I could not make full use of them. If the Government provides loans and subsidy I may be able to do my production as well as business. Government should purchase our material which can be used for Government purposes by giving correct market price; otherwise our debts will increase and suicides will be the only option let open for us. During the recent years there are a large number of suicide deaths in our Community due to indebtedness.

My Suggestions:

- Government should give working capital and margin money to all weavers.

- Government should provide cotton to the weaver on subsidized price.
- Government should purchase our products or arrange market facility.
- Our handloom clothes must be exhibited in appropriate exhibitions.
- Handloom workers should be provided personal loan for consumption purposes when needed.
- Every worker must get Rs. 1000 pension after attaining 50 years of age.
- Training should be provided to the weavers to use new technologies.

Bathula Venkata Laxmi (Padmashali)

My name is B. Venkata Laxmi, 59 years age never went to school. I had learnt 'Maggam' work from my father and mother before my marriage. After my marriage I came to Warangal, my husband's place and joined him in the profession. I found the occupation gradually losing its charm. Suddenly due to some health problem my husband has died. I continued this profession even after my Husband's death. I continued the work later. Now I am also doing "Beedi Rolling" work to earn some additional income, along with weaving cloth.

We are five members in the family two sons, two daughters and myself. Elder son (26) studied degree and doing a private job. My two daughters 34 and 30 years already got married. Youngest son (19) stopped studies in 10th class and doing Gumastha (store clerk) work. My husband and my father lived mainly on this profession throughout their entire life and now I am doing it. I may be the last person in my family to do the traditional occupational work as my children had chosen a different path consciously and never wanted to return back to the hereditary profession although they know the work very well.

We have our own house with tap, bathroom, latrine and current facilities. Recently we have bought Gas (L.P.G) and T.V. As all the neighbourhood women are Mahila group members they are friendly. I have also utilized the opportunity to join a Mahila group. Though in the beginning I was able to work for more number of hours doing outside jobs now I am unable to do 'maggam work' regularly. Hence I am doing Beedi rolling work to get assured income. Earlier my husband used to manage the family well, but after his death, the burden fell on my shoulders. I have to feed my 4 children and look after their studies also. I told my problem to my relatives who are in "Bewandi". They responded positively and asked me to come over there. I went there, and did labour work in a weaving Karkana. First they gave me training in cotton rolling (Kandelu Chuttuta) work, after they gave training for other works. They provided me facilities but did not give me any regular job. I have to do whatever work they entrusted to me. They provided all raw material and equipment and we have to go there and do the work there. They pay the wage for our work. We had the opportunity to weave lungis, towels, nawar, hand kerchiefs, baniyans etc., we had to weave 10-20 at a time meager long cloth. After work we separate them one by one. We only get wage as per the quantity of work and no other benefits are available. We have to work daily there as per specifications. Naturally we give importance to quality but whatever material they give we produce cloth with that material. After some years I came back to my native place keeping in view of the studies of my children. I intended to do this work here in my village also but no one has encouraged me to do this work here and take my services. All looms are kept idle as there was no work availability and everybody had a hard time in the village. I thought of going back to Bewandi as I didn't find any work, but I learnt beedi rolling work and started doing this work. Since then I have been doing Beedi rolling work for my livelihood.

Till today Government has not given any help or encouragement to me. For this work I don't need any working capital. I collect it from the middle man or Broker who gives raw material, such as tendu, leaves, and tobacco in particular measurements. After making Beedis I handover them daily upto 15 bundles of Beedis. If any damage occurs we have to bear the loss. They pay 90 paisa per one Beady bundle. We are facing many problems with the Brokers. They extract more work and pay less. There has been a lot of exploitation. There is no one to regulate and stop the exploitation including the government. The labour welfare department hardly takes interest. Government must recognize the problem and help us otherwise the exploitation will carry on. Actually I am still interested to do my 'maggam weaving' work but government should create a condition to offer work by providing working capital and margin money to work independently. Government should provide personal loans and raw material and other equipment; there is a need to revive every handloom society and show work to them. Government should market the products and make regular payment. As individuals cannot purchase raw materials and sell their products on their own, Government should take the entire responsibility and help revive the handloom industry. Otherwise the persons like me will be at loss and turn to other works which are equally bad and exploitative. Handloom work has a glorious past which employed thousands, but now it has become a burden on our head because of non-policy or negative policies of the Government.

6

Meru- *The Tailoring Community*

The traditional occupation of Meru Communities is tailoring or stitching clothes and dress making. A Meru works for himself or for other tailors. Clients usually come from with in the locality or neighborhood. Some Merus also sell ready-made clothes from their shops or at weekend markets. The Merus are skilled at dyeing fabrics and Meru women are expert at embroidery. The Merus profession is poorly regarded and held in some contempt: a village proverb runs, "the tailor's boy will sew as long as he lives." Agriculture and daily-wage labour are some of their subsidiary occupations.

The community now has a number of designers, professionals and entrepreneurs. Although this community regards education as important, girls are not sent to school. The Meru are monogamous and practice adult marriage, though there are some instances of child marriage. Although they have some community Associations or councils to exercise social control especially in rural areas they are not common throughout all the regions. The Meru, before beginning their day's work in the morning commonly bow to their tools of the trade-Scissors, sewing machine and needle- and pray to them for a bountiful livelihood.

Tailoring is also as old as the profession of Weaving Cloth and it is still growing in villages and towns. Earlier long time ago, Tailors used to stitch clothes by hand, but sooner sewing machines appeared which made the job of a Tailor more rewarding. Though for a long time only Meru or Darji Communities were involved in the profession as one or more families used to live in the village to fulfill the tailoring needs of the village concerned. But over the years, the profession is being modernized and began to attract other castes and communities to do the job. In case of those families which are drawn from inside the community are trained hereditarily within the families concerned and those from outside the communities get themselves trained outside and start sewing units. With the growth of the profession individual community-based family enterprises also ventured to modernize themselves in many cases for surviving the competition. But those who entered fresh from outside, began to convert the occupation into a 'commercial undertaking' by opening Tailoring shops or firms with application of new techniques in designing and stitching the clothes. New kind of designing in dress making became big business now. As new fashions are emerging, 'ready-made dress making' became a big industry and began to flourish the markets with new fashionable materials with latest designing. All these development made the profession 'modern' but the original 'Meru' community in the process had lost their grip on the profession. In this background it has been attempted to collect first hand information relating to the socio-economic conditions and issues relating to their traditional occupation of the respondents of Meru Community.

Sample and Size of Family

Table 6.1 indicates that the study covers 180 Meru families drawn from Rural and Urban areas. 53.33% (96) families were drawn from urban areas, while 46.67% represent rural areas. Age-wise data indicates that about 66.67% of respondents (120) belong to 26-45 age-group, 16.67% (30)

households belong to 46-55 age-group, while another 16.67% (30) households belong to 56 and above age group. Some respondents (6.67%) were found to be even above 66 years of age amongst the sample.

It may be observed that a large majority of families (68%) of three to four member families, while 20% families had only 2 members in the families. In case of others, 3.33% had five members in the family, while another 3.33% had 6 and above members in their respective families.

Table 6.1 thus indicates that a large majority of the respondents were young and middle-aged, mostly drawn from urban areas with an average membership in their families between three and four. The sample also covers other age-group and rural based households with family members both at minimum level and also large-number of membership in their respective families to that extent the sample is ideal and representative.

Table 6.1
Size of the Family

Sl. No	Age	Place	Single	Two Members	Three Members	Four Members	Five members	Six Members & Above	Total
01.	Up to 25	Urban	-	-	-	-	-	-	-
		Rural	-	-	-	-	-	-	-
02.	26-35	Urban	-	12 (40) (33.33)	6 (20) (25)	6 (20) (6.25)	-	6 (20) (100)	**30 (100) (16.67)**
		Rural	-	-	-	30(100) (31.25)	-	-	**30 (100) (16.67)**
03.	36-45	Urban	-	-	-	42 (100) (43.75)	-	-	**42 (100) (23.32)**
		Rural	-	-	6 (33.33) (25)	12 (66.67) (12.5)	-	-	**18 (100) (10)**
04.	46-55	Urban	-	-	-	-	12 (100) (100)	-	**12 (100) (6.67)**
		Rural	-	-	12 (66.67) (50)	6 (3.33) (6.25)	-	-	**18 (100) (10)**
05.	56-65	Urban	-	-	-	-	-	-	**-**
		Rural	-	18 (100) (50)	-	-	-	-	**18 (100) (10)**
06.	66 & Above	Urban	6 (50) (100)	6 (50) (16.67)	-	-	-	-	**12 (100) (6.67)**
		Rural							
Total			**6 (3.33) (100)**	**36 (20) (100)**	**24(13.34) (100)**	**96 (53.34) (100)**	**6 (3.33) (100)**	**6 (3.33) (100)**	**180 (100%) (100%)**

Education of Family Members

Table 6.2 indicates the educational attainment of family members of the sample households. The members of families, who include the respondents, their spouses, parents, brothers and sisters, sons and daughters. Those who live together in a house were taken into consideration as a family unit and data were collected from the family members. As far as the respondents are concerned, 18.75% were illiterates, 17.39% studied upto 5th class, and 36.59% between 6th to 10th class and 57.15% had intermediate qualifications to their credit. Among the family members the younger generation (sons and daughters) seen to be all literates and educated including 8.74% (54) of them graduates and even holding the professional degrees like B.Tech and M.B.A. The parents of the respondents had a minimum education; while 13% (12) were illiterates the spouse of respondents had almost identical educational levels. Some of them had education upto intermediate level, while a large number of them (68.75%) were illiterates. The educational situation in these Meru families indicate that the elders in the family were less educated, their forefathers were almost illiterates, while the younger generation being prone to education reached new heights to become professional graduates. There has been clear shift in the attitudes of these families as the present generation clearly thinks that education is of high priority.

Table 6.2

Educations of Family Members

Sl. No	Relationships with the Respondent	Illiterate	1-5 Classes	6-10 Classes	Inter	Degree	ITI/Other Technical Courses	Others B.Tech/ MBA	Total
01.	Respondent	18 (10) (18.75)	24 (13.33) (17.39)	90 (50) (36.59)	48 (26.67) (57.15)	-	-	-	**180 (100) (29.12)**
02.	Father	6 (50) (6.25)	6 (50) (4.35)	-	-	-	-	-	**12 (100) (1.94)**
03.	Mother	6 (100) (6.25)	-	-	-	-	-	-	**6(100) (0.97)**
04.	Wife	66 (42.30) (68.75)	24 (15.39) (17.39)	48 (30.77) (19.51)	18 (11.54) (21.42)	-	-	-	**156 (100) (25.24)**

05.	Son	-	48 (29.63) (34.78)	72 (44.45) (29.27)	6 (3.70) (7.14)	6 (3.70) (50)	-	30 (18.52) (71.43)	**162 (100) (26.22)**
06.	Daughter	-	36 (37.5) (26.09)	30 (31.25) (12.20)	12 (12.50) (14.28)	6 (6.25) (50)	-	12(12.50) (28.57)	**96 (100) (15.54)**
07.	Brothers/Sisters & Others	-	-	6(100) (2.43)	-	-	-	-	**6(100%) (0.97)**
	Total	**96 (15.54) (100)**	**138(22.3) (100)**	**246 (39.80) (100)**	**84 (13.59) (100)**	**12 (1.94) (100)**	-	**42 (6.80) (100)**	**618(100%) (100%)**

Generational Shift of Occupations

Unlike the other artisan groups there has been some significant shift in the occupational pattern of the respondents. About 96.67% of respondents practicing the traditional occupation as their primary activity, while the remaining 3.3% were in other related traditional occupation. It may be observed that the respondents were found to have been consciously chosen their main occupation which essentially stands as their hereditary traditional occupation, while there has been a lot of a variation in the occupation of their children. As it has been found that around 40% of the respondents (sons & daughters) children were still pursuing education at various levels, those who had already completed their education joined various jobs which indicate non-traditional pattern. While the last four generations and much earlier adopted predominantly the same hereditary traditional occupation, the present generation seems to be shifting drastically. It may be seen from Table 6.3 that only 26.67% of respondents joined their forefather's profession, while 5% in other related traditional occupations, 18.33% were in modern occupations. The remaining was in studies and all of them prefer to join other than their traditional occupation. The respondents are of the opinion that their children should become professionals or Government officials so that they need not lose the benefits of the modernization of economy.

Table 6.3

Occupation

Sl. No		Same Occupation	Other Traditional Occupation	Modern Occupations including Government Jobs	Other Jobs	Others/ Studies	Total
01.	Respondent	174 (96.67)	6 (3.33)				180 (100)
02.	Respondent's Father	162 (90)	18 (10)				180 (100)
03.	Respondent's Grand Father	162 (90)	12 (6.67)		6 (3.33)	6 (3.33)	180 (100)
04.	Respondent's Grand Father's Father	156 (86.66)	12 (6.67)		12 (6.67)	12 (6.67)	180 (100)
05.	Respondent's Son	48 (26.67)	09 (5.0)	33 (18.33)	10 (5.56)	80 (38.89)	180 (100) (100)

Education and Length of Occupation

There has been a greater shift in the occupational pattern, the main motivating factor seem to be the education. As it may be found that the higher the education amongst the people of the community, the greater the chance of moving towards modern occupations. Thus those who have no education or less education seems to be continuing in

Table 6.4

Education and Length of Occupation

Sl. No	Education	0-5 years	6-10	11-20	21-30	31-40	41-50	51 & above	Total
01.	Illiterate	-	-	6 (33.33) (9.09)	6 (33.33) (20)	-	-	6 (33.33) (100)	18 (100) (10)
02.	0-5 Classes	6 (25) (33.333)	-	-	6 (25) (20)	-	12 (50) (100)	-	24 (100) (13.33)
03.	6-10 Classes	6 (6.25) (33.333)	30 (31.25) (71.43)	42 (43.75) (63.63)	12 (12.5) (40)	6 (6.25) (100)	-	-	96 (100) (53.34)
04.	Inter	6 (14.28) (33.333)	12 (28.58) (28.57)	18 (42.86) (27.28)	6 (14.28) (20)	-	-	-	42 (100) (23.33)
05.	Degree	-	-	-	-	-	-	-	-
06.	Others	-	-	-	-	-	-	-	-
	Total	**18 (10) (100)**	**42 (23.34) (100)**	**66 (36.67) (100)**	**30 (16.67) (100)**	**6 (3.33) (100)**	**12 (6.66) (100)**	**6 (3.33) (100)**	**180 (100%) (100%)**

the same traditional occupation, while the younger generation with sufficient education, preferring to continue in higher education or join other than the traditional occupation. The data given in table 6.4 confirms the general understanding. The short period of their service in the traditional occupation indicates the higher rate of their education they possess and the longer the service in traditional occupation indicating the lower level of education.

Stated Occupation of Children in relation to Migration

There may also be found from the data that those who migrate to urban areas with or for higher education, tend to join modern occupations other than their traditional occupation. Those who stayed back in the villages did not shift their occupations. Those who stayed back in urban areas witnessed gradual shift in their pattern of education and occupation. The educational dropout of the family members of the respondents has the direct bearing in their occupational status. Those who have not dropped out from education found invariably shifting towards other occupations.

Occupation of women in the Family

It may be observed from table 6-5 that women in 43.33% of families of the sample respondents stayed back in the traditional occupation of their spouses and supported them by sharing the work. In 33.33% of families it may be found that the women joining some other occupation, other than the occupation of their respective husbands. The remaining 23.33% found either in education or keeping idle at home as house wives. Thus may be found women shifting towards education and other non-traditional occupation. Those who have stayed back in the traditional occupations learnt the skills of the trade by observation and those who had shifted to others occupations however had some training.

Table 6.5

Occupation of Women in the Family

Sl. No	Age	Involving in Occupation	Doing other work	Idle/unmarried/ Housewife	Total
01.	Up to 25	-	-	-	-
02.	26-35	30 (38.46) (38.46)	48 (6.08) (80.0)	-	78 (100) (43.34)
03.	36-45	42 (53.84) (53.84)	12 (15.38) (20.0)	24 (30.77) (57.14)	78 (100) (43.34)
04.	46-55	-	-	6 (100) (6.25)	6 (100) (3.33)
05.	56-65	-	-	12 (100) (12.50)	12 (100) (6.66)
06.	66 and above	6 (100) (7.70)	-	-	6 (100) (3.33)
	Total	**78 (43.33) (100)**	**60 (33.33) (100)**	**42 (23.33) (100)**	**180 (100%) (100%)**

Assets

It may be found from the available data that only 3.33% of respondents living in rural areas had some agricultural land which they prefer to cultivate seasonally. 90% of respondents (162 out of 180) had their own house, while 10% did not possess any house of their own. Around 3% had Bullocks, Fowls and other birds to their credit. 48% of the respondents had owned some vehicles, while half of them had scooter or motor cycles. 92% of respondents had bathroom and latrine facility in their respective homes. All the respondents had power connection, drinking water facility and gas connection. Only 6% of house did have TVs in their home. Only 13.33% had Radios, while other (only 10%) had Rice Cookers in their respective houses. 6% of respondents had subscribed to the news papers. In all, the asset position indicates moderate development of the families in relation to other artisan groups.

Place of Work

It may indicate that 43.33% of the respondents established their sewing units in their own houses, while 36.67% had opened a separate shop of their own outside their house and the remaining 20% had adopted the same occupation but joined some tailoring firm as wage employees.

Investment Particulars

It may be observed that 12.5% of the respondents had set up 'workshops separately which needed investment. It shows that 43.25% had invested upto Rs. 10,000/- while 21.88% had an investment ranging from Rs. 10,001 to 50,000/. 9.37% had invested in between Rs. 50,000/- to 1 Lakh and around 3% had invested between 1 lakh and 2 lakhs. The investment has been made mainly on converting a part of their house or renting an accommodation and converting it as a show-room-cum work place, purchase of sewing machines, other tools, raw materials and others. As most of them were self employed, they need a separate shop floor for the purpose of work. Most of the respondents seen to have purchased the machines and other materials required from nearby towns and cities.

Source of Investment

About 70% of the respondents had said that the investment they made was from their savings only, while only 12% had secured bank loans. The remaining 18% had secured the required amounts from various sources including chit funds, relatives, companies and money lenders. The later part of investment seems to have been made by taking short term loans. Access to banks is limited but it is relatively higher in comparison to other OBC artisan groups. Tailoring has been considered more or less a white collared artisan and it carries relatively higher status than others. Tailoring also had seasonal impact as during the marriage and festival season they have more work and during these periods they work even for extra hours. In case of non-seasonal times they hardly get work. But those who have contacts and had sound public relations invariably get work during all times. Sometimes some of the respondents also found undertaking piece work, working for others and also doing repair works. Like some of the other OBC service or artisan communities, Meru community people were not involved in ceremonial jobs.

Government Schemes

Table 6-6 indicates that Government schemes are 'distant dreams' to most of the Meru households, only 3.33% of the Meru households could get 'Sewing machine' under Aadharna schemes, while 12.22% of respondents could get bank loans. The artisan credit card scheme, Government pension scheme, occupational schemes and others were not within the reach of these families.

Table 6.6

Government schemes

Sl. No	Government Schemes	Available	Not Available	Total
01.	Artisan Credit Card	Nil	180 (100)	**180 (100)**
02.	Aadarana Scheme	6 (3.33) (100)	174 (96.67)	**180 (100)**
03.	Bank Loans	22 (12.22)	158 (87.88)	**180 (100)**
04.	Govt. Pensions	Nil	180 (100)	**180 (100)**
05.	Occupational Pensions	Nil	180 (100)	**180 (100)**

Role of Community Associations

There has been mixed reaction towards the role of Community Associations though the Associations were found useful for celebrating social and cultural events, they fail to work as pressure groups to gain benefits from governments. These Associations however fix the rates of stitching for various works relating to dress making including shirts, pants etc., and everyone is expected to follow them. This kind of fixing the minimum rate for stitching had helped them maintain their income levels. There was also a problem of multiplicity of Associations existing resulting in leadership clashes and division among rank and file. But in any case, in the overall sense, the Associations could play only a little role to earn benefits to its community.

It may be seen that the female members in the family join various DWAKRA or SHG which are beneficial to the families to some extent. 42% of spouses of the respondents had the benefit of joining the groups and organizations carrying their activities successfully. As the Government extends benefits such as loans with nominal interests and in easy installments repayments, it helped most of the families during the difficult situation.

Occupational Problems

The main problems faced by Meru community seem to be 'stiff competition' they encounter from readymade shops and subsequent fall in their work orders and lowering levels of income. New fashions, design, styles, combinations etc., all made these traditional tailoring community outdated and outmoded. The emergence of high profile Tailoring shops made the customers shift their loyalties and the traditional tailors with no attractive 'show room' facility lose their grip on their trade. Further raw materials need for stitching and designing also made them raise prices to their disadvantages. More and more competition from their own counterparts also resulted in 'reduction' in work orders. Despite the fact that a most of their over-work during the festivals and marriage seasons, income range according to them has been not satisfactory.

Major Solutions

The main suggestions made by most of the respondents include mainly that government should come forward to offer work orders relating to Hospitals, Uniforms of Residential Schools, Corporation, Municipalities, Factories and other Departments. Such a huge work should be able to provide lot of employment and work to this community and help them earn their livelihood. Further government should set up Special Economic Zones or apparel parks and offer them to these community people for establishing local readymade units. Government should also provide sewing machines and equipment under Aadharana scheme. There should be liberalization with regards to bank loans, subsidies and margin money etc. there is a need to establish 'Tailoring cooperatives' by grouping Meru community people on the lines of DWAKRA Groups and help them organize themselves. Most of the respondents also suggested that free and compulsory residential education should be given to their children. Training in Designing and modern stitching need to be given as several of the respondents had multiple suggestions for improving their personnel life. They have also claimed that their profession has brought prospects and unless government comes forward with a 'policy framework' and extend necessary facilities they lose the 'advantage' of the same.

Profiles and Select Case Studies

Panthagani Kavitha

My name is Panthagani Kavitha, belong to Meru Caste. I am 42 years old. I live at Gopala Swamy Temple, Warangal City. My Family members including my husband works as a Tailor. We are having two children, one son aged 14 years studying 9th class and one daughter aged 16 years studying intermediate 1st year. My Husband did not go to school at all but I studied up to 10th class and later married and stopped studies. For generations together my family members are depending up on the caste profession, but there has not been much qualitative development.

We possess a small RCC house at Gopalaswamy temple, Warangal and we don't have any agricultural land or any other property. We have minimum facilities in our house like toilets, electricity, gas for cooking and others. We did not get any help from government, neither any subsidy nor any loan. As I am a member in DWAKRA Group and have been friendly with other caste members, we help each other, whenever we need help.

Myself and my husband has been doing this tailoring work together since last 10 years. I also do my household work along with tailoring work. I did not get any training from any training centre but learnt it from my elders in the family. Later myself and my husband started one tailoring shop in our own house with four stitching machines with a capital investment of Rs. 50,000/- for infrastructure facility and Tailoring material. Later I have taken the assistance of other two members for stitching the ladies and gents dresses. They are part-time workers. These part-time workers belong to Meru Caste.

In the village, we get less rate for stitching the dresses than in cities. We get Rs. 150/- per pair after deducting the material charges to stitch a male dress and it takes a minimum 4 hours time. My husband stitches male dress and I stitch for women. I also know the embroidery work. I know new designs in embroidery but the amount that customers pay is less and as a result it as getting difficult to run the shop. In our caste the literacy rate is less and most of us are not able to find jobs in government. Most of the public are moving towards readymade dresses. These problems should be overcome only by the assistance of government or other agencies. In marriage season and on festival days we get some amount of good work but on other days the work is very less. Due to this we cannot afford to lead a normal life. It becomes difficult to run the shop while paying current bill and remuneration to the workers.

To sum up the following are some of the problems

- Due to readymade dress shops we are not getting work.
- No government orders received by us to stitch school uniforms and other dresses used in the offices for IV class employees or drivers etc.,
- No grant, subsidy or loans from government
- It is difficult to run this shop with workers due to lack of work availability in the market.

- In tailoring work mostly we have to sit and work and due to this we are getting knee pain, limber pain, and eye problem.

Suggestions to overcome the problem:

- Government should provide land to open the shops.
- It should provide personal loans from the Bank.
- Orders may be placed for school uniform and for other official dresses required in Hospitals, Police Department, Industries etc.,
- Free education facility to the children.
- Free medical checkup and medicines.
- Pension of Rs. 1000/- to the elders who crossed 50 years age.
- Training facilities should be extended to the women workers and provide grants to open the shops.

Ramagiri Krishna Swamy

My name is Ramagiri Krishna Swamy. I am 43 years old and from Kanagarthi Village, Odela Mandal, Karimnagar District. For the last 15 years I am doing the (Stitching) Tailoring Work. I have not undergone any training in this field, but learnt it from my father and grandfather.

We are three members in my family. Myself, my wife and one son. I studied up to 7th class and discontinued and started Tailoring job. My wife 38 years old studied up to 5th class and stopped education due to poor economic conditions. Though we have not studied well, we are now giving importance to our son's education. He is now 19 years old and doing degree 1st year.

I am having my own RCC building, but no agricultural land. We have some facilities like Bathroom, and Electricity connection. I own two sewing machines. Myself and my wife both are involved in Tailoring work. My wife is a DWAKRA

Group Member. She is the 2nd Leader of that DWAKRA Group named Sai Meghana Mahila Society. We borrowed some amount from money lenders at the time of establishing the shop.

We are living near bus-stand and it is accessible for all facilities. We have friends from other castes people and neighbours who are friendly. I opened a shop in my own house in the front room with partition with two sewing machines and one over lock machine and other tools are available in my shop along with thread bundles and needles, cloth, taps etc. my wife also works with me and stitch Ladies dresses, blouses etc., and I stitch male dresses, trousers, shirts, drawers, banyans etc., There are plenty of readymade shops which attract customers towards them and rob our work. Due to readymade shops we are losing our work, It is a paradox that other community members also opening the tailoring shops where in our caste members are working as wage labourers. In 1984, Government has sanctioned one sewing machine but after that we did not get any assistance. No government is supporting our profession. As a result of 'not getting sufficient work', we lost our regular income. As there has been a gradual fall in our income, it became difficult to lead our livelihood.

Professionally we are busy during the festivals and marriage season but we get very less work on other days. We will be doing some patch work of repairing old dresses whenever we are free from stitching new dresses. As we have no other skills there is no alternate for us. It became difficult to pull on in the profession. As the cost of the input materials used for stitching dresses is also growing. We get little margins to our works. We get only Rupees 100 to 150 per day after deducting the cost of the material used for stitching a dress. Sometimes it is so happening that we have to go to Money lender very often for consumption loans, paying high interest which is causing mental agony.

Most of the villagers are also going for readymade dresses in the city while middle aged are getting stitched dresses in the city only. Most of our caste members are illiterates of semi-literates are not able to get any government or private jobs. Modernization of economy has not helped us in any way; instead it ruined our lives robbing our work and incomes. At present we are in deep crisis.

Our Specific Problems

Lack of Government support to caste people; Non availability of loans and subsidy for material purchased; Health problems coming across like knee pain, back pain, eye-sight problem. Ladies are not getting main work except part time work like stitching buttons.

In view of the above we suggest that government should make it a rule to provide work orders for Stitching school dresses, uniforms of other workers; Materials may be provided on subsidy; Old age pension may be granted. Bank loan with only a little or no interest may be granted to open the shop; shopping complexes may be constructed and Tailoring cooperatives may be setup; textile parks may be opened to provide full time employment to our community, training in fashion designing and stitching modern dresses may be given. Unless government comes forward and initiate certain measures. Our community will lose the dignity it used to carry and alienate us from the field.

Madishetty Suresh

My name is Madishetty Suresh, age 42 years. My native place is Damera Village, Elakaturthi Mandal of Karimnagar District. But I am living at Hanamkonda taking a single room rented house and I am doing Tailoring work. For the last 20 years I am doing this profession.

We are four members in my family-myself and my wife and two children. I have studied up to 10th class and discontinued due to poverty. My wife 32 years of age studied up to 10th class and my elder son 12 years studying 7th class and younger son 9 old years studying 5th class.

In my native place we have our own house (tiled one) constructed by my parents. We did not get any assistance from Government. We did not have any agricultural land. I have one scooter, water tap, bathroom, latrine, current, cooking, gas facility and sewing machine also. I have friends from other castes also and all the neighbours are helpful to me.

Occupational Details

I have started Tailoring work in my village Damera. Initially I struggled for 3 years. As there was no handful work I have joined in other as piece-rate worker. Even this arrangement also could not help, so later I have shifted my family to Hanamkonda, a neighbouring city. I took a room on rent and put up a Tailor shop. I have started the shop in the year 2006, named as 'codex'. I individually started this shop and do the work on my own.

The shop area is 10/20 sq feet and I have spent 60,000 for machines and 15,000 for raw materials and 5000 as capital amount. I did not get any assistance from Government. I took some loan from my relatives and I personally invested some amount out of my savings. Now I am paying interest towards the loan taken. For quite some time I could not get full income as expected and I always felt bad about the question that I am in debt, and how long should I carry it?

I have 2 stitching machines, 1 Juke machine, one over lock machine, 4 Scissors, 4 Stools, 1 Iron box, 2 Fans, 3 Tube lights filled in the room, mirror, with in the shop. There are hangers, tapes and other materials required for stitching. I do stitching work of those customers who visit the shop. I stitch Shirts and Trousers most and during the marriage season we have full work and also during the school admission days I have full work. In other days when I do not have much work, we also do patch work. Whenever there is more work I employ on part time basis one person of the same caste, so that he could work along with me well. Every day I work for 10 or more hours from morning 09:00 am to 08:00 pm.

I get Rs. 400-500 a day on an average apart from the charges of maintenance of shop and raw materials. The expenditure comes to nearly 100-150 rupees. We did not get any financial assistance from government.

Our Problems

Housing accommodation problem; lack of Government loan and subsidy on materials; insufficient earnings; lack of training in fashion designing; heavy competition from outsiders, other than our community; lack of education etc.

We have represented our problems several times to Government and public representatives but nothing has been done. There is a 'Federation' specially created for our community but due to lack of funds it is unable to extend loans to tailors. In view of this there is a need for creating a single window facility for easy loans through societies, subsidy and margin money for setting up shops, stitching of uniforms needed for schools, hospitals and other Government organizations be entrusted to our society, free medical insurance, supply of raw material on subsidy basis through societies etc, Government should also evolve a policy for developing apparel parks and provide employment to the community members.

Komekula Srikala

My name is Komekula Srikala aged 47 years. I have passed VII class. I got married at the age of 16 years. My native place is Managuru of Khammam District. My husband's name is Shankaraiah of Warangal District. I came to Warangal after marriage. Before marriage I learnt Tailoring work from my parents at Mangoor. My husband also does Tailoring work. I am working as Tailor for the last 18 years. My husband is not well educated. He passed only VIII class. We have two children, one son and one daughter. My son aged 20 years and daughter 16 years. My son has studied upto X class and daughter passed inter but no one has got any employment outside. They also help us in tailoring work. We could not send them to higher education due to lack of money, so put them to work to earn their livelihood.

We do not have our own house. Financially my husband's family is poor. We, took a room for rent initially by paying a monthly rent of Rs.600/-. Over the years there is a hike in the rent payable. We shifted the house in between for want of more accommodation. And due to this now we are paying more rent to the house which comes to Rs.1200/- per month.

We have several problems in our family. My husband is not taking care of the family. He do not take work seriously and always found roaming here and there in other villages, not working and not taking care of the family. The entire family burden has been laid in my shoulders. My neighbours are good with helping nature. They also do the Tailoring and agriculture work. Some of them also sell the vegetables. My mother gave me a Sewing machine and I learnt the skill from her which is now fetching the livelihood of my family.

Daily I work from morning 9 am to 10 pm. I do not have any rest. I used to go out in search of work. Now there has been lot of competition amongst the Tailors. As I work hard I could get 5000 to 6000 rupees per month. Initially, I used to take loans from money lenders for family expenditure and I have to pay the interest which is very heavy i.e., sometimes 10% interest.

Now I joined as a member of a DWAKRA Group and I took 6000 rupees loan which I could get through Bank. Now I purchased an electronic Sewing machine for stitching. It is nearly 10 years as a member of the DWAKRA Group I could manage well finally I could get Rs. 25000 as loan from the Bank and I used that amount for my children's education and health.

It is very difficult to carry on the Tailoring work and also to look after the children in addition to household work. My husband is a drunk and it is difficult to lead a life when men do not work in the family. Now the rates of stitching material are very high. Cost of living increased. Due to this we are unable to purchase vegetables even.

Generally we get much work during festival season and marriage season and very little on other days. On these days there will be lot of work and it is very difficult to look after the household work. During the unseasonal days we hardly get work and many a time we need to take consumption loans invariably. If Government helps us giving loans it will be helpful to some extent.

I strongly feel that Government should provide us free Sewing machines as part of Aadharana Scheme and assist us in opening a shop. It should provide Housing facility and fee concession to our children.

The Tailoring workers generally get health problems such as Back Pain, Kidney Pain and also Knee Pains. As such Free Health Check Up, Medicines and other facilities are to be provided by the government. For senior citizens, old age pensions are to be given.

We should be trained in modern technology & Stitching. Modern Sewing Machines are to be supplied. Pension scheme need to be implemented. Health care and free medicines are to be provided. Government should extend necessary support especially stitching of all categories of dress materials required for Government servants, School children. Medical apparels and uniforms for other officials of various departments should be entrusted. If the situation continued like this, the future life of this community will be at a risk.

Raparthi Sampath

My name is Raparthi Srinivas, age 40 years. My native place is Veenavanka of Karimnagar District. For the last 10 years I am doing this tailoring work as our traditional occupation. I completed intermediate and stopped further education due to poverty. My wife studied up to intermediate. She is of aged 37 years and we are having one son aged 8 years studying 3rd class and another son aged 7 years studying 2nd class. I am only the person working for the family now doing tailoring work. My ancestors also did the same profession. My grandfather and my father also had practiced the same profession. I have not undergone any training to carry on this profession and learnt it from my parents, family members and elders.

We don't have any agricultural land. My wife is a member of DWAKRA Group and we are friendly with other caste members and neighbours. The building which I own having minimum facilities such as Toilet, Water Facilities, Electricity, and a Gas Stove and I am living here in the village since my birth.

I started a small shop in my house having minimum requirement for shop The villagers will come to me with dress material to stitch them. We stitch Trousers, Shirts etc., previously it was good and we used to get good income from this profession. Tools required in my occupation include; Sewing Machine, Tapes, Scales Counter Table, Stools, Chairs, Iron Box, Thread Bundles, Buttons, and other arrangements in the shop are required. Myself and my father together work in the Tailoring shop. Daily we are able to get around Rs. 400/- only. We take only 400 Rupees for stitching a pair of dresses. Even then despite charging less most of the public go for readymade dresses. But now a days it is becoming difficult to fulfill the minimum needs of life because firstly, most of the villagers are preferring city tailors. Secondly, most of them are going for ready-made dresses as a fashion of today.

Even though both my father and myself are working in our shop, we are not getting full time work and due to this the income which we earn has become insufficient to meet the minimum needs of the family. My wife is also extending support especially by doing the patch work like stitching buttons and undertaking sundry work. We also undertake dress repair work to earn some money.

It is observed that other caste members also doing the same job of tailoring and some of them have opened their tailoring shops where in the other members including the members of my caste are also found working as piece-rate workers. Since there has been lot of competition, we are not able to get sufficient work.

Here are some of our problems

1. We are not getting any financial assistance from the government.
2. No subsidy on the materials purchased.
3. No bank loans are available.
4. Negative effect of availability of readymade dresses on our work.
5. We face Health problems like knee pain, eye sight and nervous problem.

Our Demands include:

- Government should extend necessary financial assistance, subsidy on purchase of materials etc,.
- Government should entrust the work for stitching dress and uniforms to school children, police officials etc so that we can have good work.
- Provide training in modern skills and designs.
- Provide free education to children, scholarships, provision for free health check up.
- Pension scheme for senior citizens to be provided by paying at least 1000 Rupees per month.

7

Mangali- *The Barber or Nayee*

Mangalis are known as Nai are barbers. The name, Nai, is a corrupt form of the Sanskrit word napika, or 'one who cleans nails'. The traditional occupation of the Mangali is cutting hair, beard and nails, shaving, cleaning ears, extracting teeth, setting sprains right and lancing boils. They also perform some rituals and other important duties in connection with marriage, matchmaking and other family celebrations.

Though they interact closely with all other communities, and despite a patron-client relationship, they are still regarded as a low caste community due to their occupation. Higher castes generally do not accept food and water from the hands of the Nayi and they in turn do not accept the same from some lower castes such as the Chamar (tanner), Balmiki (sweeper) and Mochi etc.,

Each region has a distinct name for the Mangali- especially in North, they work as barbers and keep animals but a large-scale occupational change is taking place. The literacy rate of the Mangali is quite low although it has improved a lot in the past few decades. The Mangalis are Hindus and worship all Hindu gods and goddesses. The

Mangali also give special prominence to their regional deity. The major festivals observed by them include Navratri (nine sacred nights) and Dussehra. They share all the major centres of pilgrimage with other Hindu castes.

The practice of cutting hair, shaving the body, cutting nails and filing them were services that the barbers offered for centuries. Even a cursory look at the work ethic of the barbers, their expertise and their philosophical moorings, indicate that the barbers contributed enormously to social progress by setting up the basic philosophy of health and well-being. In fact, the word 'mangali' means 'that which is good and positive'.

A barber's knowledge begins with an understanding of the relationship between skin and hair. The next stage is to learn to operate a very sophisticated knife, which, if not wielded correctly, could cut and badly injure the body. This skill has to be learnt in childhood itself. Learning to shave and to cut hair involves enormous skill.

The barber's knife had many uses, the evidence of which is extensively present in villages even today. It served a socio-medical purpose. Apart from being an instrument for shaving the body, it is also a surgical instrument. In the absence of sterilized surgical Knives and scissors, the barber's knives and scissors were the main source of surgery in our village system.

The Mangali women were the best midwives, who had perfected the method of making a woman's labour easy and bearable. They were experts in cutting the umbilical cord after delivery. The Mangalis were a community possessing advanced skills, who could handle highly sophisticated instruments like the Knife, Scissors, Nail cutters, and so on. Even children could shave without injuring the most significant parts of people's bodies. The following tables provide field data collected from a sample of Mangali households for a detailed analysis.

Size of Family in relation to age

Mangalis are popularly named as Nai Brahmins are found everywhere spread over the entire state. Out of the sample of 216 families, 55.56% (120) were chosen from rural areas, 25% (54) from urban areas and 19.44% (42) from rurban or semi-urban areas. Age-wise the sample constitutes 8.33% (18) under 25, 44.44% (96) between 26-35 age, 27.77% (60) from 36-45 age group, 11.11% (24) from 46-55 age group, 2.77% (6) from 56-65 age group. While 5.56% (12) from 66 and above age group category. As far as family members are concerned, a large majority, 41.67% (90 out 216) had four members in their families, 22.22% each had three and five members each in their families respectively, while two-member families were 11.11% and single member families were only 2.78%. The overall picture presents that the sample predominantly constitutes rural based younger and middle aged with ideally 2+2 families. The nature of sample is found to be representative in character as there are some uniform tendencies all over age-wise, family strength-wise and rural-urban contexts.

Table 7.1

Sample of Size of Family in relation to age

Sl. No	Age	Place	Single	Two Members	Three Members	Four Members	Five members	Six Members & Above	Total
01.	Up to 25	Rurban	-	-	-	-	-	-	-
		Urban	-	-	-	12 (100) (13.33)	-	-	12 (100) (5.56)
		Rural	-	6 (100) (25)	-	-	-	-	6 (100) (2.78)
02.	26-35	Rurban	-	-	18 (75) (37.5)	6 (25) (6.66)	-	-	24 (100) (11.11)
		Urban	-	-	-	18 (100) (20)	-	-	18 (100) (8.33)
		Rural	-	12 (22.22) (50)	6 (33.33) (12.5)	30 (55.56) (33.34)	6 (11.11) (12.5)	-	54 (100) (25)
03.	36-45	Rurban	-	-	-	6 (33.33) (6.66)	12 (66.67) (25)	-	18 (100) (8.33)
		Urban	-	-	6 (33.33) (12.5)	-	12 (66.67) (25)	-	18 (100) (8.33)
		Rural	-	6 (25) (25)	-	6 (25) (6.66)	12 (50) (25)	-	24 (100) (11.11)

04.	46-55	Rurban	-	-	-	-	-	-	-
		Urban	-	-	-	-	6 (100) (12.5)	-	6 (100) (2.78)
		Rural	-	-	12 (66.67) (25)	6 (33.33) (6.66)	-	-	18 (100) (8.33)
05.	56-65	Rurban	-	-	-	-	-	-	-
		Urban	-	-	-	-	-	-	-
		Rural	-	-	6 (100) (12.5)	-	-	-	6 (100) (2.78)
06.	66 & above	Rurban	-	-	-	-	-	-	-
		Urban	-	-	-	-	-	-	-
		Rural	6 (50) (100)	-	-	6 (50) (6.66)	-	-	12 (100) (5.56)
Total			6 (2.78) (100)	24 (11.11) (100)	48 (22.22) (100)	90 (41.67) (100)	48 (22.22) (100)	-	198 (100%) (100%)

Education of Family Members

Out of the total 798 members in the sample families, a majority of members of the families of the respondents are found to be educationally weak and unimpressive. In all only 0.75% of the respondents (6 out of 798 family members) seem have become graduates-they too are found amongst the sons of the respondents concerned. 10.52% are found to have reached upto intermediate level, while another 6.75% had done certificate courses such as ITI and others. 15.79% of the family members are found to be illiterates, among them predominantly found are female members of the family such as spouses and mothers. In all 45.86% had education in between 6th to 10th class, while 21.80% had upto 5th class or less education. It seems there has been large scale dropout at the school education level of the respondents family members. As far as the respondents themselves are concerned. 5.56% were illiterates, while 19.44% had studied between 1st to 5th classes, 55.56% studied between 5th and 10th class and around 16% reached intermediate education? For various reasons, it may be found that education is not within their reach and in case of earlier generations of the respondent's forefathers joining educational institution has been a rare experience. Hence Mangali community continues to be ill-educated and illiterate.

Occupation

Table 3 indicates that for four generations, the respondent, his father, grandfather and great grandfather all were doing the same traditional occupation without any exception. This trend has witnessed sudden change during the present generation only 39.08% of the respondent's sons seem to have adopted the same profession. However 40% are found to be still persuing education, whose occupation will be different from their father's profession, since their parents were not inclined to see them as barbers. 13.79% have already joined a government job, while 6.89% had joined some modern occupation.

Table 7.2

Education of Family Members (Cumulative)

Sl. No	Relationships with the Respondent	Illiterate	1-5 Classes	6-10 Classes	Inter	Degree	ITI/Other Technical Courses	Others	Total
01.	Respondent	12 (5.56) (9.52)	42 (19.44) (24.14)	120 (55.56) (30.50)	36 (16.66) (46.16)			6 (2.78) (16.67)	**216 (100) (27.07)**
02.	Father	6 (100) (4.76)							**6 (100) (0.75)**
03.	Mother	24 (100) (19.05)							**24 (100) (3.00)**
04.	Wife	78 (39.39) (61.91)	12 (6.06) (6.90)	102 (51.52) (28.82)	6 (3.03) (7.69)				**198 (100) (24.82)**
05.	Son	6 (3.44) (4.76)	54 (31.05) (31.03)	60 (34.49) (16.95)	6 (10.34) (23.08)	6 (3.44) (33.33)	6 (3.44) (50)	24 (13.80) (66.66)	**174 (100) (21.81)**
06.	Daughter/ Daughter-in-law		66 (42.30) (37.93)	72 (46.15) (20.34)	12 (7.70) (15.38)			6 (3.85) (16.67)	**156 (100) (19.55)**
07.	Brothers/Sisters			12 (50) (3.39)	12 (50.0) (7.69)				**24 (100) (3)**
	Total	**126 (15.79) (100)**	**174(21.80) (100)**	**366 (45.86) (100)**	**84 (10.52) (100)**	**06 (0.75) (100)**	**06 (0.75) (100)**	**36 (4.51) (100)**	**798 (100%) (100%)**

Education and Length of Occupation

Education has become no bar for the respondents to carry on their traditional occupation. Most of the respondents had trained under their fathers concerned and joined the profession as and when needed while dropping out from education. It has been said by the respondents that sometimes during the Sundays and evenings, their sons used to assist their father to attend to the work of waiting

Table 7.3
Occupation

Sl. No		Occupation	Other Traditional Occupation	Modern Occupation	Govt. Job	Education	Total
01.	Respondent	216 (100)					216 (100%)
02.	Respondent's Father	216 (100)					216 (100%)
03.	Respondent's Grand Father	216 (100)					216 (100%)
04.	Respondent's Grand Father's Father	216 (100)					216 (100%)
05.	Respondent's Son	68 (39.08)		12 (6.89)	24 (13.79)	70 (40.22)	174 (100%)

customers while also persuing education. Almost all the male children with a few exceptions had learnt the skills and techniques of their profession in the early age itself. Further analysis indicate that some of the children after dropping out their school seem to have migrated to nearby towns and cities where their relatives are found and practice their traditional profession there in various saloons. Thus the wide spread drop out from education has been continued without break even in the present generation.

Table 7.4
Education and Length of Occupation

Sl. No	Education	0-5 years	6-10	11-20	21-30	31-40	41-50	51 & above	Total
01.	Illiterate	-	-	6 (50) (7.69)	-	6 (50) (46.15)	-	-	12 (100) (5.55)
02.	1-5 Classes	-	6 (14.28) (10.0)	18 (42.86) (23.07)	-	6 (14.28) (46.15)	12 (28.58) (100)	-	42 (100) (19.44)
03.	6-10 Classes	18 (12.68) (75)	42 (29.58) (70.0)	6 (4.22) (46.15)	3 (2.11) (50)	1 (0.70) (5.56)	-	-	142 (100) (55.56)
04.	Inter	6 (16.66) (25)	6 (16.66) (10.0)	12 (33.34) (15.39)	12 (33.34) (33.34)	-	-	-	36 (100) (16.67)
05.	Degree	-	-	-	-	-	-	-	-
06.	P.G & Others		6 (100) (10.0)						6 (100) (2.78)
Total		24 (11.11) (100)	60 (27.78) (100)	72 (33.33) (100)	30 (13.89) (100)	13 (6.02) (100)	12 (5.56) (100)		216 (100%) (100%)

Occupation of Women in the Family

Nai or Mangali work is a major occupation in Telangana and Andhra Pradesh. Although Nai or Mangali women also found involved a shaving of head of female in pilgrim places, it was all to found to be a male job. An analysis of the available data relating to the occupation of women in the family indicate not even a single women in the family are doing the traditional work of the family. The respondents narrated that certain female members in their relations families does the job elsewhere. However in the present study a large number of women in the family are found doing other odd jobs other than the Nai work. Young and middle aged women go out for work in farms, markets, shops and private offices and other. Five percent of women are found working in construction and other physical labour activity while all other doing some sort of 'blue collared work'.

Occupation of Young

Young boys prefer to stay away from work in case educated or persuing education. But on certain occasions, especially during the holidays and Sundays where there will be more number of customers visiting the shops, doing work will help the families. It has been noticed that some youngsters (around 24%) had started modern saloons of their own, after receiving some training in Hyderabad and (two persons) from Mumbai city in modern hair dressing. Of these in all, 6 persons have set up two 'beauty parlours' jointly. As many a beauty parlours are now coming up and being started by upper caste men and women with high profile equipment and much advertised cosmetics. The youngsters in the Nai families found it difficult to compete with them in investment and mode of modernisation. There has been a tendency developed in amongst the public that visiting a beauty parlour managed by a non-nayee family with a modern air condition facility is prestigious than visiting a Nayee shop. This has made the youth in the Nayee families frustrated.

Family Assets

It has been found from the sample households that none of the families are found to be holding any agricultural land to their credit. Long ago Nayee families were found to be holding some land in villages but had lost over the years. Now no one does the cultivation work nor take it up as a supplementary work. 92% of the sample households own a house of their own of varying degrees. 8% were found in the rented places. Owning Bullocks, Chicks fowls or other birds also rare in these families. Only 69% of families had drinking water facility at home, 91% bathroom facility and 65% latrine facility. 92% had power supply facility, while 86% had cooking gas at home. 83% own T.Vs, 27% Radios and 6% sewing machines, which ladies in the families operate to earn some money. 3% had rice cookers and around 6% subscribe to news papers to be used in their shops for customers. The overall assessment of amenities and facilities available in the houses of Nayee sample households indicate 'deprivation' trend regarding essential amenities and every day especially women in the families face problems to discharge their daily core activities.

Source of Employment

Table 7.5 indicates that out of these who had own account enterprises or employment, 60.72% work in or own saloon shops including a couple of beauty parlours, while 39.28% are found to be doing the work from their own houses. They convert a part of their house as a saloon, shop and do the job. Some of them in rural areas also visit 'houses' of the regular customers to do the job. Most of the upper caste landlords or rich peasants in the villages call for the Nayee to the homes to get the work. In such situation some 'rich customers' in the village maintain their family Nayee like family Dhobis. It may be found that the 22.22% of the respondents are under wage employment doing the same traditional job in some saloon owned by others on piece rate basis. In most cases the availability of work depends upon the type of public relations they maintain and also the 'confidence' of the customers they gain for their regular visits to the 'saloon shop' or home visits. During the Sundays and non festival holidays however most of the Nayee get full overtime work.

Table 7.5

Sources of Employment

Sl. No	Respondent's Occupation	Self Employment	Society	Wage Employment	Total
01.	Saloon Shop	102 (68) (60.72)	-	48 (32) (100)	**150 (100) (69.45)**
02.	House	66 (100) (39.28)	-	-	**66 (100) (30.55)**
Total		**168 (77.78) (100)**	-	**48 (22.22) (100)**	**216 (100%) (100%)**

Investment Details

It may be noticed that those who 'create their work place' at their homes need less investment than those who set up a separate 'saloon shop or a parlour' of their own. Separate saloon shops are located in rented places and need remodelling as per the level of investment they propose. Those who operate from their home and set up a part of their house had different levels of 'shop arrangement'. Some sample respondents in villages get it done in open place or under a shed infront of their house. Some in open place in nearby their house under a tree. Around 18% of the respondents had such arrangement mostly in villages. In urban and semi-urban areas however only 6% of respondents had set up such open shops. Normally these Nayees also visit homes or manage mobile shops. A 'mobile shop' is nothing but carrying the minimum 'Nayee tools' required in a specially designed bag (which are most commonly used everywhere) and does the job wherever possible in private houses. Under a tree or a nearby a market or four-road square/cache etc., All these Nayee families require to invest around Rs. Five hundred to Rs. 5,000/-. Around 20% of respondents spent even upto Rs. 10,000/-. Those who setup separate shops need to invest more. Among them 62% spent upto Rs. 20,000/-. 26% spent upto Rs. 40,000/-. While the remaining 12% had spent upto Rs. 1.0 lakh. Two (less than 1%) of the respondents own 'beauty parlour' in this category. The investment they made has been spent towards on shop remodeling, decoration, in shop facilities and amenities including Air conditioners, equipment and tools, gadgets, mirrors, high chairs and variety of cosmetics and beauty aids in the shop. As such more and more investment they need in setting up modern parlours. As they need to compete with the rich parlours owned by those other than their community people and chain shops. The competition is heavy during the recent years and to face this the respondents said that they need more investment and also additional training in the job.

Most of the respondents had repeated that they get the needed supplies of modern gadgets/cosmetics/others through 'Agents' who deliver at the shop or home or from the open market. Necessarily a large majority of the Nayee shop owner-respondents (up to 90%) approach the Agents belonging to their own community. These agents deliver the goods and introduce new items coming in the market at reasonable rates, many a time lesser than open market rates. The agents get the supplies from 'outside cities' would have latest and day to day knowledge in the new arrivals in the market and after ascertaining their utility and superiority' they procure and promote them through their shops or home deliveries. This is more convenient to the Nayees. The respondents had said they will be able to keep themselves 'upto date' with the new products and their utility through the agents. The respondents also said that they get the supplies on credit which could be paid later as per the convenience and even in installments in case of equipment and instruments.

Source of Investment

It may be observed in table-6 that 66.67% of respondents (among them 20% from urban areas and 80% from rural areas) had used their own savings or money from their own sources towards investment for setting up the 'shop' either at home or at a separate place. Only 12%, they too belong to urban areas had the facility of getting bank loans for setting up 'saloons or parlours'. It may be observed that 57.89% belong to urban areas that use the sources like societies or chit fund companies for loans. This seems to be peculiar as far as Nayees are concerned in relation to other OBC Communities pursuing traditional occupations. 2.77%, all belong to urban areas had approached money lenders to take loans to be used as investment for setting up their respective shops. Like other artisan and service communities, Nayees also had to bear the brunt of the problem of money lenders imposing high rates of interests. Since they had no other alternative source of financial assistance or a loan, Money lender is the only institution available to them for extending support. As 20.22% of the respondents are working as 'wage employees', the owners of the shops, 90% of them belong to Nayee community looks after the need for investment. The source of investment needed for setting up the 'saloon or Nayee shops', indicate that though the community for centuries doing the job as a traditional occupation had to look out for investment to modernize their shop and face new 'unexpected problems'. As others enter the field making business especially corporate and other Branded like Reliance Beauty Parlour companies. The traditional shop keepers hardly consider them as competitors become they can neither able to compete with them nor able to offer them the variety of services available there. In any case the Nayees community is gradually loosing the only 'employment source or income source' which was an exclusive area of occupational source of this community.

Table 7.6

Source of Investment

Sl. No	Source	Urban	Rural	Total
01.	Own	28 (20.0) (47.83)	112 (80.0) (100)	**140 (100) (66.67)**
02.	Bank	12 (100.0) (12.5)	-	**12 (100)**
03.	Society/Chit Fund Company	11(57.89) (11.46)	8 (42.11)	**19 (100) (8.80)**
04.	Shop Owner/Other	36 (100) (37.50)	-	**36 (100) (30.56)**
05.	Money Lenders	9 (100) (9.37)	-	**9(100) (2.77)**
Total		**96 (44.44) (100)**	**120 (55.56) (100)**	**216 (100%) (100%)**

Ceremonial Jobs

Like Chakali community, Nayee community has also certain traditional ceremonial jobs to fulfill in the Hindu society. During the time of marriages, birth and death ceremonies, house warming ceremonies etc, Nayee are expected to do 'certain rituals' and once some of the rituals were considered as most important and essential things everybody to observe. Though their jobs are considered 'impure in nature' but ceremonially they become important. The impure becomes pure in the families where the ritual's take place become pure and blessed one. Only those Nayees who were 'attached' informally with the families for other purposes were asked to carry on the rituals for which they are specially paid. Earlier for long Nayees used to get regular income in cash and kind in the villages for the work done. But due to modernization, the traditions are found to be changing, attitudes and approach towards life has been found changing and traditional rituals 'gradually disappearing'. This has been taking place in a faster mode in urban areas followed by semi-urban areas and rural areas. Modernization has also effected the mindset of the impure rituals undermine their status and they also in term started avoiding. Hence both the sides, there has been some change and such ceremonial jobs found fast disappearing.

Table-7 indicates the 'variation' between urban and rural areas in this regard. Though in all areas urban, semi-urban and rural areas, these rituals are followed with a degree of difference. Only 22.22% urban Nayees find such ceremonial jobs in urban areas, regularly while 77.78% get rarely. In contrast to rural areas 80% of Nayees will get such jobs to fulfill the traditional obligations, while 20% rarely get. In semi-urban or rurban areas the situation is mixed as 64.28% get such assignments while 35.71% rarely get. In all 62.50% of respondents regularly get those jobs while there has been a gradual change in urban areas than in rural areas. Though the transformation may be for good or bad, it is a bad news for a Nayee who lose the income which they earlier used to get.

Table 7.7

Ceremonial Jobs

Sl. No	Place	Regularly Available	Rarely Available	Not Available	Total
01.	Urban	12 (22.22) (11.76)	42 (77.78) (63.16)	-	54 (100) (25.0)
02.	Rural	96 (80.0) (76.48)	24 (20.0) (5.26)	-	120 (100) (55.56)
03.	Rurban	27 (64.29) (11.76)	15 (35.71) (31.58)	-	42 (100) (19.44)
Total		135 (62.50) (100)	81 (37.50) (100)	-	216 (100%) (100%)

Government Schemes

Only 5.56% of respondents, who were drawn from urban areas, could find the benefit of getting bank loans while all the rural and remaining urban respondents did not have access to bank loans. It has been found that they approach private sources such as money lenders, chit fund compliances, which are easily accessible to them than the government financing agencies or Banks Schemes like Artisan credit card, Aadharana, Government Pensions, occupational pensions etc., were not available to them despite the fact that they are in need of it.

Table 7.8

Government Schemes

Sl. No	Government Schemes	Available	Not Available	Total
01.	Artisan Credit Card	-	216 (100) (20)	**216 (100) (20)**
02.	Aadarana Scheme	-	216 (100) (20)	**216 (100) (20)**
03.	Bank Loans	12 (5.56)	204 (94.44) (20)	**216 (100) (20)**
04.	Govt. Pensions	-	216 (100) (20)	**216 (100) (20)**
05.	Occupational Pensions	-	216 (100) (20)	**216 (100) (20)**

Community Associations

Community Associations exist in rural and urban areas separately with state level bodies. They very often represent various issues to appropriate bodies including the 'Bankers' but their demands were hardly met. Associations though focus more on cultural and social issues in which there will be wider participation of the members of the community but demands of economic and political nature hardly undertaken on priority basis. There was some sort of indifference on the part of members of the community and the 'leadership' of these bodies also does not continuously represent and exert needed pressure. As a result of it associations have become less significant.

Main Occupational Problems

Like other OBC Artisan or service communities, the perceptional and articulation levels of the problems concerned has been 'limited' even in the case of Nayee respondents. They face several day to day problems and in the course of discussion they pointed out that their conditions are deteriorating over the years, they cannot properly identify the same and articulate them to find suitable solutions. Both rural and urban respondents had the same problem and they were found not in a position to identify the causes for the deteriorating conditions. Some of the problems mentioned are indicated in table 7.9 such as not having regular work, non-availability of regular wages, negative attitude of houses/ shelter owners to rent it for opening a 'saloon shop' as they think it a bad thing etc., Lack of needed directions to Banks to extend loans, lack of Government policy towards helping these people in establishing saloon shops, lack of subsidized supply of cosmetics, competition from modern shops and corporate into the field, lack of pensions support etc., are some of the problems they have mentioned. Most of the respondents felt that they do not want their children to enter into the occupation like them and precisely with this reason they began to get their children educated. The youth in the Community also think that this is not a 'honourbale job' and they prefer it only as a last resort, though they have learnt the skills of the trade since their childhood itself. In all, it may be found that socio-economic conditions of this community are awful and need special attention of the Government.

Table 7.9

General Occupational Problems (Cumulative)

Sl. No	Response	Rural	Urban	Total
01.	Not having Work/Business regularly	90 (48.38) (15.30)	96 (51.62) (13.92)	**186 (100) (14.55)**
02.	Daily wages not viable	102 (65.38) (17.35)	54 (34.62) (7.83)	**156 (100) (12.21)**
03.	Not getting shutters to open shops	-	90 (100) (13.04)	**90 (100) (7.04)**
04.	Lack of Banks to provide loans	102 (47.22) (17.35)	114 (52.78) (16.52)	**216 (100) (16.90)**
05.	Government is not extending help to set up the shops	48 (34.78) (8.16)	90 (65.22) (13.04)	**138 (100) (10.80)**
06.	Lack of subsidized supply of tools and cosmetics	42 (31.82) (7.14)	90 (68.18) (13.04)	**132 (100) (10.33)**
07.	Competition from Modern Shops/Corporate Intrusion	42 (70.83) (17.35)	42 (29.17) (6.09)	**144 (100) (11.27)**
08.	Lack of Pensions	102 (47.22) (17.35)	114 (52.78) (16.52)	**216 (100) (16.90)**

Occupational Demands

As it has been observed that the 'demand articulation' of Nayee Community has not been matching to the level of intensity of their problems. The general demands as expressed by them include: pension facility to old-age and handicapped in the community, provision for tools and investment support, provision for land allotment and provision for individual loans with separate budgetary support, Free education to children etc., are some of the demands expressed by them. They demanded that government should interfere and evolve a policy to extend necessary help and support to readdress their problems.

Table 7.10

Occupational Demands (Cumulative)

Sl. No	Response	Rural	Urban	Total
01.	Pension Facility	102 (47.22) (22.37)	114 (52.78) (22.62)	**216 (100%) (22.5)**
02.	Provision for supply of tools and investment support	90 (41.67) (19.74)	126 (58.33) (25)	**216 (100%) (22.5)**
03.	Provide Land and Accommodation in Shopping Complex	72 (44.44) (15.79)	90 (55.56) (17.86)	**162 (100%) (16.88)**
04.	Provide Individual Loans by sparing separate budget.	108 (50) (23.68)	108 (50) (21.43)	**216 (100%) (22.5)**
05.	Free Education to the children from the community	84 (56) (18.42)	66 (44) (13.09)	**150 (100%) (15.62)**

Profile and Case Studies of Select Artisans

Vijjagiri Raju

My name is Vijjagiri Raju, aged 42 years. I live in Jammikunta Village, Mandal Jammikunta, Karimnagar District. For the last 30 years I have been doing this profession. My grandfather, father and myself completely depended on this profession. I haven't taken any training; just I watched my father and learnt my work. My family makes a livelihood while completely depending on this profession.

We are 5 members in my family, my wife and three children. I have studied upto 7th class in my village. Due to financial problems I stopped my studies and doing this profession since12 year of my age. My wife aged 38 years studied upto 3rd class. She also works as a domestic servant in a nearby house. My eldest son 18 years studied 10th class. Second son 16 years studying intermediate and third and youngest son is in 9th class. I encourage my children to go for higher studies and get good jobs. We have our own house built with our own money. We haven't got any help from Government. We don't have any agricultural land, but we have some domestic animals. Ours is a tiled house and it has facilities like bathroom, current, gas etc. I have a bicycle. I read newspapers outside. My wife is a DWAKRA group member. I have friends in other castes also. We have good neighbours and friendly. I have been living in this village since my birth.

I have setup my own shop. Prior to my setting up of my own shop, I used to do my profession at home. But I could not get many customers there, so I have taken a shop for rent at Bus Stand and set up my own Barber shop. While using my own money I purchased the equipment and tools needed. But I have taken loan from money lenders for other family purposes. I am the only person in the family to do work in my shop. I open my shop at 6'0 clock and after cleaning it, I start my work daily. I take 40/- Rupees for cutting, 20/- for shaving and Rs. 30/-for trimming and Rs. 10/ - for face cleaning and for Gandhi cutting (clean shave) 30/ - rupees. Normally I get Rs.150 to 200 daily. Sometimes I do not have much work and get only a little. I am only the earning member in the family. In our caste in most cases only male persons do our profession. I am the leader of our 'Nayee Brahmana Sangam' I hold the post of "secretary" to our Sangam. Due to work of my Sangam I keep one person in shop and go out to perform Sangam work. Many times I represented the government about the problems of caste people. I fought on behalf of the caste people to solve the problems. In the year 2004 Government helped us on the scheme of "Aadharana" to provide some tools to do the profession. Till today we haven't get any other help from any government. Many times government ministers and political leaders promise to do some help but they have not done anything. Governments did not formulate any policy to develop our caste people. In this profession, in villages we do not have any competition. The reason is in rural areas only our caste people do this work and they distribute the houses by themselves to do their work. But in urban areas other caste people also doing this work. So, there is heavy competition here. Our caste people due to financial problems and also not getting sufficient work had to go for daily wage works in other caste people's saloon shops. To set up a shop generally our caste people spend 50 to 80 thousand. Whereas the other caste people spend Rupees 2 to 3 lakhs with lots of decorations and attract customers to earn more. Now most of the people are going to beauty parlours. Once upon a time they used to come to us for different kinds of cutting and showing. Now, all the people are going to beauty parlours for "facial" and Bridal preparation. Even ordinary people are not coming to our shops for these special purposes.

We feel that

1. Government should extend us helping hand keeping in view of the problems of our caste.
2. Government must help us to set up our own shops giving capital amount and subsidies and allot commercial place.
3. To purchase raw material, government must provide subsidy.
4. Our children should be given free education and health facility.
5. Modern training should be given.
6. Government should give us jobs in jails, hospitals, temples where our services are required and it should not be given to other caste people.

Giddemari Ramanna

My name is Giddemari Ramanna S/o Sammaiah. I am 37 years and my native place is shayampet Mandal of Warangal district. I am working as a Barber ever since I attained the age of 20 years. My father, grandfather and great grandfather did the same profession. We did not have any regular training in hair cutting but we have learnt it by ourselves through observation.

We are four members in my family. Myself, my wife and two children, I did intermediate and due to financial problems dropped out from studies and entered into the profession. My wife (32) passed 10th class and she is a housewife. My son is 12 years old studying 7th class and my daughter is 10 years old studying 6th class. My wife is a DWAKRA group member. We have started Nai Brahmin society and carry some social activities too, apart from doing our traditional occupation.

I have small tiled house constructed by me. No Government help has been received by me at any time. We have drinking water tap, bathroom, latrine, current, cooking gas. We are living in our native place only and did not move anywhere. We are having neighbours belonging to other castes and had good friendly relations with them.

I am working in a friend's saloon. My work starts from 8 am and we share the amount received from the customers. We do hair cutting, beard cutting, and face cleaning, freshing, washing and muscle rubbing. Sometimes we have good work and on other days we do not have enough work. We go back to homes with empty hands on some days. We collect 40 rupees for hair cutting, 30 rupees for beard cutting, 40 rupees for trimming and 15 rupees for face washing. I do not have enough money to open a shop on my own. Government did not give me any loan or land to open a shop and also any subsidies to purchase the material required. I had always had a dream that I should have my own shop and lead on independent life. But my dream never comes time. I consider that if I get the loan from government, I could lead my life comfortably by opening a shop. Even though I studied upto Intermediate, I could not get any job. There is a competition in our profession. Other caste members are also opening the saloon and they are opening beauty parlors which causes injustice to our caste members. While other caste members open beauty parlors they do not do the work. They employ our caste members to work in it and they earn the profit with our labour.

Generally I earn daily an amount ranging from Rs. 150-175, a meager amount insufficient to lead good life. Government will select some of the barbers to work in temples to cut the hairs of devotees. They are appointed on contract basis. Sometime, get also get part-time employment in Hospitals, Prisons to work there. We have given a representation to Government to appoint us on regular basis but there was no response.

Our major Problems Include:

1. The income which we are getting is insufficient and we cannot charge more as we may lose even this.
2. There has been lot of competition between the workers due to unemployment.
3. Other caste members are entering into our profession depriving our opportunities.
4. Influence of beauty parlor on urban citizen is more and they are attracted towards them ignoring our services.
5. Government is not recognizing the profession to assist and offer support to improve our conditions.
6. Lack of financial assistance to open hair cutting saloons.
7. No pension to senior citizens of our caste.

8. Due to financial problems our children are not going for higher education.

9. Health problem are arising in the profession. i.e., Backache, Knee pain, eye problem etc., and no medical facility have been provided.

We have submitted a number of representations to government, but nothing has been done till now. We sincerely hope that government should come forward and extend necessary support to resolve our problems.

1. Government should provide land and Bank Loans to open the shops.
2. Subsidy to get the materials required.
3. Government should organize community cooperative societies and provide financial assistance.
4. Government should restrict the others entry and should not allow to open saloons by other caste people.
5. Several of our caste members are leaving villages to shift for cities in search of other employment and in such cases government should extend necessary support to them.
6. Pension facility should be extended to senior citizens.
7. Free education and medical facilities should be extended to our children.

Mogilicherla Suresh

My name is Mogilicherla Suresh. Age 30 years native of village Kanugulagedde, Mandal Huzurabad, District Karimnagar. I am a Barber. I learnt this profession from my father. When I was studying 10th class I began this profession. Now my age is 30 years and I have been doing this profession for the last 15 years.

We were 8 members in our Joint family, but at present we three, my wife, daughter and myself are living separately. Now I am working in a shop. My wife does homework. I have a daughter aged 3 years. I had discontinued in the middle of Intermediate studies and my wife also studied Intermediate. Due to financial problems I had to dropout from studies and continue the profession. We all, grandfather, father, brother and myself had to do the same traditional occupation, almost for the same reason. My grandfather and father used to go to customers houses and do the work. But my brother and myself opened a shop and doing the work.

We own a tiled house. We built it with our own money. Government hasn't given any help. We don't have any agricultural land. We have Current, Latrine, Bathroom, drinking water tap facility at our house. Neighbourhood is very good. We do not have drainage facility and due to this we need to clean our open drainage canals every week.

All our neighbours belong to the same 'mangali' caste. The name of the street itself is 'Mangali wada' as all residents are of same caste people. Most of the streets are being called with caste names and hence our street is being called as 'Mangali Street'.

Most of the people in my family did not go for higher studies for the last two decades. In my family I am the only person studied up to Intermediate. I began work at home after I stopped studies. I did the barber work at home in the beginning when my father was engaged in visiting houses and did the work. I used to do the work as a helper to my father in the first day. After my marriage, my responsibilities have been increased and I joined my brother to work in a Barber shop owned by others as a paid workers. After some days we have earned some money taken a shop for rent for Rs. 1500/- per month and started doing work independently. We have purchased the material required for the shop by taking loan from private money lenders. After some days of work we have cleared loan by taking chits. Daily, I had to travel 6 KMs by bicycle from my village to reach the shop located in a nearby town. Normally I open shop at 7'0 clock in the morning and close it at night 9 or 10 clock. On Tuesdays the shop is closed every weak and that day we clean our shop and materials. My brothers and myself do the work collectively. The rates to be charged at the shop are decided by our caste society. We all have to follow the rates as fixed by the society. They impose fine on those who violate the rules of the society. On an average, daily after excluding all expenditure of shop (including current bill) we earn 100 rupees or more each as the case may be on some days we get more money. Sometimes due to lack of work we do not get anything and cannot pay daily chits. We charge for cutting Rs. 40/- for beard Rs. 20/-, for trimming Rs.30/-, Gandhi cutting (that is "Gundu") 40/- and baby cutting (small children) 30 rupees. We have all necessary materials in the shop like two Big Mirrors front and back, 3 Cutting Chairs, one Bench, one chair, 8 Combs, 2 Trimming Machines, Powder Tin and other etc in our shop. We got some government aid in 2004 and secured some tools under the scheme of "ADARANA" and except that we haven't get any help from Government.

Our Problems Include:

1. Till today, we haven't got any help from Government.
2. Neither the Government nor the Banks are giving any type of loans to set up shops. Also not giving any loan to purchase shop materials and raw materials.
3. Government is not providing training to set up modern saloons.
4. Our caste occupation has been considered as low and looked down as unclean work and no action is being taken at any time on those who treat us low and discriminate.

Our needs include:

1. Banks should give personal loans to individuals and to our caste societies liberally.

2. To set up Barber shops Government must provide a free place and free current facility and provide capital amount and required subsidies.
3. Government must provide free education to our children.
4. Government should provide training on new techniques in our profession.
5. Our caste people should be entrusted with the cutting work available in Police Department, Hospitals and Temples etc.

Nagavalli Krishna

My name is Nagavalli Krishna S/o Pappaiah. I am 48 years. My native place is Siddapoor village, Hasanparthy Mandal of Warangal District. I came to Hanamkonda town 25 years back in search of work and living at Hanumannagar, Hanamkonda and I had inherited my profession from my father, my grandfather. I did not undergo any training but learnt the skills from my father and has been working as a Barber since 28 years.

We are 5 members in my family, my wife, one daughter and two sons. I did intermediate and discontinued due to financial problems. My wife 40 years old and studied up to 8th class and discontinued. My elder son 23 years presently doing M.B.A and my younger son aged 21 years doing B.Tech, my daughter 22 years doing M.Com. My wife is a DWAKRA Group member

I have constructed RCC building in my native place. I do not have Bicycle or Scooter. No tap for drinking water. I get the water from outside I have Bathroom, Latrine, Current, Cooking Gas facility at home. We are living at Hanamkonda since last 25 years. We are living amongst the residents of other "backward castes" they are friendly with us. They do not have any caste feelings. We mingle and live together.

From 20th year of my age I have started practicing traditional occupation by setting up a Saloon shop at Hanumannagar at Hanamkonda. I did not receive any professional training anywhere. There are two workers in my saloon shop. I took some amount as a loan from a money lender on the basis of interest and started the shop. I have to pay 2% interest per month on the principal amount which I took as loan. I could not clear the loan amount by paying in installment along with the interest. I could not pay the rest of the amount as my children are studying in school and colleges I have to pay huge amount towards tuition fee.

I purchased the material required for the shop with a private loan as I did not get any loan from the government Banks. I earn daily around 300 Rupees excluding the other expenses. It is very hard to live with that little amount. We started a small cooperative chit society with some members with a share amount prescribed. Each member has to pay the prescribed amount on every Tuesday. There will be bidding and someone who needs the money will take the amount and repay regularly with nominal interest as prescribed through our Nai Brahmin society. We requested government to sanction loan but no use. I have two workers in my shop they will get their share for the work turned out by them. They will work from morning 8:00 am to evening 8:00 pm and sometimes we also do work after 8:00pm along with me every Tuesday the shop will be closed as a prescribed Holiday

We do not have good earnings for the work we do and there is no other alternative for us. Further our work is also done by the other caste members as they have opened beauty parlours and saloons and our caste members are working there as wage earners. The owners are getting more money and the workers are paid only 150/- per day. As a result there has been lot of competition and fall in our incomes. Our problems include:

1. No regular work in the shop
2. Modern instruments are not available in our shop.
3. No help from the Government side.
4. Health problems arise due to hair cutting.

Our needs include

Government should assist us in providing Bank Loan and subsidy in purchasing materials. It should provide land for opening shops and Beauty Parlors, stipend and scholarships to our school going children's, free education and old age pension should be provided. Technical training should be provided to our caste members so that they can improve their sills further and make use of emerging technology to compete well with others.

8

Kanchari- *The Brass Worker*

Kanchara and Kanchera are a caste of metal workers (Thusrston, 1909), who derive their name from the work Kanchu meaning Bronze. The locals also address them as 'Kancharollu'. They suffix Achari equivalent to the Brahman Acharya. They work on bell-metal and make all kinds of household utensils. They are experts at working with alloys of copper, lead and brass. The Kanchari is one of the five subgroups of the Vishwabrahman. The five sub groups trace their descent from five sons of Vishwakarma (the architect of the gods). The Truastras, who are brass makers or metal workers, are said to be the Kanchari, who are distributed all over Telangana and Andhra Pradesh. The Kanchari are notified as a socially and educationally backward community and are grouped under Backward Class 'B' group along with Vishwabrahman (Backward Classes Commission, 1970).

The Kancharis are vegetarian. Their staple food is rice. The norm among the Kanchari is the nuclear family. Joint families are very few. The Kanchari women enjoy a low status compared to men in all walks of life. They participate in all the social, religious and ritual activities along with their men folk. Their women do only household work. The

Kanchari are a landless community. Their traditional is brass smithy and primary occupation is working in karkhanas (factories) and making household utensils with metals. Only a few of them do petty business. Their subsidiary occupation is agricultural labour. The Kanchari favour formal education for their children. The drop out of school going children is due to socio-economic reasons. They favour modern Medicare and family planning. To examine the socio-economic conditions, work conditions of Kanchari community in details, field work undertaken. The details are given below:

Sample & Size of the Families

Kanchari communities are one of the smaller communities found in Telangana and Andhra Pradesh states. Only one or two families exist in major villages or a group of cluster villages. They are found relatively in select towns and cities. Population wise it is a minority backward caste community and they are also found moving from place to place. Due to this, a sample of 72 households has been chosen to investigate into their issues and problems. Out of 72 families chosen, 33 families (45.83%) have been selected from urban areas and the remaining 39 families (51.17%) have been selected from various villages studied. Out of the 72 families chosen, 57 families (79.17%) belong to the age-group of 36-65. Among them 24 families (33.33%) belong to the age group of 36-45, 15 families (20.83%) belong to the age-group of 56-65. About 3 families (4.16%) representing rural areas were drawn from '66 and above age-group'. It is significant to observe that 29.17% (19) of families had more than five members in the families, while 41.66% (30) had four members in their respective families. 29.17% (24) of families had 2 to 3 members in their family. Larger families are found urban areas than rural areas.

Education of Family Members

As in the case of other OBC artisan groups 23-58% of family members were found as illiterates, 49.55% have education ranging between 1-10th classes, 11.32% studied intermediate or ITI certificate course, and only 6.60% had studied upto graduation. 0.94% went for other studies. Women in Kanchari families are found to be less educated than men and children had more education than the elders in the respective families. As far as the respondents themselves are concerned, 25% are found to be illiterates, while 29.17% each had education between 1 to 5 classes and 6-10 classes respectively. 8.33% are found to be graduates but surprisingly carrying on the traditional hereditary occupation.

Table 8.1
Size of the Family

Sl. No	Age	Place	Single	Two Members	Three Members	Four Members	Five Members	Six Members & Above	Total
01.	Up to 25	Urban	-	3 (100) (33.33)	-	-	-	-	**3 (100) (4.16)**
		Rural	-	-	-	-	-	-	-
02.	26-35	Urban	-	6 (66.67) (66.67)	-	-	3 (33.33) (25)	-	**9 (100) (12.5)**
		Rural	-	-	-	-	-	-	-
03.	36-45	Urban	-	-	3 (25) (33.33)	6 (50) (20)	-	3 (25) (33.33)	**12 (100) (16.67)**
		Rural	-	-	3 (25) (33.33)	9 (75) (30)	-	-	**12 (100) (16.67)**
04.	46-55	Urban	-	-	-	-	-	3 (100) (33.33)	**3 (100) (4.16)**
		Rural	-	-	-	6 (50) (20)	6 (50) (50)	-	**12 (100) (16.67)**
05.	56-65	Urban	-	-	-	6 (100) (20)	-	-	**6 (100) (8.34)**
		Rural	-	-	3 (25) (33.34)	3 (25) (10)	3 (25) (25)	3 (25) (33.34)	**12 (100) (16.67)**
06.	66 & Above	Urban	-	-	-	-	-	-	-
		Rural	-	3 (100) (25)	-	-	-	-	**3 (100) (4.16)**
Total				**12 (16.67) (100)**	**12 (12.5) (100)**	**30 (41.66) (100)**	**12 (16.67) (100)**	**9 (12.5) (100)**	**72 (100%) (100%)**

Occupation adopted during the last Four Generations

As in the case of other artisan groups, Kanchari community people continue to adopt the same age-old occupation during the last four generations. There has been change only in the case of the sons' of the respondents as only 16.67% had adopted their father's profession. The

Table 8.2
Education of Family Members

Sl. No	Relationship with the respondent	Illiterate	1-5 Classes	6-10 Classes	Inter/ITI	Degree	Other	Total
01.	Respondent	18 (25) (25)	21 (29.17) (23.23)	21 (29.17) (22.58)	6 (8.33) (16.67)	6 (8.33) (28.57)		**72 (100) (22.64)**
02.	Father	15 (22.73) (20.83)	33 (50.00) (36.67)	18 (27.27) (19.35)	-	-	-	**66 (100) (20.75)**
03.	Mother/Wife	42 (63.64) (58.51)	15 (22.73) (16.67)	9 (13.64) (9.68)	-	-	-	**66 (100) (20.75)**
04.	Sons	-	24 (33.33) (26.67)	21 (9.68) (22.58)	12 (16.67) (33.33)	15 (20.83) (71.43)	-	**72 (100) (19.81)**
05.	Daughter	-	3 (7.69) (3.33)	24 (61.54) (25.80)	18 (30.77) (50.0)	-	3 (4.17) (100.0)	**39 (100) (12.26)**
Total		75 (23.58) (100)	90 (20.30) (100)	93 (29.25) (100)	36 (11.32) (100)	21 (6.60) (100)	3 (0.94) (100	318 (100%) (100%)

remaining 4.17% were found in other traditional occupations, 3.33% in various modern occupations, 8.33% work in Government service and other 8.33% in various physical works as wage labour. 45.83% of the sons of respondents were in studies. Thus only during the present generation there has been change or shift in the occupation.

Table 8.3
Occupation

Sl. No		Same Occupation	Other Traditional Occupation	Modern Occupation	Government Job	Other Occupation	Others	Total
01.	Respondent	72 (100) (24)						72 (100) (20)
02.	Respondent's Father	72 (100) (24)						72 (100) (20)
03.	Respondent's Grand Father	72 (100) (24)						72 (100) (20)
04.	Respondent's Grand Father's Father	72 (100) (24)						72 (100) (20)
05.	Respondent's Son	12 (16.67) (4)	3 (4.17) (100)	12 (16.67) (100)	6 (8.33) (100)	6 (8.33) (100)	33 (45.83) (100)	72 (100) (20)
Total		**300 (83.33) (100)**	**3 (0.83) (100)**	**12 (3.33) (100)**	**6 (1.67) (100)**	**6 (1.67) (100)**	**33 (9.17) (100)**	**360 (100%) (100%)**

Education and Length of Occupation

Table 8.4 indicates that more than half of the respondents had been in the occupation between 21-40 years, while 16.66% of respondents had more than 40 years of experience in the profession. Around 16.67% of respondents with relatively better education (which include graduates) have joined the occupation recently with 0-5 years of experience. Another 8% of respondents with education under 10th class have been in the occupation between years 6-10. This offers a predictable discouraging situation as 6 graduates had to join the same occupation for want of better job. They had learnt the skills of the trade from their respective fathers despite being in education and for lack of other opportunities they seem to have joined their father's occupation temporarily as they explained.

It may be observed that there was been wide-spread dropout at the school education level in case of both the respondents generation and his forefathers generations.

Table 8.4
Education and Length of Occupation

Sl. No	Education	1-5 years	6-10	11-20	21-30	31-40	41-50	51 & above	Total
01.	Illiterate				9 (50) (50.0)	6 (33.33) (40)		3 (16.67) (50)	**18 (100) (25)**
02.	0-5 Classes	3 (14.29) (25.0)	3 (14.29) (50)		3 (14.29) (16.67)	6 (28.57) (40)	3 (14.28) (50)	3 (14.28) (50)	**21 (100) (29.17)**
03.	6-10 Classes		3 (14.29) (50)	9 (42.86) (100.0)	3 (14.29) (16.67)	3 (14.28) (20)	3 (14.28) (50)		**21 (100) (129.17)**
04.	Inter	3 (50) (25.0)			3 (50) (16.67)				**6 (100) (8.33)**
05.	Degree	6 (100) (50.0)							**6 (100) (8.33)**
	Total	**12 (16.67) (100)**	**6 (8.33) (100)**	**09 (12.50) (100)**	**18 (25.0) (100)**	**15 (20.83) (100)**	**6 (8.33) (100)**	**6 (8.33) (100)**	**72 (100%) (100%)**

Occupation of Women in the Family

Out of the 72 sample respondent families, women in 21 (29.17%) families have been found sharing the work of their family enterprise. 16.67% of respondents were found doing other works, other than the family business. As far as the other 54% of the families are concerned. Women are found to remain idle as house wives.

Table 8.5

Occupation of Women in the Family

Sl. No	Age	Involved in the family Occupation	Doing other work	Idle/ Housewife	Total
01.	Up to 25			3 (100) (7.69)	**3 (100) (4.17)**
02.	26-35	6 (40) (28.57)		9 (60) (23.08)	**15 (100) (20.83)**
03.	36-45	15 (62.5) (71.43)		9 (37.5) (23.08)	**24 (100) (33.33)**
04.	46-55		12 (66.67) (100)	6 (33.33) (15.38)	**18 (100) (25)**
05.	56-65			9 (100) (23.08)	**9 (100) (12.50)**
06.	66 and above			3 (100) (7.69)	**3 (100) (4.17)**
	Total	**21 (29.17) (100)**	**12 (16.67) (100)**	**39 (54.17) (100)**	**72 (100%) (100%)**

Investment Details

Table-8.6 indicates that 25% of respondents spent upto Rs.10,000/- towards various aspects such as construction of shed, purchase of raw material, tools and machines etc., 54.76% of respondents spent upto Rs. 50,000/- towards construction of shed, purchase of raw material, purchase of tools etc., are considered the essential part of investment, while investment on machines depends upon the size of the enterprise or unit they design to undertake. They purchase the raw material from local markets, on cash or credit basis. It may be observed that outside transactions are limited. Since most of the family enterprises are 'tiny' in nature and they cannot afford more and the level of investment will be generally marginal.

Table 8.6

Investments Details

Sl. No	Amount	Shed/Hut/House/ Shop	Raw Material	Tools	Machine	Others	Total
01.	1-10,000	9 (14.29) (12.5)	15 (23.81) (12.5)	36 (57.14) (50)		3 (4.76) (100)	63 (100) (25)
02.	10,001 - 25,000	54 (39.13) (75)	54 (39.13) (39.13)	30 (21.74) (41.67)			138 (100) (54.76)
03.	25,001- 50,000	9 (17.65) (12.5)	3 (5.88) (12.5)	6 (11.76) (8.33)	33 (64.71) (100)		51 (100) (20.74)
Total		72 (28.57) (100)	72 (28.57) (100)	72 (28.57) (100)	33 (13.10) (100)	3 (1.19) (100)	252 (100%) (100%)

Source of investment

It has been noticed that public institutions including Banks fail to extend loans to these Kanchari artisans groups. This is true in case of both rural and urban artisan households. It has been noticed that these households whether use their won or other family funds or approach the only source they think available to them was local money lender. Data in table 8-7 indicate that half of the respondents had to take loans from money lenders with higher rate of interest. The modus operandi as has been found in this regard was they take loan at the start of establishing the unit, and each month they pay installment of capital amount along with interest rate. Most of the time the 'interest rate' will be higher than Bank or other public institution loans. Apart from this they also take 'incidental' or short term loans for purchase of raw material to make products on the basis of orders received and once the products are finished and the customers make payment. The 'short term' loan taken from the money lender will be returned with interest once the goods are taken away by the customer and make complete payment. Short term or incidental loan carry relatively higher rate of interest than the 'long term' loans. Sometimes the shop keepers from where the raw materials are regularly purchased also provides it on credit basis but on a 'special rate' and specific 'terms and conditions' laid down by him. Sometimes the customers pay advance for the products they intend to get which will be used for the purchase of raw material and other things required for preparing the product. It has been observed in the course of discussion with the sample respondents that not only, the 'establishment charges', but the raw material' also will be expensive and they cannot normally afford to pay from their savings or funds. This has been regular feature and every time they need to 'worry' about the 'investment' needs. As banks and other public institutions consider them 'out of coverage objects', they loose Government subsidies, margin money etc., linked to the bank loans.

Table 8.7

Source of Investment

Sl. No	Source	Rural	Urban	Total
01.	Own/Other Family Members	15 (41.67) (41.67)	21 (58.33) (58.33)	36 (100) (50)
02.	Money Lender	21 (58.33) (58.33)	15 (41.67) (41.67)	36 (100) (50)
Total		**36 (50) (100)**	**36 (50) (100)**	**72 (100%) (100%)**

Production Plan

Normally the Kanchari households get three categories of work: one, they go to shop keepers and get orders for the products which they sell or the shop keepers themselves place orders to them. When there was demand in the market they get their work done by these artisans and seek products required. These works constitute 41.67%, second, individual customers who approach them with needed products and with or without payment of advance they seek products for their use. Third, the artisans household themselves produce some products on the basis of 'demand in the market' or on the basis of needs of regular customers and display it at their residence for sale. These orders constitute a marginal 8.23% of the total products. The Table 8-8 thus indicates that local customers are important for them for getting regular work orders. Sometimes shop orders are bulk but the 'regularity' may be a causality in the while affair. There is a general complaint that they themselves do not get government orders as 'contactor-lobbies' other than the community people who operate swallow everything. As there were no separate 'cooperative societies' for Kanchari households, collective production and sales are also lacking. Thus table-8 indicates that there has been a lot of uncertainty in the trade and several Kanchari families are always found on the lookout for work.

During the festival or marriage seasons, there will be more work orders than the regular times. It may be found that 70.83% of the total work they get during the seasons and the remaining 29.17% during the half season or regular times. It has been found that both men and women in the family go for other works whenever they don't get sufficient work. In urban areas they do all sorts of work when they find no 'orders for their products'. It may be seen that there has been gradual fall of work orders and as a result many of these families are found displaced looking out for odd outside jobs.

Table 8.8

Production Plan

Sl. No	Response	Main Items
01.	Shop Orders	30 (41.67)
02.	Local Customer Orders	36 (50.0)
03.	Outside Orders	06 (8.33)
	Total	**72 (100)** **(100)**

Government Schemes

Table-8.9 indicates the details relating to the availability of Government schemes extended for the benefit of these artisan households. The two Government Schemes such as Artisan Credit card and Aadharana schemes could not be extended to these people as no one in the sample could get such a benefit. Government pension also did not reach them. Only 12.50% of respondents could get bank loans or other financial assistance. 8.33% of women in the families could get the benefits of the DWAKRA programmes as they have become members of DWAKRA groups. It has been found true even in the case of these Kanchari community people that 'general welfare of development programmes' meant for poor may not reach all. Unless specific focus is laid on these communities, their automatic development cannot be possible. Thus the impact of Government Programmes on this community has been either marginal or negative.

Table 8.9
Government schemes (Cumulative)

Sl. No	Government Schemes	Available	Not Available	Total
01.	Artisan Credit Card	-	72 (100)	**72 (100)**
02.	Aadarana Scheme	-	72 (100)	**72 (100)**
03.	Bank Loans	9 (12.50) (60.0)	63 (87.50) (15.10)	**72 (100)**
04.	Govt. Pensions	-	72 (100)	**72 (100)**
05.	DWAKRA	6 (8.33)	66 (91.67)	**72 (100)**
06.	SBH Loans	9 (12.5)	63 (87.5)	**72 (100)**
Total		**15 (3.47)**	**417 (96.53)**	**432 (100)**

Community Associations

Kanchari Community also has an Association supposed to look after their welfare. It has been found that the associations mainly focused its activities on cultural issues rather than economic or occupational issues. The associations were neither successful in organizing their members properly nor served to raise their level of consciousness to articulate their demands. Sometimes due to the 'leadership failure' also there was 'negative development' sidelining the main issues?

Occupational Problems and Issues

Table 8.10 provides a long list of issues and problems faced by the Kanchari community. The respondents were asked to identify their problems in order of their intensity but most of them did not understand the question. The responses were neither uniform nor seem to be based on the 'intensity' of the problems they faced. A large majority of respondents had said that lack of availability of work negligence by the society in general and the government in particular, lack of government policies towards their occupational development, lack of availability of raw materials, lack of capital, lack of insurance support, lack of financial assistance by banks, failure to provide free education to the children in the families, lack of marketing facility, negative attitude of government officials etc., are the major concerns and problems of Kanchari Community. The problems are almost uniform to both rural and urban kanchari community families.

Table 8.10

Occupational Problems in order of their Preference (Cumulative)

Sl. No	Response	1	2	3	Total
01.	Lack of availability of work, negligence by society	12 (100) (16.67)	-	-	**12 (100) (5.53)**
02.	Lack of minimum support price	12 (40) (16.67)	12 (40) (16.66)	6 (20) (8.33)	**30 (100) (13.89)**
03.	Lack of Govt. support towards occupational groups	21 (38.89) (29.16)	15 (27.78) (20.83)	18 (33.33) (25.09)	**54 (100) (25)**
04.	Lack of availability of raw materials and capital	9 (25) (12.50)	15 (41.67) (20.83)	12 (33.33) (16.67)	**36 (100) (16.67)**
05.	Lack of insurance support and caste associations	6 (25) (8.33)	9 (37.5) (12.50)	9 (37.5) (12.5)	**24 (100) (11.11)**
06.	Lack of Bank Financial support	-	3 (50) (4.17)	3 (50) (4.17)	**6 (100) (2.78)**
07.	Failure to provide education facility to children	-	6 (50) (8.33)	6 (50) (8.33)	**12 (100) (5.55)**
08.	Lack of Marketing Facility	-	3 (50) (4.17)	3 (50) (4.17)	**6 (100) (2.78)**
09.	Lack of Training Programmes of Modern Machinery	6 (40) (8.33)	3 (20) (4.17)	6 (40) (8.33)	**15 (100) (6.94)**
10.	Degradation of trade practices	3 (4.17) (25)	3 (4.17) (25)	6 (40) (8.33)	**12 (100) (5.56)**
11.	Lack of Negative attitude of Government Officials	3 (50) (4.71)	3 (50) (4.17)	3 (50) (4.17)	**9 (100) (4.16)**
Total		**72 (33.34) (100)**	**72 (33.33) (100)**	**72 (33.33) (100)**	**216 (100%) (100%)**

Solutions to Problems

Based on the problems identified by the respondents, they were further asked to suggest the solutions for resolving the problems they face. The responses indicate the variation in their perceptional levels and lack of clarity and direction. Most of the suggestion made were either 'general' in nature or in a 'disproportionate form'. These include provision for economic support, subsidized supply of raw materials, need for specific governmental policy for their welfare, support from political parties and leaders, financial support from banks, provision for regular (alternate) employment and proper implementation of government welfare programme while covering all Kanchari Community families. The suggestions are uniformly applicable to both rural and urban respondents.

Table 8.11

Solution to Problems

Sl. No	Response	Rural	Urban	Total
01.	Providing economical support	9 (60) (25)	6 (40) (16.67)	**15 (100) (20.83)**
02.	Subsidized supply of raw materials	12 (80) (33.33)	3 (20) (8.33)	**15 (100) (20.83)**
03.	Need for a specific government policy	3 (50) (8.33)	3 (50) (8.33)	**6 (100) (8.34)**
04.	Support from political parties and leaders	3 (100) (8.33)		**3 (100) (4.17)**
05.	Financial support from Banks	6 (66.67) (16.67)	3 (33.33) (8.33)	**9 (100) (12.5)**
06.	Providing alternative employment	3 (16.67) (8.34)	15 (83.33) (41.67)	**18 (100) (25)**
07.	Proper implementation of government welfare process	-	6 (100) (16.67)	**6 (100) (8.33)**
Total		**36 (50) (100)**	**36 (50) (100)**	**72 (100%) (100%)**

Profiles and Case Studies of select Artisans of Kanchari Community

Rudroju Kedari

I am Rudroju Kedari aged 60 years. I live at Rayapura Colony, Mandal Hanamkonda and District Warangal. I am in the profession of Brass Smith since 45 years. I learnt it from my father I don't have any training from any Institute. I have entered this occupation when I was 16 years of age. My grandfather and father did the same profession as an hereditary occupation.

We are four in my family. My wife, my son and daughter-in-law. I studied up to 5th class and discontinued due to poverty. My wife 50 years old also studied up to 5th class and got married to me. She is a housewife and assists us in my house and sometimes preparation of articles.

We have a tiled old house with 3 rooms and with minimum facilities. We don't have any Tap and Latrine facility at home. We have a provision for current, T.V and a Gas Cylinder. My son aged 30 years studied upto 10th class and will assist me in my work and my daughter in law aged 28 years studied up to 10th class works in the house.

My native place is Unikicherla but we migrated to Hanamkonda when I was 10 years old. Here we came long back of 50 years to have our livelihood. We have a house-cum-workshop shed and myself and my son are working together in the shed. We have purchased the tools required on our own. We did not get any financial assistance from government. We produce various Brass articles and sell them.

We prepare bronze utensils like glass, plates, bowls, buckets etc., and also repair the old articles. We also prepare the articles on orders. Seasonally during marriage and festival days we have good work but other days we don't have enough work. Now-a-days most of the public are not using bronze utensils and going for other plastic and machine made steel articles. No Government assistance or subsidy is available. We purchase required raw material from Warangal from wholesale shop and prepare the articles required. In good olden days even till seventies and eighties people used to purchase the articles prepared by us only but now-a-days they are purchasing readymade articles. Sometimes we recycle the old articles and produce new one. For this purpose we buy older articles and recycle them and even on customers demand when they seek the replacement of their old articles, we recycle them and produce new one as per their specifications. Even though I am doing this work for the last 40 years, I am unable to open a separate shop on my own as I did not have any money to open it. The Modern tools available are of high cost and we are unable to purchase them. The coal which we use in the production of articles for fixing is also of high cost and not easily available as it has been regulated material. We do work for minimum of 8 hours a day along with son and my wife who assist me in my work. Even then we were still not in a position to earn more. Due to rising raw material cost, the profit margin has been reduced to our disadvantage. Hence despite hard work there is fall in our income. As things stand it is hard to lead our life.

The Issues include:

1. No capital amount for the establishment of workshop.
2. No training facilities to update our skill.
3. No machinery available to maintain the workshop.
4. Need financial assistance from government and corporations.
5. Need Bank loan and subsidy from government side.
6. Need Educational and Hostel facilities to our children.
7. Government should encourage establishment of Brasssmiths workshops in industrial estates separately.
8. We need marketing facility so that we may able to get good price to the articles prepared by us.
9. Pension scheme to senior citizens needed.

Gajjela Venkat Narsaiah

My name is Gajjela Venkat Narsaiah. I am 65 years old. My native place is Siricilla Village, Siricilla Mandal of

Karimnagar District. My profession is Bronze work and I am doing the work since 50 years. I have started doing this work at the age of 15 years.

We are five members in our family. Myself and my wife and three children. I am illiterate and from my early age I started helping my father in this work. My wife 55 years old and she is also illiterate and assists me in my work. My elder son 35 years studied up to 10th class but doing the same profession. My second son aged 33 years studied upto Degree and doing the some other work outside. My younger son aged 32 years discontinued his Degree and did a diploma course in designing. He is also helping me in my work. My elder son with his family is staying with us. We are all living together.

We have our own house (RCC) and having three rooms. We have amenities like drinking water, tap, bathroom, toilet facility, cooking gas, T.V, at home. We have one scooter; we do not have any agricultural land. Since birth we are living here in Siricilla. We have neighbours from other castes and live harmoniously.

I have set up a workshop in my own house doing the work. We work with Bronze, Copper, prepare idols and statues of Gods which will be installed in temples. We use coal to heat the materials. We also do other ornamental material works used in Temples. We use coal to heat the metals. Now-a-days coal has been a regulated commodity. We get it in the open market but with a higher price. This is an additional investment for us. We get the required raw material from the Hyderabad city. We borrowed the required money from money lenders and purchased the tools to prepare our articles. We liquefy the copper and bronze metals and get models as required. We also purchased required tools to operate a small furnace to heat the material and then mould it in required shapes. We do not get local orders but we get orders from city and also outside mostly required for temples. We get the orders directly from temple managements. We have to prepare the material carefully. They provide us some amount in advance which will not be sufficient for us to get the required quantities of raw materials and meet other expenditure. The management of temples pays us through cheques after supplying the temple materials to them.

My younger son draws designs required to meet the needs of the temples asp per their specifications. Although he is qualified in designing he could not get any job outside. He joined a job in some firm but they did not pay him reasonable salary and due to this he has left the job. Later he could not find a better job and returned back home to assist us in our work. Now he is assisting with me along other at my home. He designs and prepares the model idols of Gods and Goddesses. He also formulates designs of animals like Elephant, Camels and also make door designs, roof designs etc., and we does the metal melting and shaping works to prepare the final products. It is a highly skilled work to shape the idols of Gods. But no one recognizes our skill and workmanship even though we stick to the time to deliver the products on time. Actually it takes a long period of preparing the material. But we do it fast as more number of family members is involved in the work. We are not getting any loan from anybody either from bank or other financial agencies. We work generally 8-10 hours in a day. Due to the intricacies involved in the product preparation which produce gases and heat. We invariably get Health problems. Though we have represented Government has not provided us any land to open a workshop and materials on subsidy. As we do a specialized activities and in the whole of Telangana state, there are only few like us preparing 'metal idols'. Government should provide us employment to work in temples so that we continue to get income and recognisation. Now we are not being recognized by any agency as a skilled worker and our workmanship go unnoticed as nothing is recorded anywhere in temple about the 'makers' of the idols which everyone pray. Now we hardly get work as modern workshops have come up. As we know only this work, if we do not get sufficient work we starve. Presently we are in a fix as we love the hereditary profession and supplied hundreds of small and big idols of Gods and Goddesses to several temples cannot leave this profession despite not getting sufficient work. We cannot even go for any outside labor work after doing such kind of 'divine work of preparing idols'. We feel that there is no future for us in this trade and we feel complete alienated. We feel that government should help us and protect our workmanship.

Kodurupaka Lakshmaiah

My name is Kodurupaka Lakshmaiah native of Kanagarthi Village, Odela Mandal of Karimnagar District. I am 60 years old and I am doing this Brass work from my 16th years of age. I learnt the occupational skills from my father. I have passed 10th class and discontinued and started doing the work. My father, grandfather and great grandfather and many ancestors had continued the tradition without any break.

We are three in our family. My wife aged 45 years studied upto 5th class and my son aged 13 years studying 9th class. My wife does household work and also assists me in my work. I own a house. It is a small tiled house constructed by myself and not received any financial help from Government. It is having only minimum facilities like Bathroom, Toilet and Cooking gas stove. I do not have any agricultural land.

Kanagarthi is a major panchayat village and there are 10 families of my caste doing the work. I prepare Brass articles like glasses, plates, and cooking utensils. I do not have any separate workshop but I converted a part of my house as the workshop. We purchase raw bronze material from Karimnagar/Warangal District, recycle them and prepare new articles on orders booked by the customers. The articles prepared in my house will be sold in the villages. The city people do not give importance to these utensils. I sell the articles produced by me in my village and also neighboring villages traveling by riding a bicycle. Now-a-days most of the people are purchasing plastic materials and as such due to this we are losing the work. It is so happening that we are not getting sufficient amount to lead our daily life.

The materials which are prepared sometimes unable to sell even after visiting a number of villages to sell the products. We also sell them in our house to those who approach us. If the materials are not sold we get loss, I have taken a loan from a money lender and invested it on the tools and raw materials and I need to repay it with the profit I have earned. But in the event of getting loss it will be difficult to repay the loan amount to the money lenders with interest. We are not getting sufficient returns despite working hard and investing our labour. There is no other source of income we have and we hardly know any other work.

At the end I would reiterate that

1. Day by day the profession has been losing its importance. We are not getting value for our labour
2. We are not getting any other jobs and Government is not taking care of my profession.
3. We don't have any capital amount to start any business or carry on any other income generating activity.

We have already lost our hopes on our future, but we still feel that government can intervene and do something, especially:

1. Government should help us by providing Bank loan interest free or with a little interest.
2. Subsidy should be given for the purchase of raw material.

3. Separate Production –cum- Business areas should be developed by the government and allot sites to us so that we can produce and sell the material prepared.
4. Government should provide market facilities to the materials prepared.
5. Free medical assistance is to be provided and Workers aged above 50 years must be given pension to lead their livelihood.

Kodurupaka Laxmirajam

My name is Kodunupaka Lakshmirajam. I am 50 years old. I hail from Kanagarthi Village of Odela Mandal and District Karimnagar. I learnt the Brass work from my father and maternal uncle and started working from the age of 16th year. I have not undergone any training. My ancestors did the same occupational work for a few hundred years and I am also continuing the hereditary occupation.

There are five members in my family. My wife, my mother and two children. I studied upto 3rd class. My mother aged 80 years and my wife is 45 years, illiterate helps me in my work. My daughter 22 years doing BSc final year and my son 18 years doing degree 1st year. I wish my children to get higher education and get some good job. I have got a small house with two rooms constructed by me and no Government assistance is given. I have minimum facilities of drinking water, toilet, current and cooking gas cylinder and minimum utensils.

I am doing the Brasssmith work since 35 years. I am doing the work from my own house by sparing a certain portion of the house for my workshop purpose. I produce the utensils with Copper, Bronze and Aluminum. The household utensils used in the villages like glass, bowls, plates etc are prepared by us and sold to the villages. We purchase all the raw materials required such as raw Copper,

Bronze etc., from open market we produce various kinds of utensils with that material. We also prepare Boilers, Buckets, Tumblers and other materials used in house. We get orders from the regular customers or shop owners and some others who directly purchase the available utensils from us.

Customers who require products pay advance and place orders to prepare the utensils. We then prepare the articles and hand over them. Then we collect the balance amount. We don't have any new technology or equipment and no formal training in using the new technology. We do the hard manual work with traditional tools and it takes longer time to produce articles. We repair the old utensils and other articles as asked by the public with low payment.

We need Tejab, Yelligaram, Sutte, Patkar, Gannu, Sangadi, other materials to liquefy the metals. Later we mould the articles into required shapes. The articles prepared by us are standard one and durable for several years. I do not engage any outsider for labour assistance. Now-a-days as the new technology has been emerging and factories are producing modern products, we are finding it difficult to get the work needed. To start a shop or small industry, we need heavy investment nearly to the extent of at least 1 lakh which we cannot afford. No Government is extending any loan facility or subsidy facility or providing us any raw material. This is the state of affair of our community and its occupation.

In our caste very few people are well educated. Only few members who are countable on fingers are doing some job either in the Government or private sector. I took an amount of 30,000 on loan basis for purchasing the equipment and raw material required. Now I am unable to repay the loan. We are not earning sufficient amount to make our livelihood. Now a days there is no importance to the utensils produced by us. My father and my forefather did the same job when there was lot of demands for our products but the future generation cannot do the same job because there is neither any demand nor we receive assistance from government. We do not have any competition in our vocation as other castes people do not do this work. So only our caste people come forward to do this job. But there is heavy competition from factory production. For the last two generations our conditions are further deteriorated. We are not getting any pension. It will be better if Government provides pension to the old age people who have crossed 50 years. There are also Health problems, so health care should be provided to us.

We feel that Government should provide free education to our children, medical aid to our families and loans and subsidies to our caste workers. In order to lead a better life Government should extend necessary help.

Kandukuri Sudhakar

My name is Kandukuri Sudhakar 40 years old. I am residing at Lashkar Bazar, Hanamkonda Mandal of Warangal District. Since birth I am staying here. I started undertaking this profession since 20 years. I started this work at the age of 20. We are 6 members in our family, myself, my wife, father, mother and two sons. My father aged 62 passed 7th class and discontinued and started doing this Brass work. My mother is illiterate and now 56 years old. I studied upto 7th class and discontinued. I started helping my father after discontinuing my studies. My wife 32 years old studied up to Inter and now helping the family and looking after the household duties. My elder son aged 14 years studying 8th class. My father did the same profession and I am continuing the same traditional occupation and after dropping art from school in the middle.

We are having our own RCC building. There are three rooms in it. We do not have any agriculture land. I have one scoter, Drinking water facility, Bathroom, Toilet, Current, T.V, Cooker and other facilities we have at our home.

I do Brass work and undertake welding by using gas. I did not get any training for this work. I learnt it from my father and I am doing this work alone. I do not have separate area for workshop I am doing it now from my home. I purchased a gas welding machine. I need to cut the metal in required shapes and for this I have to purchase the cutting machine. For this purpose I need capital amount. As I do not have the required money and I could not purchase a cutting machine. Whenever the cutting is required, I send the material for other workshop for cutting and pay for it. I need to spend additional amount for transport and pay for cutting charges and it has been a time consuming process. In the absence of a cutting machine customers are also avoiding me for giving work. In rainy season and winter season I do not have much work. On unseasonal days we go for outdoor work. I purchased the tools required and even for that no financial assistance required from Government. I did not get any help at all from Government side. In my work children are not associated because it is a hazardous work doing with gas. Any miscalculation may lead to a disaster. Women also will not participate in this work. Generally I work for 8-10 hours a day when there is work. During the work we also consume electric power and Government charges the 'power tariff' on commercial basis. The cost of unit rate in this regard will be more than domestic use. Competition is more in this work especially from big workshop. They use their influence and public relations and monopolies the work available. We need subsidy for the material purchased and there should be an agency to sell our products. No bank is providing loan to our caste members. In villages there is no work for the profession. Most of our caste persons are migrating to the cities and doing some other work.

In our caste the literacy rate is less and most of those enrolled invariably dropout at school level and very rare go for higher education. As a result only a handful of our caste members are found in government service. Among my relatives I found not even a single person in Government service. As 'big units' with higher capital and modern machines are coming up there has been a steep fall in our demand and we are experiencing 'loss of work and incomes' and there is a shift in our occupation towards joining construction sites as labour'.

As things stand today we have only a limited number doing their work due to non-availability of capital amount and non-availability of work. Government and other agencies should extend necessary support to our units. Old people cannot work and if they don't work they loose their livelihood. There is no pension scheme to old age people. If things are moved like this there will be hardly any future for us.

9

Kammari- *The Black Smith*

Traditionally, the Kammaris are iron-smelter workers and miners. The name Kammari is derived from the Hindi word aag, meaning fire, and from the association with the furnace used for smelting iron ore. They also call themselves Kammari (or Blacksmith from the word loha, meaning Iron) and believe that their caste has existed from the beginning of the world. Their traditions teach them that the first Kammari made the ploughshare with which the first Bullocks furrowed the primeval soil.

The traditional occupations of the Kammari are Iron melting and manufacturing of agricultural implements like axes and ploughshares, mattocks, and sickles. Today, the metal for making these implements is purchased from the market. Iron implements are readily available too which has caused a good number of Kammari to turn to agriculture, animal husbandry and unskilled wage labour. Some Kammaris, like those of Madhya Pradesh, are proficient in making wooden masks as toys for children. Hunting and collecting forest produce are their subsidiary occupations.

The most serious engineering skills of India are located in three communities-the ironsmiths, the carpenters and the goldsmiths. These communities brought in a revolutionary change in agrarian production. All these caste communities suffer from the social stigma of Shudra existence. Iron smithing seems to have pre-Aryan existence; hence it continues to be a shudra occupation all over the country. Historically, the skill of using metals to make tools must have been perfected much before the onset of Indus valley Civilization. The artisan communities and their tool based engineering skills work as a record of their own history.

The process of smithing iron has several stages. The process of smithing has contributed to the process of agrarian revolution in several ways. How the Indian Social Forces, before the Aryans invaded the country, discovered the importance of iron is a part of history. The process of melting iron and the working out of the smithing process, especially in terms of caste and the Indian civil society, has not been discussed in any significant way in any of our historical writing. The entire development of the smithing technology is a part of the knowledge system of the Ironsmiths (Kammaris in Telugu country, and equivalent castes in all the linguistic states).

This entire village based iron-melting spot is known as Kammari Kolimi in Telugu. The Kammari is a highly knowledgeable person who knows about the properties of iron that he (iron smithing in the villages is primarily a male task) to handle. He knows at which points of heating the iron melts in the hearth, and knows how iron should be moulded to build agrarian instruments or early industrial tools like the Sickle, the hammer, the spade, and so on. The hammer that was made out of this process has been the most powerful industrial instrument that shaped not only India but the whole world. However, the iron smithing science put the Indian civilization on its legs as it helped to construct a whole range of wood technology for improving the process of production in India.

Apart from Iron, Wood and pot making, the artisans of India also possess enormous skills in Gold and Silver smithing. The knowledge of this engineering though, was not very useful for the productive process as it constructed a cultural and economic value-based wealth in India.

Children begin working with their parents at an early age. Literacy is poor among this rural community, though more recently they have begun sending their children to school. Like most Hindus, the Kammaris are restricted by custom or law to marry within a specific caste but within this grouping they are divided into several clans and sub-clans. Marriages are permissible between these units or clans. The Kammari folk songs tell about their lives as artisans and farmers. They also have many folk tales and dances.

The Kammaris are traditionally are skilled at making and repairing agricultural implements like the Sickle, Spade, Hoe, Axe and Plough, as well as Buckets, Pans, Knives, Scissors, Grills and Cages. They also fix iron shoes on the hoofs of bullocks. Some of those living in cities work in Government and private service or industrial work. The landless among them are increasingly are migrating to urban centres in search of employment. They supplement their income by selling bullocks and cattle. Some of the Kammari practice share-cropping and work as daily-wage laborers. In some towns and cities, some Kammaris own workshops that are fitted with modern machinery for making fine implements. Literacy is low, but their attitude towards formal education is highly favorable. They are a fervent Hindu community, worshipping Ram and the goddess Kali.

Like Carpenters, Kammaris the Blacksmiths are important artisans needed in villages and also towns. As most of the agricultural implements apart from wood, are made of iron (and some both wood and iron), the primary Iron work is mainly done by the Kammari families. The man does the main work but women do assist and help the male members in some works. Like Carpenters, Blacksmiths were also part of earlier jajmani system in the village and they too were attached to farmer families in the village. They manufacture various agriculture implements and also do repairs to most items every year. For the repairing work done, they are paid in kind in the shape of grains at the time for harvest by the farmers to whom they were attached. For the fresh manufacturing of goods and articles, they are paid in cash. Primarily Blacksmiths produce goods for the consumption of the villagers in case of rural areas and nearby localities in case of urban areas. The entire transaction in urban areas is done in the form of cash. As there has been new 'implements' coming in over the years and also mechanization is taking place, the 'works' which were to be done by Blacksmiths earlier have been reduced and as a result they face severe shortage of work and thereby fall in their income. Some Kammari families, who could mobilize funds and invest in 'Lathe and Welding machines' were found to be in a position to get orders for work but such enterprises are found 'limited'. Installing Lathe machines and Moulding implements need heavy investment and also need special training to run the machines. Only in big villages and towns such units are found and among them many outside communities other than 'Kammari' communities starting setting up such units taking, away their 'traditional opportunities' with this background a field study has been undertaken to analyze the socio economic and work situations of the Kammari community in Telangana and Andhra Pradesh.

Sample and Size of the Family

Table 9-1 indicates that out of 129 sample households chosen from Kammari Community 58.14% (75) belong to urban areas and the remaining 42.86% (54) belong to rural areas. A large number of respondents belong to the (51.48%) age-group of 46 and above. There were also around 11% of respondents belong to above the age of 'and above' 66. 23.26% of respondents belong to the age group of 20-35. It is significant to notice that more than 20% of families had more than five members in the family. While 58% of families had three to four members in the family, around 18% were two-member families. The overall picture of the data presented in table 9.1 indicate that a majority of the sample of Kammari community respondents were drawn from urban areas, middle aged group and had more than four members in the family.

Education of Family Members

Table-2 indicates that the educational background of family members. It shows that about 28.48% of family members (of the total 453 family members) were illiterates. 51% of family members had education between 1 to 10th class. Only 5.30% were graduates and 3.97% has technical degrees to their credit. As far as the sample respondents themselves are concerned, out of 129, 23.25% (30) were illiterates, while only 4.65% (6) had completed graduation. Most of the elder female persons including almost all the spouses of the respondents were illiterates. In all it indicates that educationally the Kammari community members were 'weak'.

Occupation of Five Generations of Family Members

Table 9-3 indicates the details relating to the occupational background of five generations of the respondents family. It may be significant to observe that the father generation, grand fathers, great grandfather's generation and the respondent has followed the hereditary occupation without any break or shift. However when it comes to the respondents son's turn, only 13.04% of them had adopted the hereditary profession, while others had already 'shifted' to other occupations after completing their studies. Around 10% of grown up male children however shifted to other traditional occupations, while another 10% shifted towards modern occupations. It is also significant to observe that for five generations, no single member of the respondents could get the opportunity to join the government service. 'Modernization' has not reached these communities and its impact on their occupational life has been very much negligent in job absorptions, while the pace of 'modernization' on the other has been very slow and dragging.

Table 9.1

Size of the Family

Sl. No	Age	Place	Single	Two Members	Three Members	Four Members	Five Members	Six Members & Above	Total
01.	Up to 25	Urban	-	3 (50) (12.5)	3 (50) (8.33)	-	-	-	**6 (100) (4.65)**
		Rural	-	-	3 (100) (8.33)	-	-	-	**3 (100) (2.33)**
02.	26-35	Urban	-	3 (16.67) (12.5)	3 (16.67) (8.33)	12 (66.66) (30.78)	-	-	**18 (100) (13.95)**
		Rural	-	-	-	-	3 (100) (20)	-	**3 (100) (2.33)**
03.	36-45	Urban	-	-	-	6 (66.67) (15.38)	3 (33.33) (20)	-	**9 (100) (6.97)**
		Rural	-	3 (14.28) (12.5)	6 (28.57) (16.67)	9 (42.86) (23.08)	3 (14.29) (20)	-	**21 (100) (16.28)**
04.	46-55	Urban	-	-	6 (40) (16.67)	6 (40) (15.38)	-	3 (20) (25)	**15 (100) (11.63)**
		Rural	3 (20) (100)	-	12 (80) (33.34)	-	-	-	**15 (100) (11.63)**
05.	56-65	Urban	-	6 (28.57) (25)	3 (14.29) (8.33)	6 (28.57) (15.38)	6 (28.57) (40)	-	**21 (100) (16.28)**
		Rural	-	-	-	-	-	3 (100) (25)	**3 (100) (2.33)**
06.	66 & Above	Urban	-	3 (50) (12.5)	-	-	-	3 (50) (25)	**6 (100) (4.65)**
		Rural	-	6 (66.67) (25)	-	-	-	3 (33.33) (25)	**9 (100) (6.97)**
	Total		**3 (2.33) (100)**	**24 (18.60) (100)**	**36 (27.91) (100)**	**39 (30.23) (100)**	**15 (11.63) (100)**	**12 (9.30) (100)**	**129 (100%) (100%)**

Table 9.2
Education of Family Members

Sl. No	Relationship with the Respondent	Illiterate	0-5 Classes	6-10 Classes	Inter/ITI	Degree	Other Technical Courses	Total
01.	Respondent	30 (23.25) (23.25)	27 (20.93) (32.14)	27 (44.19) (38.77)	9 (6.98) (17.64)	6 (4.65) (25)	-	**129 (100) (28.48)**
02.	Father	3 (100) (2.33)	-	-	-	-	-	**3 (100) (0.67)**
03.	Mother	6 (100) (4.65)	-	-	-	-	-	**6 (100) (1.32)**
04.	Wife	66 (51.16) (51.16)	33 (25.58) (39.29)	21 (16.28) (14.29)	9 (6.98) (17.65)	-	-	**129 (100) (28.48)**
05.	Son	12 (12.5) (9.30)	6 (6.25) (7.14)	42 (43.75) (28.57)	9 (9.37) (17.65)	12 (12.50) (50)	15 (15.63) (83.33)	**96 (100) (21.19)**
06.	Daughter	9 (12.50) (6.98)	18 (25) (21.43)	21 (29.17) (14.29)	15 (20.83) (29.41)	6 (8.33) (25)	3 (4.17) (16.67)	**72 (10) (15.89)**
07.	Others	3 (16.67) (2.33)	-	6 (33.33) (4.08)	9 (50) (17.65)	-	-	**18 (100) (3.97)**
	Total	**129 (28.48) (100)**	**84 (18.54) (100)**	**147 (32.45) (100)**	**51 (11.26) (100)**	**24 (5.30) (100)**	**18 (3.97) (100)**	**453 (100%) (100%)**

Table 9.3
Occupation of the Family Members

Sl. No		Caste Occupation	Other Traditional Occupation	Modern Occupation	Government Job	Others/ Study	Total
01.	Respondent	129 (1000 (24.15)	-	-	-	-	129 (100) (19.73)
02.	Respondent's Father	129 (100) (24.16)	-	-	-	-	129 (100) (19.73)
03.	Respondent's Grand Father	129 (100) (24.16)	-	-	-	-	129 (100) (19.72)
04.	Respondent's Grand Father's Father	129 (100) (24.16)	-	-	-	-	129 (100) (19.72)
05.	Respondent's Son	18 (13.04) (3.37)	15 (10.87) (100)	15 (10.87) (100)	-	90 (65.22) (100)	138 (100) (21.10)
	Total	**534 (81.65) (100)**	**15 (2.30) (100)**	**15 (2.29) (100)**	**-**	**90 (13.76) (100)**	**654 (100%) (100%)**

Education and Length of Occupation

Table 9.4 indicates that educational background of the respondents in relation to the length of service of their occupation. It shows that education has been nothing to do with the choice of occupation. It has been noticed that some of the respondents (4.65%) could complete graduation but could not get any job and joined their hereditary occupation for the last two years. Likewise 6.98% of respondents who completed 'intermediate', but could not get other job, had to join the rank and file of their forefathers as Blacksmiths. Out of the remaining 67% of respondents who had education between 1 to 10 classes had to invariably enter into this occupation and have been in the profession for long. Around 24% of respondents had been in the profession for more than 31 years and some of them even for the last 50 years. Thus literate or illiterate, educated or not educated, the situation as far as Blacksmiths are concerned had to invariably retain their hereditary occupation, mainly because of their bad economic position and lack of other alternative.

Table 9.4

Education and Length of Occupation

Sl. No	Education	0-5 years	6-10	11-20	21-30	31-40	41-50	51 & above	Total
01.	Illiterate	-	3(10) (33.33)	12 (40) (33.33)	9 (30) (23.07)	-	-	6 (20) (100.0)	**30 (100) (23.25)**
02.	0-5 Class	3(11.12) (16.18)	-	3 (11.11) (8.33)	9 (33.33) (23.07)	9 (33.33) (75)	3 (11.11) (33.33)	-	**27 (100) (20.93)**
03.	6-10 Class	-	6 (10.53) (66.67)	21 (36.84) (58.33)	21 (36.84) (53.86)	3 (5.26) (25)	6 (10.53) (66.67)	-	**57 (100) (44.19)**
04.	Inter	9 (100) (50.0)	-	-	-	-	-	-	**9 (100) (6.98)**
05.	Degree	6 (100) (32.82)	-	-	-	-	-	-	**6(100) (4.65)**
	Total	**18 (13.95) (100)**	**9 (6.98) (100)**	**36 (27.91) (100)**	**39 (30.23) (100)**	**12 (9.30) (100)**	**9 (6.98) (100)**	**9 (6.97) (100)**	**129 (100%) (100%)**

Stated occupation of Children of Respondents

Table-9.5 indicates that only 13.05% of children prefer to join fathers occupation during the present generation. All of them were being drawn from urban areas. Significantly the children of all the respondents drawn from rural areas had either found in studies or joined other occupations such as agricultural labour. A large number of respondents who migrated from rural to urban areas were either found in studies or joined some or the other occupation other than their hereditary occupation.

Table 9.5

Stated Occupation of Children

Sl. No	Place		Same Occupation	Modern Occupation	Labour	Others/ Study	Total
01.	Rural	Migrant	-	-	-	-	-
		Local/ Non Migrant	-	-	21(36.84) (87.50)	36 (63.16) (41.38)	**57 (100) (44.19)**
02.	Urban	Migrant	3 (8.33) (16.67)	-	3 (8.33) (12.50)	30 (81.34) (34.48)	**36 (100) (27.91)**
		Local/ Non-Migrant	15 (41.67) (83.33)	-	-	21 (58.33) (24.14)	**36 (100) (27.90)**
Total			**18 (13.95) (100)**	-	**24(18.61) (100)**	**87 (67.44) (100)**	**129 (100%) (100%)**

Occupation of women in the Family

It is significant to observe that 66.67% of women in the families have been preferred to be idle not doing any outside work as per the family norms. 9.52% of women preferred to join other work, breaking the norm while only 23.81% of women in these families had been drawn into the same occupation by their spouses. These women belong to the age-group of '36 and above'. This indicates that age is no bar for the women to join some or the other occupation, but for the family norms young women however not inclined to join in any of the occupational work of the Blacksmith.

Blacksmith has been a male-oriented occupation for long but women still assist men mainly in 'hammering operations'. Men do the moulding or sharpening or other jobs of the mutual instruments. All the men and women in the profession were found to have received training under their parents and not received any formal training from anywhere.

Table 9.6

Occupation of Women in the Family

Sl. No	Age	Involved in Occupation	Doing other work	Idle/unmarried/Housewife	Total
01.	Up to 25	-	3 (25) (25)	9 (75) (10.71)	**12 (100) (9.52)**
02.	26-35	-	3 (9.09) (25)	30 (90.91) (35.72)	**33 (100) (26.19)**
03.	36-40	9 (50) (30)	3 (16.67) (25)	6 (33.33) (7.14)	**18 (100) (14.29)**
04.	40-55	18 (40) (60)	3 (6.67) (25)	24 (53.33) (28.57)	**45 (100) (35.72)**
05.	56-60	-	-	9 (100) (10.71)	**9 (100) (7.14)**
06.	60 and above	3 (33.33) (10)	-	6 (66.67) (7.14)	**9 (100) (7.14)**
	Total	**30 (23.81) (100)**	**12 (9.52) (100)**	**84 (66.67) (100)**	**129 (100%) (100%)**

Assets

An analysis of the available data indicates that only 9.30% (12 out of 129) of Kammari sample households had owned some agricultural land of their own. 74.41% of respondents own a house, while there was mixed position with regard to other assets/amenities such as Power, Tap, Bathroom, Lavatory facilities, TV, Sewing Machine, etc.,

It may be found that all the respondents had their 'own account enterprises or self-managed enterprises' and their primary occupation being blacksmith and has no other secondary occupation. Most of the Kammari families had converted a part of their own house into a 'production/floor area', while 32.56% of respondents had separate workshops as an 'annexed' of the house or somewhere in the town and city.

Investment Details

The available data collected from the respondents indicates that 30% of them had invested only upto Rs. 10,000/-, while 44% of respondents had invested upto Rs. 25,000/- 13.18% of respondents had invested upto Rs. 50,000/. Only 0.78% (3) of respondents had invested between 1 lakh and above. It may be observed that 79.07% of respondents had used their own funds as investment which was between

5000 to Rs. 30,000/-. It is surprising that Banks did not reach these Kammari community people as only 2.33% of respondents could take loans from Banks. Money lenders had their sway over these people as 18.06% of respondents had taken loans from them. This has been the case mainly with the respondents drawn from urban and rural areas.

Tble 9.7

Source of Investment

Sl. No	Source	Urban	Rural	Total
01.	Own	54 (52.94) (72.0)	48 (47.06) (88.89)	**102 (100) (79.07)**
02.	Bank	3 (100) (4)	-	**3 (100) (2.33)**
03.	Money Lender	18(75) (24)	6 (25) (11.11)	**24 (100) (18.60)**
Total		**75 (58.14) (100)**	**54 (41.86) (100)**	**129 (100%) (100%)**

Production Plan

Normally Kammari families involve their own family members in the production or repair operation and do not take outside support. Unless and until there are 'heavy orders' and excess work available. During those times they employ their own Caste men part time payment basis. Customers will visit their 'places or localities' or workshops and get their things done. Most of them buy the required products on the spot as sometimes the required quantities of products are readily available. Kammari families mainly depend upon local orders of individual customers or shop keepers. Individual consumers pay advance for the products only in advance shop keepers generally do not pay any advance. In that case to 'place an 'order' for a product shop keepers do not need to invest but expect that the producer himself invest money on raw materials used and other spares.

Due to supply of industrial goods which are available in the open market, people are preferring them for want of variety in product range and quality component and due to this Kammari families are found to be struggling to get orders. In rural areas also due to 'mechanisation' and limited use of plough and bullock carts and various others traditional agricultural implements, most of them had lost their livelihood and had to search for alternate employment. Those who had stayed back in the village looked out for agricultural work or whatever paid work available to them. In the urban areas 'sophisticated cutting machines' had replaced the Blacksmith men and they have become popular. Due to this those Kammaris who work with hand tools had lost the opportunity. It may also be found many of the Kammari families joining the construction industry doing various odd job. Most of the respondents had said that they had to search for seasonal work and move from one place to the other, based on the availability of work, while alienating themselves from their traditional work.

Unlike other OBC Communities such as Kamsali, Rajaka, Mangali, etc., Kammari community has no ceremonial functions to attend and offer their services except providing new implements to the agricultural families during the agriculture season. But such opportunities has become rare now and due to the widespread use of Tractors and others Machines in agricultural operations. Now in many areas these Kammari men and women are looked down and had lost the earlier esteem.

Government Policies and Schemes

Government has not evolved any specific policy or welfare scheme with regards to these communities and their occupations. The general welfare and development schemes such as Artisan credit card system, Aadharana scheme, Pension Schemes etc did not reach these groups. The coverage of these schemes was found very limited. Bank loans had become distant dreams as only 2.33% of respondents had access to Bank loans. Majority of the respondents said that they have approached the Banks for loans, but could not pursue further because of many restrictions, the Bank officers imposed.

About 7% of respondents approached money lenders for loans and secured the same. The respondents had said that these communities over the years had looked down and hardly considered for extending any support by others. Due to the failure of Banks to cover these people, they had lost whatever the facilities such as margin money, subsidy etc., as they were linked to Bank loans.

It has been found that 48.8% of respondent's families had availed the facility of joining a DWAKRA or other self-help groups and participating in its programmes. This facility has benefitted some families to obtain loans and manage savings for utilizing the same for various family purposes.

In the overall sense, the government schemes only had a little impact on the lives of these communities with some exception here and there.

Table 9.8

Welfare schemes

Sl. No	Schemes	Available	Not Available	Total
01.	Artisan Credit Card	-	129 (100)	**129 (100) (20)**
02.	Aadarana Scheme	-	129 (100)	**129 (100) (20)**
03.	Bank Loans	3 (2.33)	126 (97.67)	**129 (100) (20)**
04.	Govt. Pensions	-	129 (100)	**129 (100) (20)**
05.	DWAKRA/SHG	63 (48.87)	66 (51.16)	**129 (100) (20)**
06.	Money Lenders	9 (7.0)	120 (93.0)	**129 (100)**
	Total	**66 (10.23)**	**579 (89.77)**	**645 (100%)**

Role of Associations

It has been found that Community Associations are not strong and organized well to protect their interests. Most of the Associations favour to focus mainly on social and cultural aspects of their caste, while doing little towards exerting pressure on political leaders and government officials for getting economic benefits. Several of the respondents had said that due to bad leadership and its failure, Associations could not play any significant role in representing their problems. Most of the Association does not have any economic agenda to bring up their communities with their programmes.

Occupation Based Problems

Respondents were asked to mention their three main occupational problems in order of intensity. There was mixed opinion and respondents were not clear in their perception and also in their order of intensity of the problems. Most of the respondents mentioned their normal problems as it occurs to them, without giving any deep thought to it. There was also lack of clarity as the order of preferences was jig-jag and 'specific trend' could not be found out. However the data given in Table 9.9 will provide some general understanding about the major occupational problems and the general perception or respondents towards the same. The problems mentioned were: Capital (Investment) Problems, Non-availability of subsidized raw material, issues relating to quality of the products, corruption among government officials in extending modernization, benefits, lack of other alternate employment, lack of technical education and occupational training, lack of proper implementation of welfare schemes, exploitation by readymade industrial goods and products, lack of minimum support price and insurance. Other problems also mentioned during the course of discussion include lack of subsidy for tools, lack of Bank loans, lack of education, lack of occupational or accident relief pensions, failure of community associations to represent the problems, caste discrimination, lack of unity amongst the members of the community and their unorganized nature and failure of leadership etc., Majority of the respondents had also said that due to the 'heavy physical nature of work' involved in the occupation using metals, hammer, fire etc., they very often get heart diseases, joint pains, eye sight problems, skin allergies, hearing problems and others and medical expenses made many a families indebted, creating other unforeseen problems. According to them these problems were found accumulating over the years and solutions were hardly found. The result was all round deterioration of their conditions.

Table 9.9

Occupational Based Problems in order as mentioned (Cumulative)

Sl. No	Problems	1st Order	IInd Order	IIIrd Order	Total
01.	Capital Problem	24 (80) (18.60)	3 (10) (2.38)	3 (10) (2.27)	**30 (100) (7.75)**
02.	Raw material Problems	18 (60) (13.95)	9 (30) (7.14)	3 (10) (2.27)	**30 (100) (7.75)**
03.	Quality Maintenance	-	9 (42.86) (7.14)	12 (57.14) (9.09)	**21 (100) (51.42)**
04.	Corruption among Government bodies	9 (16.67) (6.98)	24 (44.44) (19.04)	21 (38.89) (15.91)	**54 (100) (13.95)**
05.	Lack of Government support	33 (64.70) (25.58)	3 (5.88) (2.38)	15 (29.41) (11.36)	**51 (100) (13.18)**
06.	Lack of Modernisation	9 (33.33) (6.98)	3 (11.11) (2.38)	15 (55.56) (11.36)	**27 (100) (6.98)**
07.	Lack of other alternative employment	6 (18.18) (4.65)	12 (36.37) (9.52)	15 (45.45) (11.36)	**33 (100) (8.53)**
08.	Lack of technical development and occupational training	12 (44.44) (9.30)	9 (33.33) (7.14)	6 (22.22) (4.56)	**27 (100) (6.98)**
09.	Lack of Market Facility	9 (42.86) (6.98)	6 (28.57) (4.76)	6 (28.57) (4.56)	**21 (100) (5.42)**
10.	Exploitation of Ready Made Industrial Products	3 (12.5) (2.33)	9 (37.5) (7.14)	12 (50) (9.09)	**24 (100) (6.20)**
11.	Lack of Minimum support price and lack of insurance facility	6 (8.69) (4.65)	39 (56.52) (30.95)	24 (14.79) (18.18)	**69 (100) (17.83)**
Total		**129 (33.33) (100)**	**129 (32.56) (100)**	**132 (34.11) (100)**	**387 (100%) (100%)**

Solutions to Problems

Most of the respondents did not give suggestions dealing with the specific occupational issues and problems. But during the course of discussions, they have said that they need Governmental intervention with regards to all the problems mentioned by them earlier. Government should evolve specific policy to save them from the deteriorating conditions. Table 9.10 indicates the trend of their specific suggestions. Apart from those mentioned in the course of their discussion, the suggestions include provision for regular alternate employment, provision for financial assistance and subsidies, evolving protective discrimination policy to provide the facility of 'product reservation and provision for issue of work orders relating to Government' work exclusively for them, provision for free technical educational, occupational training etc., Most respondents had felt that 'nothing would change' in their life, unless Government comes forward and do something as above and help them.

Table 9.10

Solutions to Problems

Sl. No	Response	Rural	Urban	Total
01.	Provision for regular alternate employment.	24 (34.78) (44.44)	15 (65.22) (60)	**69 (100) (53.49)**
02.	Provision for Financial Assistance and Subsidies	15 (50) (27.78)	15 (50) (20)	**30 (100) (23.26)**
03.	Product Reservation and Government Orders	9 (60) (16.67)	6 (40) (8)	**15 (100) (11.62)**
04.	Provision for Free Technical Education Occupational Training	6 (66.67) (11.11)	3 (33.333) (4)	**9 (100) (69.81)**
	Total	**54 (41.86) (100)**	**75 (58.14) (100)**	**129 (100%) (100%)**

Future Perspective

Although during the course of discussion, many of the respondents were 'skeptical' about the prospects of their occupation, all of them however said that their children should not enter into this occupation. They said that over the years they have witnessed only the degradation of their socio-economic conditions and accumulation of their problems. Still however 13.95% of respondents find that 'future' may be 'hopeful' for them if things change, but 86.05% of respondents said categorically said that their future is not 'hopeful.' Both urban and rural respondents without any exception have said that nothing may save their occupation. Unless a specific policy framework is created and their problem are understood and addressed in proper perspective their 'degradation process' will continue to play havoc with their lives.

Table 9.11
Future Prospects

Sl. No	Response	Rural	Urban	Total
01.	Hopeful	3 (16.67) (5.56)	15 (83.33) (20)	**18 (100) (13.95)**
02.	Not Hopeful	51 (45.95) (94.44)	60 (54.05) (80)	**111 (100) (86.05)**
03.	**Total**	**54 (41.86) (100)**	**75 (58.14) (100)**	**129 (100%) (100%)**

Profiles and Case Studies of Select Kammari Respondents

K. Kumaraswamy

My name is Kumaraswamy aged 55 years, studied upto 2nd class. My native place is Nagampalli, Mandal Nallabelli of Warangal District. Due to certain financial problems I left my village and went to Pochammakunta of Hanamkonda in Warangal District. I came here long before 10 years. I learnt Black Smith work from my parents. My grandfather and great grandfather did the same profession.

We are four in our family, myself and my wife one son and daughter-in-law. My son aged 26 years studied upto 10th class and married. His wife stays at home and do not work. She discontinued her studies. My wife is 45 years old illiterate. She also looks after the household work.

We are living in a rented house. It is RCC building and we do not have any pet animals. I have one Bicycle. The facilities in the house include bathroom, latrine and cooking gas. I do not have any T.V, Sewing Machine, Cooker, or Refrigerator. I read news paper outside.

I have a workshop at home itself. We have good relationship with the neighbours. We live together friendly and help each others. I got my own welding machine. I am also doing welding work at home. I get the iron material from Warangal town itself. I brought the tools from my native place and I purchased some of the newly emerging tools when I opened the shop.

I prepare Grills, different types of Shutters and also the material needed for house construction, shed work and other office materials with different Designs, Doors, Windows and other equipment required for the house construction. The amount we get out of this work is not sufficient to our family expenditure as many works are not available due to heavy competition from big workshops and readymade articles.

We need some capital investment towards purchase of machines and raw materials. We do not have sufficient backup as our family's economic position is weak. I had to borrow the amount whenever needed from outside money lenders. For this we have to pay exorbitant rates of interest which becomes heavy burden on our part.

Generally we start the work in the morning around 8:00 am and carry it up to evening 6:00pm. The material which we prepare and sell from home as well as outside away in Bazar or Market.

Government or any other agencies are not extending any help to us. We have to depend on our work. Our livelihood depends on the work done by us and source of work is essential. When my father was doing the work and looking after the workshop there was no competition and there was availability of plenty of work. Now due to the arrival of new technology and new machinery several big workshops have come up, the labour component is reduced and it is affecting our work. As such we are not getting good amount of work and there is no value to our work.

Government is not providing its work to us. It gives the work orders to only big contractors otherwise there should have been plenty of work which would have been sufficient to us. As a result of loss of work we have left with no alternative expect to go out for daily wage physical labour outside. We are facing harsh times and everyone in the family feel frustrated. If we get regular work, there will be happiness. If they are followed by the festivals or community functions in the family, we spend some time with our Community and family members and feel further happy and such occasions which however are not many and rare over the years.

As part of welfare programme, we expected that government to provide some help but it is not doing anything. We feel that

1. Government is not coming forward to provide individual loans.
2. No tools are provided by government on subsidy basis.
3. No training facility in modern technology.
4. We expect that Government should allot Budget to our caste members to purchase raw materials and tools.
5. Government should provide subsidized power for welding work.
6. Government should provide Health Card to our communities members for free Health checkup and issue medicines.
7. Government should also recognize our skill and encourage our art.
8. Government should provide free residential education to our children and help the coming generations in our community.
9. Government should evolve a specific suitable policy exclusively meant for artisans and help them survive in their traditional occupation or show suitable alternate employment.

Kanchalla Krishna Murthy

My name is Kanchalla Krishnamurthy 58 years old studied up to intermediate. My native place is Mucherla Nagaram of Hasanparthy Mandal District Warangal. I came to Hanamkonda, Hanumannagar 20 years back in search of work. My father and grandfather were also doing the Blacksmith work. My wife is 45 years and studied upto 10th class and works at home. I have one daughter and one son. My son is 25 years old completed Degree but doing presently the same Kammari work and looking for a job. My daughter is 25 years old did MBA but unemployed and she is looking for a job.

I have one RCC building with reasonable amenities like Bathroom, Latrine, water facility, electricity, T.V, Radio. We do not have sewing machine or a refrigerator we do not have any pet animals. We read the news paper outside wherever is available. In my native place I got one acre of dry land which I gave it for lease and out of it I get some food grains.

I am living at Hanuman Nagar since 20 years. The neighbours are friendly to me and extend help necessary in needful occasion. I have setup a workshop and I do welding work. I prepare some articles like Iron chairs, Tables, Almarah etc. with iron and sell them in the market. I prepare Shutters, Gates and other materials used in the building construction work. My work also depends on seasons. Sometimes I am busy and on some other days there may not be any work. I work in the workshop from 10:00 am to 5:00 pm. I need more raw materials to work. I purchase iron and other material on whole sale basis and I also purchase other materials from various shops required for preparing the articles. We also prepare the iron articles and sell them in the market. Sometimes we have full work at hand in the seasonal days and on other days especially in unseason we do not have enough work. On seasonal days we take the help of one or two persons drawn from my community and I will pay Rs. 250/- per day to them.

My Problems Include:

1. I do not have much capital to invest and setup a good workshop.

2. I did not get any loan from Bank or Government as they demand sureties and imposed several conditions.

3. I earn an amount which is insufficient to my daily life.

4. I have no other source of employment whenever I do not get any work.

Needs:

1. I need some help financially from Government and also from other.

2. I need the amount to purchase tools and materials needed in the workshop on subsidy rates from Government.

3. We need health protection, scholarships and hostel facilities to our children.

4. Government should assist us by supplying electricity on subsidized rates to the workshop. Training facilities in new technologies to be extended.

5. Some times while doing welding works accidents occur and Government should extend help necessary and provide relief such a insurance etc.,

6. Pension and other welfare schemes are to be extended to our aged professionals.

Eluvaka Brahmachary

My name is Eluvaka Brahmachary. My age is 40 years studied up to 10th class and discontinued due to financial problems. I learnt Blacksmith work from my parents. My forefathers also did the same profession. I am doing the Blacksmith profession for the last 24 years in my village.

My wife aged 35 years studied up to 5th class and discontinued. My wife works in the home. We are four in my family. Myself, my wife one son and daughter. My son aged 21 years studying B.Tech and my daughter 18 years studying Intermediate. Our children assist me in my work. Whenever they are free I wish that my children get Government employment in future and I do not want to see them in my profession.

We have our own small house. We do not have any pet animals. We have Bathroom, Latrine, Toilet facility, Cooking Gas, Radio, Sewing machine, Cooker and no Refrigerator. I read news papers outside.

We don't have any agricultural land. Living only on the income which I get from Blacksmith profession. When there is no work we go to Agriculture work as labourers. Since my birth I am living in this village. All the agriculturalists and village people come to us for Blacksmith work earlier.

Blasksmith is an ancestral profession. We required prepare our own required produce the articles with iron. We purchase the iron material from Warangal. Some customers will pay the money in advance and some others do not pay. Some customers who visit us also sell the old material and exchange it with the new material and some public will get their old one and get repaired and we do all such needful works in making, repairing and selling etc., we recycle the old materials and articles which we collected through exchange and produce new articles out of it.

In the villages we help the cultivators by supplying agricultural implements which we produce at home. We undertake repairs whenever their implements get spoiled. We also prepare chairs, iron tables and other articles useful in the house and also other materials required for new buildings. Previously we used to get rice or other food grains towards our products on exchange basis but agriculturists who take work from us had stopped such transactions. The income we get is not sufficient to meet the needs of our daily life. During the agriculture season we have handful of work but on other seasons we don't have much work to do.

As I am doing the work since a long time I also improve our products for the benefit of our customers. Now new technologies have come up. Traditional tools have been replaced by machine tools. Agriculturists are using Tractors and other mechanical implements and we have not received any training to repair the new machines etc., As a result we lost our work and subsequently the income.

Our Problems Include:

1. We are doing the traditional work which is not suitable for present day conditions.
2. We have received no help from Government and no subsidy for materials required.
3. Due to the emergence of new technologies and use of tractors and other modern machines, our work has been reduced and most of us have become jobless especially in villages and we had left with no alternative work.
4. We do not have Welding machine and unable to purchase it due to lack of money and capital.
5. We do not have appropriate professional organizations of our own and no one is taking care of us.

Our Suggestions Include:

Government should provide us financial assistance and arrange Bank Loans; Free medical checkup and old age pensions to our caste members. Free residential education to our children. Guarantee minimum employment by entrusting government works. Extend necessary social support to carry on our profession or show suitable alternate employment.

K. Ravindra Chary

My name is K. Ravindra Chary 42 years of age completed

I.T.I. My native place is Parkal Mandal, Peddakodapaka Village. I came to Bheemaram 16 years back in search of work. I did apprenticeship after completing I.T.I Trade and now working as a Blacksmith. My wife is 35 years old, studied upto 6th class and working at home. I have two children, one daughter 15 years studying 9th class and one son 13 years, studying 7th class.

I have own house with minimum facilities like Bathroom, Toilet, Water Facilities, Electricity, gas, T.V, Radio. I do not have any Agricultural land and no pet animals.

I have started one workshop at Gopalapuram in a rented building. I do both welding and Blacksmithy, The workshop is fitted with traditional welding, drilling and other implements and tools. I prepare gates, shelters, windows, doors and other household materials in the workshop. I prepare the articles in the design as ordered by the customers. I get the raw material from the wholesale shop from Warangal. I need modern welding machine, welding sticks, cutting machine and some other tools required to do my job of welding in a better way. But I may need to purchase them soon.

Normally the customers who visit us place the orders and give some amount as advance. After the completion of work I would collect the rest of the amount and hand over the products to the concerned customers.

We get little profit for the material we produce. We pay Rs. 400/- per day towards labour to each person employed for providing assistance and they attend to the work from morning 9: am to evening 05:00 pm and sometimes more. To start a shop we need huge investment and presently whatever is needed we take from the money lenders and we will try to repay the amount by taking amounts from chit bidding. We continuously take membership in some chit fund company and pay monthly subscription for the same. Whenever we need finance we lift the chits and get the amount.

Many a time we prepare the articles with our own investment and sell them in the market. Sometimes we do not get much profit out of the sale of the products. The members of other castes are also opening big workshops with huge investment and heavy machinery. They take the help of our caste-members, who are paid wages as they work as labourers. This will be painful to our caste members. Due to this there has been lot of competition and those who invest more and use modern machines are able to do well and we remain as sufferers in the whole process. Sometimes accidents occur in the work and we do not get any help from the government nor any organizations.

Our Problems Include:

1. We did not receive any loan from any Bank or Society, in spite approaching them several times.
2. We did not receive any material on subsidized rates.
3. No order has been received from any government departments to prepare the materials required by them.
4. No Financial assistance from any agency.
5. No Association has been formed on the basis of occupation to fight for our cause.
6. No Accidental Insurance or benefits secured from government.
7. No pension scheme is implemented for the benefit of workers in the trade.
8. No medical assistance is provided by the government.

In view of the above problems, we had represented many times to the Government to provide financial assistance in the form of loans, subsidies, margin money and sought Government works to ensure full employment. We also demanded quite often that the government to provide children's education loan, free hostel facilities etc., we have also asked for a provision for a Training facility in new technologies and provision for supply of machinery and equipment. Finally we also demanded marketing assistance to our products. Despite many representations over the years we have not received any help from the Government. In fact there is no specific policy or programme meant exclusively for our welfare. Unless Government considers our issues and problems seriously, we have little future in our profession.

Vemunuri Ramesh (Kammari)

My name is Vemunuri Ramesh 28 years old, studied upto 10th class and discontinued due to bad financial position. My native place is Nekkonda Mandal Deekshakunta of Warangal District. I did not have any work in my village so I came to Hanamkonda in search of work. Now I am living at Hanumannagar in Hanamkonda. I came here 6 years back in search of work. My father used to take up Iron works and I am doing the same Blacksmith work now. My forefathers used to do the Blacksmith work. We prepare necessary tools and spares required for the agriculturists apart from producing household goods.

My father now aged 80 years studied upto 3rd class and did Blacksmith work in our village. My father worked as a Black Smith all his life-long and now he is unable to work due to his old age. Health is also not cooperating him to do and hence taking rest at home. My mother 65 years old, illiterate and works in the home. I have my own RCC building with ordinary facilities. I do not have any agricultural land or other sources of income. I have water facility with borewell and also Latrine, Bathroom, Cooking gas stove and T.V. I read the news paper outside borrowing from others. My neighbors belong to other castes but live friendly and help each others.

As part of my work I also do the welding work. I do most of work with Iron rods and iron material. My profession is based on using iron material. I purchase the iron and other material from wholesale shops at Warangal.

I have the tools required for welding such as a traditional welding machine, cutting machine, welding sticks, Tape and other material required for my work. When there is more work which I cannot do on my own I take the assistance of other workers available outside and I pay Rupees 300/- per day to them. We work for 10 hours per day and sometime we spend more time on the basis of availability of work. Sometimes we may not be able to get any work at all.

I prepare iron material implements and furniture. I also prepare household Gates, Windows, Fencing material, Chairs, Tables and other required articles on order. There has been some demand for building works especially iron grills and other products.

Need capital amount to open a big workshop. I have already taken some loan from private money lender with higher interest and I am finding it difficult to repay the amount. Hence I need a bank loan and a subsidy. Till now I have not received.

We actually need Government help or subsidy on materials we have not secured orders to work for Government buildings or furniture required in government offices; Government should purchase materials required from individuals like me and provide us work; Marketing facilities are also to be created by the Government, so that we can supply our products on demand; Government should provide training to us in modern techniques and use of new technologies; Free education to our children; Health cards and free medical aid; Pension scheme to senior citizens etc.,. We have been making these demands over the years but till now our demands are not met and we are facing lot of difficulties. Government should consider resolving our problems as part of its social welfare activity and cannot ignore its responsibility towards the development of artisans like us.

10

Vadrangi- *The Carpenter*

The Vadrangis are an occupational caste of carpenters and wood carvers. They make Furniture, Wooden ploughs, Harrows, and other agricultural tools as carpenters for village and town people. They trace their descent from the god Vishwakarma who is believed to be the all-accomplishing divine architect and carpenter who makes weapons and celestial chariots to the gods. It is believed that Vishwakarma created two groups of people- the Vadrangi who work in wood and the Kammari, who could work in iron, apart from others.

The Vadrangis live in both joint and nuclear families. The Vadrangis have a rich oral tradition of folksongs, dances and tales that they often share with other communities. Social control is handled by elders and respected members of the community.

The Carpenter's work requires tremendous craftsmanship. The most revolutionary outcome of the Carpenter's Engineering is the plough, which could furrow the land with the help of bull and buffaloes power. The Carpenters also took the help of the Ironsmiths to construct necessary instruments for moulding the wood into a plough. The plough that was carved out by the carpenters, the iron rod that the ironsmith fitted to the plough, and the Mala mode of tanning of the bulls and the buffaloes to use their strength for production resulted in the development of what is called 'agriculture'.

The second most important contribution of the carpenter was that of the construction of the wooden parts of the Bullock Cart. If the ironsmith constructed the Iron instruments of the bullock cart, the entire woodwork was done by the carpenter. Technically the most skillful aspect of the carpenter's engineering was in the construction of the wheel and the body of the cart. Constructing the whole body of the cart itself required skills and knowledge systems of an advance nature.

Vadrangi or Carpentry is primarily a male job, but in some of the families, women also do help the male members in case the work is done at home. The carpenter is an important functionary of the jajmani system in rural setup and every agricultural family needs his assistance in almost every year in repairing the wood based agricultural implements. Manufacturing of ploughs, bullock carts, boxes, doors and window frames, furniture etc., has been done by him especially during the non-agriculture seasons. For a long time under the jajamani system they were paid in kind especially in the shape of grains at the time of harvest by the farmers in return to the 'repairing' work taken from him. In most cases Vadrangis are attached to farmers families and every year they get 'grains' in proportion to the 'repairing' work done. In case of fresh manufacturing of various wood based items, carpenters were paid in cash. Hence the carpenters produce goods generally for the consumption of the 'villagers' where they stay, but sometimes sell their products outside. In urban areas, for works done, the transaction will be entirely in cash as per the rates fixed on mutual consultation. Now-a-days in both villages and towns every transaction has been done in the form of 'money or cash'.

Vadrangi (Carpenter) is an old occupation grown along with agricultural practices in rural areas. As an important functionary of the earlier jajamnai system in the village, they work for almost all agricultural families. They also produce other products like cots, tables, chairs, benches, stands etc., and sell it both in the local market and in urban areas nearby. They are also involved in large scale in urban areas in the construction of new buildings and flats and preparation of large scale wood furniture on the basis of demand. In this background a field study has been conducted to highlight the details relating to the socio-economic conditions and work situation relating to the Vadrangis living in both rural and urban areas.

Size of Family in relation to Age

For the purpose of the study the data had been collected from 135 Carpenter households drawn both from urban and rural areas. Table 10-1 indicates that 40% of families had four members each and 33.33% of families are found with three members each, 17.78% of families had five members, while 8.89% had two-member nuclear families. Only 6.66% of respondents are in the age group of 'upto 25', while around 24.15% families are in the age group of 26-35. About 20% of households belong to above 56 and above age group. It may be found that more than 60% of households belong to the urban areas as during the recent days more families are found in urban areas than rural areas as the work in rural areas continue to get reduced due to mechanization of agriculture and import of wood-based furniture. There was also large scale migration from rural to urban areas for want of work.

Table 10.1

Size of Family in relation to Age

Sl. No	Age	Place	Single	Two Members	Three Members	Four Members	Five Members	Six Members & Above	Total
01.	Up to 25	Urban	-	-	3 (50) (6.67)	3 (50) (5.55)	-	-	6 (100) (4.44)
		Rural	-	-	3 (100) (6.67)	-	-	-	3 (100) (2.22)
02.	26-35	Urban	-	-	12 (57.14) (26.67)	9 (42.86) (16.67)	-	-	21 (100) (15.56)
		Rural	-	-	3 (25) (6.66)	6 (50) (11.11)	3 (25) (12.5)	-	12 (100) (8.89)
03.	36-45	Urban	-	-	6 (40) (13.33)	6 (40) (11.11)	3 (20) (12.5)	-	15 (100) (11.11)
		Rural	-	-	6 (22.22) (13.33)	15 (55.56) (27.78)	6 (22.22) (25)	-	27 (100) (20)
04.	46-55	Urban	-	-	3 (16.66) (6.67)	9 (50) (16.67)	6 (33.34) (25)	-	18 (100) (13.33)
		Rural	-	-	-	3 (50) (5.55)	3 (50) (12.5)	-	6 (100) (4.45)
05.	56-65	Urban	-	-	3 (33.33) (6.67)	3 (33.33) (5.56)	3 (33.34) (12.5)	-	9 (100) (6.67)
		Rural	-	-	-	-	-	-	-
06.	66 & Above	Urban	-	3 (100) (25)	-	-	-	-	3 (100) (2.22)
		Rural	-	9 (60) (75)	6 (40) (13.33)	-	-	-	15 (100) (11.11)
Total				12 (8.89) (100)	45 (33.33) (100)	54 (40) (100)	24 (17.78) (100)	-	135 (100%) (100%)

Education of Family Members

Like other artisan families, Carpenter families are also educationally weak as only around 29% of families had studied upto intermediate or above. It may be seen that the present generation is interested in pursuing education as the respondents and their children had more educational achievements than their forefathers. The parents of some of the respondents are found to have studied only upto fifth class, while a large number had illiterate parents. This indicates that the present generation has understood the need for education in their families.

Occupation of the Family Members

It is significant to observe that the main occupation of

head of the family of the present generation (the respondent), his father, grandfather and great grandfather all worked as carpenters, As far as children of respondents occupation is concerned, 4.44% of them had joined modern occupations, 6.67% in government service, 80% in education, while 4.45% are found doing labour work. It is significant to note that there is a 'cultural taboo' in the carpenter families that women seldom go out for work and education. Normally they don't even share the work of men folk in carpentry work. However in 13.33% cases it has been found that women assist their men folk in some works, while 4.45% of women in these families also preferred to work outside to earn some wages. Due to change in the attitudes and culture of elders in the families and because of modern day compulsion, girls are sent to schools and adult women to paid work even outside.

Table 10.2

Educations of Family Members

Sl. No	Relationship with the Respondent	Illiterate	0-5 Classes	6-10 Classes	Inter	ITI	Degree	Others	Total
01.	Respondent	18 (13.34) (20)	45 (33.34) (46.87)	51 (37.78) (32.07)	9 (6.66) (33.33)	3 (2.22) (100)	9 (6.66) (21.43)		**135 (100) (27.78)**
02.	Father	9 (100) (10)							**9 (100) (1.86)**
03.	Mother	9 (60) (10)	6 (40) (6.25)						**15 (100) (3.08)**
04.	Wife/Husband	51 (44.74) (56.66)	15 (13.15) (15.63)	30 (26.31) (18.87)	3 (2.64) (11.11)		9 (7.90) (21.43)	6 (5.26) (8.70)	**114 (100) (23.46)**
05.	Son		15 (15.63) (12.20)	60 (48.79) (37.73)	3 (2.43) (11.11)		18 (14.63) (42.86)	27 (21.95) (39.13)	**123 (100) (25.30)**
06.	Daughter	3 (3.75) (3.34)	15 (7.85) (15.62)	18 (21.43) (11.33)	6 (7.15) (22.23)		6 (7.15) (14.28)	36 (42.85) (52.17)	**84 (100) (17.29)**
07.	Other								
	Total	**90 (18.52) (100)**	**94 (19.75) (100)**	**159 (32.72) (100)**	**27 (5.55) (100)**	**3 (0.62) (100)**	**42 (8.64) (100)**	**69 (14.19) (100)**	**486 (100%) (100%)**

Like other artisan work, the traditional skills in these families are transferred from one generation to the other by practice and male children start learning the work through observation from their early age itself.

Table 10.3

Occupation of the Family Members

Sl. No	Response	Same Occupation (Carpentry)	Other Traditional Occupation	Modern Occupation	Government Job	Labour	Others/ Study	Total
01.	Respondent	135 (100) (24.73)	-	-	-	-	-	135 (100) (20)
02.	Respondent's Father	135 (100) (24.73)	-	-	-	-	-	135 (100) (20)
03.	Respondent's Grand Father	135 (100) (24.72)	-	-	-	-	-	135 (100) (20)
04.	Respondent's Grand Father's Father	135 (100) (24.72)	-	-	-	-	-	135 (100) (20)
05.	Respondent's Son	6 (4.44) (1.10)	-	6 (4.44) (100)	`9 (6.67) (100)	6 (4.45) (100)	108 (80) (100)	135 (100) (20)
	Total	**546 (80.89) (100)**	**-**	**6 (0.89) (100)**	**9 (1.33) (100)**	**6 (0.89) (100)**	**108 (16) (100)**	**675 (100%) (100%)**

Family Assets

It has been a general tradition that carpenter families also involve themselves in agriculture as a secondary occupation wherever they possess agricultural land. In the present study it may be found that only 11.11% of respondent had tiny plots of land which they cultivate seasonally. Another 11% of families also found to have taken some land on 'lease' for cultivation. They use it for production of food-grains for their own family consumption.

It is also significant to observe that 75% of families had various facilities/amenities at home. However things like Rice Cookers, Refrigerator are found to be rare in their houses, gas facility and TVs are most favorite items most people own. Although their economic positions is not that sound, owning some of the facilities are considered to be prestigious affair which most people do not like to miss. Some of them even took loans to procure some of these items.

All the respondents consider that 'carpentry' is their primary occupation and other subsidiary occupation has been the agriculture for long which they prefer it cultivate during the rainy season mostly. It may also be found that all the sample respondents are 'self-employed' people owning their own family enterprises or units to earn their livelihood.

For a long time most of the carpenters in the villages used to produce or undertake repairs of wood based agricultural implements. But over a period of time mechanization of agriculture and applications of modern implements forced these carpentry families look out for some other products. As a result both in urban and rural areas it has been found that a large number of carpenters concentrating on the production of doors, windows, chairs, tables, cupboards, dining tables etc., which are in demand these days.

Production Area

It may be found that 90% of sample families does their work from their homes itself, while only 11.11% of household carry it by having separate workshops or sheds for doing the work. Since the work in most cases was not heavy they do it from their homes.

Investment Details

22.96% of respondents spent upto Rs. 10,000/- towards tools, raw materials and preparing 'production area' in the home for undertaking the carpentry work. 38.52% spent upto R. 25,000/- towards these establishment activities, while 32.59% had spent upto Rs. 50,000/- on these items. It is significant to observe that around 5.93% of respondents had spent upto one lakh rupees towards meeting the investment expenditure especially in those cases where a separate work shed is constructed. Purchase of tools and raw materials seem to have taken a major share of their investment expenditure.

Sources of Investment

60% of respondents seem to have mobilized their own funds towards the investment, while 13.13% seem to have depended on money lenders. The remaining 24% had found other sources to meet these expenses. Banks and other government Finance agencies had hardly helped them to meet their investment needs.

Production Plan

Carpenters at the local level generally depend upon local orders from firms and offices or orders from known people or undertake work on contract basis. 55.56% of work is drawn from known people or regular customers and the remaining work orders were secured from the local stores, firms etc.

In certain cases or whenever the carpenters do not find sufficient orders they produce small items without any orders and place them on display at homes for sales. In this case the investment will be heavy as carpenters themselves have to bear the burden. In case of other orders, the carpenters collect 'advance payment' for the purpose of raw material purchase and collect the remaining amount after handing over the finished products. This will be more convenient for them and lessen the financial burden of carpenters.

Off season activity

Carpenters do not get work during all seasons. Sometimes outside work is more lucrative than their primary work. It may be found that in rural areas during the agricultural season 44.4% respondents go for undertaking various kinds of works relating to agriculture. In urban areas many go for construction or building works. In urban areas other works such as repair works of wood furniture, fixing platforms, and stages etc, which provide them higher wages than their primary work. However in rural areas, availability of construction work is very much limited. It may be found that due to emergence of machine run workshops and import of Chinese furniture, Carpenters are found it difficult to get orders for furniture work. This has the availability of work and affected their 'earning' capacity.

Ceremonial Jobs

Traditionally the Carpenters are found assisting Hindu families in undertaking various religious or ceremonial works or rituals. During the marriages, house warming ceremonies, other family ceremonies, festivals etc., carpenters need to do certain exclusive works rituals for which they get remuneration based on the capacity of the families where the work is done. This is found both in rural and urban areas but urbanized Hindu families are found during the recent years cutting short of rituals and avoiding the work to be given to the carpenters. In rural areas however the practice is still on but they get very little payment for the work done.

Government Schemes

It has been as a general trend that carpenters were being ignored in Government policies and there is no single programme that exclusively deals with these artisans. Whatever the general schemes proposed its benefits are not found reaching them. It has been said that only 20.2% of respondents received bank loans, when approached and others found it difficult to gain access for bank loans. The schemes such as Artisan credit card, Aadharana scheme or various kinds' government pensions did not reach them. Even old age pensions have not been extended to those eligible carpenters on one or the other pretext. 97.78% of the respondents said that they have been clearly discriminated in extending government facilities and schemes. As a result of governments and banks indifferent attitude, the carpenters were denied the benefits of various schemes.

Sale of Products

It has been found that 54.7% of respondents from urban areas and 45.24% from rural areas sell their products from their house where they produce them. The respondents said that they also supply the goods on demand based on the availability of raw material. In the overall sense 71.43% of rural households said that they have total dissatisfaction about the sales. While those from urban areas it was 75% who felt that their lives are hard, due to 'marketing difficulties'. In the overall sense it indicates that 'marketing' is not that easy in the present day context of wide spread competition in the field concerned.

Occupational Problems

Table-10.4 indicates the three major occupational problems faced by the carpenters in order of their intensity. The cumulative analysis of the responses indicates that the Vadrangi in both the urban and rural areas face the problems equally and had to struggle hard for survival against all odds. Lack of clear cut policy on the part of government to extend its support to Vadrangis has been considered as the first major problem in the context of degrading conditions of the trade existing now. The second major problem has been considered to be lack of minimum support price and market facility, following by 3rd major problem supposed to be lack of availability of work due to readymade products and illiteracy and unemployment are the other major problems. Non-availability of raw material is yet another problem faced by them. It is found that whenever they get wood from the open market the urban carpenters face additional problems of harassment by forest officials for nothing. Other problems include investment problems, lack of training for use of modern implements, lack of political support, falling levels of income etc., most respondents also felt that their problems got accumulated over the years and they considered it difficult to find appropriate solutions to the problems.

Table 10.4

Occupational Based Problems (Cumulative)

Sl. No	Response	1	2	3	Total
01.	Lack of Availability of Capital	24 (88.89) (17.78)	3 (11.11) (2.22)		27 (100) (6.66)
02.	Non Availability of Raw Material	9 (37.50) (6.67)	15 (62.5) (11.11)		24 (100) (5.92)
03.	Lack of support from political parties		6 (40) (4.45)	9 (60) (6.67)	15 (100) (3.70)
04.	Failure of Bank Officials to extend necessary help	3 (25) (2.22)	6 (50) (4.44)	3 (25) (2.22)	12 (100) (2.96)
05.	Lack of availability of Modern Tools and Training	3 (14.28) (2.22)	9 (42.86) (6.67)	9 (42.86) (6.67)	21 (100) (5.19)
06.	Lack of availability of work due to readymade products	18 (42.85) (13.33)	21 (50) (15.56)	3 (7.15) (2.22)	42 (100) (10.38)
07.	Corruption among Govt. officials	6 (25) (4.44)	12 (50) (8.89)	6 (25) (4.44)	24 (100) (5.92)
08.	Lack of clear cut policy of Govt. support	15 (20.83) (11.11)	15 (20.83) (11.11)	42 (58.34) (31.11)	72 (100) (17.78)
09.	Lack of Minimum support price and market facility	15 (31.25) (11.11)	18 (37.50) (13.33)	15 (31.25) (11.11)	48 (100) (11.85)
10.	Illiteracy and Unemployment	12 (28.57) (8.89)	12 (28.57) (8.89)	18 (42.86) (13.33)	42 (100) (9.63)
11.	Lack of welfare programmes and Insurance facility	12 (8.89) (30.77)	6 (15.39) (4.44)	21 (53.84) (15.56)	39 (100) (9.63)
12.	Degradation of traditional occupations	12 (8.89) (30.77)			12 (100) (2.96)
13.	Non performance of Associations	6 (8.89) (22.22)	12 (44.45) (8.89)	9 (33.33) (6.67)	27 (100) (6.67)
	Total	**45 (33.33) (100)**	**45 (33.33) (100)**	**45 (33.34) (100)**	**135 (100%) (100%)**

Community based Problems

Table-10.5 indicate the cumulative response as community based problems and issues of the respondents. As they felt let down by the government, they thought of getting help from other sources and institutions including their own community Associations. But as expected community associations could not gear up to meet such situations and help their members. They find upper caste discrimination as most Forest Contractors and Wood depots Contractors are drawn from upper castes and they also show no sympathy towards their problems. They also find encroachment from other communities in to their occupation resulting in robbing of whatever the limited opportunities available to them is yet another problem. Lack of alternate employment, lack of welfare measures, lack of information on new development in the field, non-cooperation from officials and corruption, lack of education and availability of employment, migration, lack of market support or price support etc, are some of the other problems faced by these communities.

A large majority of respondents had said that their occupation has become hazardous as they face several health problems due to wood dust coming out, sounds it continuously create, and the physical stress it increases for hard work the occupation requires. They said that they very often get joint pains, eye sight problems, hearing problems, skin diseases etc and as a result of it they need to incur a lot of expenditure towards the same.

Table 10.5

Community Based Problems

Sl. No	Response	1	2	3	Total
01.	Lack of Help from Caste Associations	84 (93.33) (62.22)	6 (6.67) (4.44)	-	**90 (100) (22.22)**
02.	Lack of govt. support towards occupations	3 (5.26) (2.22)	30 (52.63) (22.23)	24 (42.11) (17.78)	**57 (100) (14.07)**
03.	Upper Caste Discrimination	6 (50) (4.44)	6 (50) (4.44)	-	**12 (100) (2.96)**
04.	Degradation phenomenon of traditional occupation	15 (62.5) (11.11)	9 (37.5) (6.66)	-	**24 (100) (5.93)**
05.	Lack of Clear Cut Policy of Government	-	-	6 (100) (4.44)	**6 (100) (1.48)**
06.	Other Castes encroachment in their traditional occupation	3 (100) (2.22)	-	-	**3 (100) (0.74)**
07.	Backwardness of Education	6 (12.5) (4.45)	15 (31.25) (11.11)	27 (56.25) (20)	**48 (100) (11.85)**
08.	Lack of other alternative employment	-	-	6 (100) (4.45)	**6 (100) (1.48)**
09.	Lack of help from political parties	6 (22.22) (4.45)	12 (44.45) (8.89)	9 (33.33) (6.66)	**27 (100) (6.67)**
10.	Lack of welfare programmes	9 (10.71) (6.67)	33 (39.29 (24.45)	42 (50) (31.11)	**84 (100) (20.75)**
11.	Lack of availability of traditional work	-	3 (33.33) (2.22)	6 (66.67) (4.45)	**9 (100) (2.22)**
12.	Lack of information on new developments	-	9 (60) (6.67)	6 (40) (4.45)	**15 (100) (93.70)**
13.	Corruption of forest officials	3 (33.33) (2.22)	6 (66.67) (4.44)	-	**9 (100) (2.22)**
14.	Migration/Lack of market support	-	6 (40) (4.45)	9 (60) (6.66)	**15 (100) (3.71)**
Total		**135 (33.33) (100)**	**135 (33.34) (100)**	**135 (33.33) (100)**	**405 (100%) (100%)**

Occupation based Happy Occasions

Table 10.6 indicate the occupation based happy occasions they had experienced when enquired about what would be able to make them happy in their occupation. The responses were routine and their expectations seems to be very limited. Table 10.6 reveals that the respondents feel happy when they get sufficient work, somebody recognize their skill, get minimum support price, able to perform marriages and other functions at home, celebrate festivals and attend jataras, send their children to schools and colleges, able to save something out of their earnings etc, analysis of the above indicate that during the past their life used to be happy and their occupation prosperous as their earnings used to be sufficient due to availability of regular work. They used to get reorganization of what they have produced and had high esteem of their professional skills. But now things have changed and situations becoming out of their control. In view of this they think something need to be done to save them from their precarious situation.

Table 10.6

Occupational Based Happy Occasions

Sl. No	Response	Rural	Urban	Total
01.	Availability of Sufficient Work	18 (35.69) (33.33)	33 (64.71) (40.75)	**51 (100) (37.78)**
02.	Recognizing work skill	12 (100) (22.22)	-	**12 (100) (8.89)**
03.	Getting Minimum support prices	6 (100) (11.11)	-	**6 (100) (4.44)**
04.	Celebrations of Festivals, Marriages	3 (50) (5.56)	3 (50) (3.70)	**6 (100) (4.44)**
05.	Attending Jataras	-	6 (100) (7.41)	**6 (100) (4.44)**
06.	Educating their children	-	6 (100) (7.41)	**6 (100) (4.44)**
07.	Savings	-	3 (100) 93.70)	**3 (100) (2.22)**
Total		**54 (40) (100)**	**81 (60) (100**	**135 (100%) (100%)**

Government Policy

Governments have not adopted any specific policy to resolve the problems of Carpenters. Whatever general welfare policy exists it hardly meets the specific requirements of the Carpenters. Where such general policies exist, they are not properly implemented and the officials concerned show no sympathy towards them. The carpenters complain that that the officials are 'negative' in their approach towards the problems faced by the respondents.

Due to lack of Government support and falling incomes on the one side and stiff competition faced from the Chinese products available plenty in the markets, consumers had also developed 'low esteem' towards the occupation on the other made them fix. A large majority of the respondents said that due to this they lack public support in matters concerning the readdressal of their grievances by the government. Both the urban and rural respondents felt it that way.

As a result of growing problems there is wide spread migration amongst the people of the community in search of livelihood. In most cases it was found that the respondents alone found migrating to nearby towns and cities in search of livelihoods. In most cases they leave their families and children behind and go alone. Several of the respondents had said that they had experienced out migration moving from place to place for two to three generations together without settlement anywhere. Such a kind of situation had hit the family with children dropping out from schools, increasing debts and consumption loans, economic uncertainty and disturbance in the families.

General Solutions to Occupational Problems

When asked about their genuine occupational demands to save them from their bad situation, both rural and urban respondents had expressed almost similar views. They said that they need old age pensions as well as accident-relief support, provision for supply of modern tools, occupational training and allotment of government works, offer facilities for education of their children etc.

Table 10.7 indicate the detailed responses of the respondents to meet their emerging situations which include provision for market facilities, provision for bank loans, minimum support price for their products, proper implementation of welfare programmes, controlling the readymade products, provision for supply of modern tools and training in the field provision for alternate employment, appropriate government policy support, controlling official corruption, strengthening community Associations, provision for pensions and insurance etc. All this will a go long way to help solve their problems as they felt.

Table 10.7

Solutions to Problems

Sl. No	Response	Rural	Urban	Total
01.	Providing market facilities	3 (50) (5.55)	3 (50) (3.70)	**6 (100) (4.45)**
02.	Providing Bank Loans	6 (40) (11.11)	9 (60) (11.11)	**15 (100) (11.11)**
03.	Providing minimum support price	3 (20) (5.55)	12 (40) (14.82)	**15 (100) (11.11)**
04.	Proper implementation of welfare programmes	-	12 (100) (14.82)	**4 (100) (8.89)**
05.	Controlling readymade products	3 (50) (5.55)	3 (50) (3.70)	**6 (100) (4.45)**
06.	Providing modern tools & training	9 (37.5) (16.67)	15 (62.5) (18.52)	**24 (100) (17.78)**
07.	Providing alternative employment facility	15 (27.78) (27.78)	15 (50) (18.52)	**30 (100) (22.22)**
08.	Proper policy and govt. support	-	3 (100) (3.70)	**3 (100) (2.22)**
09.	Remove corruption among govt. officials	9 (60) (16.67)	6 (40) (7.41)	**15 (100) (11.11)**
10.	Strengthening caste associations	3 (100) (5.56)		**3 (100) (2.22)**
11.	Providing pensions and insurance facility	**3 (50) (5.56)**	**3 (50) (3.70)**	**6 (100) (4.44)**
Total		**54 (40) (100)**	**81 (60) (100)**	**135 (100%) (100%)**

Future Perspective

Table-10.8 indicates their views about the future prospects of the profession. Though the response is evenly divided, majority of the rural respondents felt that they are hopeful of a better future in case their occupational demands are met as indicated in table 10.7. Urban respondents are skeptical about their future but a large number of respondents still feel hopeful that something emerges to save them from their problems.

Table 10.8

Future Perspective

Sl. No	Response	Rural	Urban	Total
01.	Hopeful	33 (47.82) (61.11)	36 (52.18) (44.44)	**69 (100) (51.11)**
02.	Not Hopeful	21 (31.82) (38.89)	45 (68.18) (55.56)	**66 (100) (48.89)**
	Total	**54 (40) (100)**	**81 (60) (100)**	**135 (100%) (100%)**

Profiles and Case Studies of select Vadrangi Respondents

Nagunuri Venkateshwarlu

My name is Nagunuri Venkateshwarlu. I am 50 years old. My native place is Dharmasagar village of Warangal District in Telangana State. Ten years back I came to Warangal in search of work. I am doing carpentry work. I learnt it from my father. I studied upto X class and discontinued due to financial problems. I am doing this carpentry work since 25 years.

We are five members in my family. My wife 45 years old, studied upto V class. She is a housewife. My daughter 25 years old did her Post graduation. My elder son 24 years old doing MBBS, and my younger son 20 years old doing his degree. My ambition is that my children should study well and do some Government job.

I have constructed one small tiled house. I do not have any pet animal. I own a bicycle, water facility and toilets are there in the house. Television is available in the house. I read newspaper outside by borrowing. I am living in Hanamkonda since 10 years and my neighbors are of different caste, but we live together friendly assisting each other.

I have procured the required carpentry Machines and tools in the open market. It needs nearly Rs.20,000/- to purchase minimum tools required for my work we go whenever we need to cut the 'wood' in required sizes we go to 'outside shops' where the cutting machines are available. Sometimes we hire for it and pay the charge towards the same. I prepare stools, chairs, Tables, Dressing Table and other furniture required in the house.

I work for all days in a month and on an average nearly I get an amount of Rs.10,000/-. I also undertake small contract works in government or private institutions to supply Furniture and sometimes Doors and windows etc., I get extra money for undertaking such works when our customers construct a new house, there will be door ceremony and the house owner will pay an amount of Rs.1116/-. But this happens occasionally.

I am always ready to do hard work without even taking any break to earn more money. I use the money for my childrens education. We get an advance amount from the customers to prepare the articles and after completion of the work they pay the balance amount as such we also require some amount to purchase the raw materials to produce the products required. We go for a loan and we have to pay the interest amount which may be a burden for us. Though I tried my level best many times to get some Bank loan but failed to get it. During certain times cases of urgency I happened to take loan from private money lenders by paying exorbitant rates of interest.

I prepare articles of house hold and other material with Teak wood, Rose wood and other types of wood which are of higher cost. In marriage season I have to take additional time to make to material and on other ceremonial days we have sufficient work. During some days however there may not be enough work and during those days I prepare some general articles by investing my own money and sell them in the open market.

Now-a-days most of the builders or house owners are going for plastic works. As the plastic material entered into the market we are loosing our work, not getting enough carpentry work, which affects our work badly. There is heavy competition as the other caste members also the started doing carpentry work and due to this also we are loosing our work. However in any case I find some work pay using my contacts and earn money.

My Problems include

No assistance from Government or any other agency; No technical training; No Bank loan or subsidy on the material purchased; No co-operative society to extend necessary help; Workers from other states are coming to our state and we are loosing our work due to heavy competition.

Suggestions

Government should extend necessary support by providing loan and subsidy; Provide technical training; provide Health and medical Assistance; Pension schemes to old age persons; Provide Free education, scholarships, Hostel facility to the children. Arrange workshop sights, wood on subsidy and marketing facility. Government should evolve a policy to protect the interests of artisans groups ad guarantee their right to employment and suitable income.

V. Srinivas

My name is V. Srinivas aged 45 years, resident of

Mulkanoor village Mandal Bheemadevarapally of Karimnagar District. 10 years back I came to Warangal in search of work. I learnt the carpentry work from my father and other elders of the family. I studied up to 10th class and discontinued due to poverty.

Now in my family we are four members. My wife is 40 years old studied up to 10th class and she is a housewife. My daughter aged 17 years studying second year intermediate and my son 14 years studying 9th class. I wish that I should bring them up and get them well educated. I want them to find good Government jobs and do not want them to join our traditional occupation.

I do not have my own house, living in a rented tiled house with only minimum household facilities. I do not have any other property. I am living at Gopalapur village and my neighbors belong to different castes but they are friendly and help each other.

I have started my own workshop namely "Balaji wood furniture works" with an investment of Rs. 1,00,000/- towards land and other material. I purchase the tools required for the carpentry work with a cost of nearly Rs. 50,000/. I prepare household wood products like doors, windows, tables, almarahas chairs and other material required to the family. I am only the person in my family doing the carpentry work. We take orders from the customers. We collect advance amount from the customers and prepare the articles required by them. After handing over the products the remaining amount will be 'collected'.

I have appointed four persons in my workshop to work along with me and daily I pay them Rs. 300/- each towards labour charges for them. I tried for Bank Loans. B.C Corporation paid me one lakh on loan basis arranged through a Bank which I have to repay in installment every month with an interest rate of 1 rupee per hundred. I secured government help of Rs. 10,000/- as margin money and a subsidy of Rs. 30,000/-. Daily we work for 8 or more hours from morning to evening and during the festival and marriage season we get additional orders and additional income. We also get some remuneration and gifts during house warming occasions, marriages, where we does certain ceremonial works or rituals.

Even though I am working for the last ten years I am unable to construct a house of my own. Since I had given priority to establish a 'carpentry workshop' I did not concentrate much as constructing my own house.

Now day's public are interested in purchasing plastic equipment and furniture which is inexpensive and attractive as such. Due to use of new machines and tools attractive materials are being produced and made available in the open market. We are unable to compete with the new trends as we do not have money to invest in new technology and modernize our workshops. Further training is required to use the new technology which we cannot afford. We have to work hard to survive the competition but we find no 'improvement over the years' in the lives of artisans and traditional occupations. Government is not taking any interest on traditional occupations and we do not have our own cooperative societies or professional organization to look after our welfare.

Though I am able to survive the competition because my contacts and also having established an independent workshop of my own, it may not be the case of large number of carpenters. Most of them do not get sufficient work and as a result, they face the problem of survival.

We have submitted many representations to Government for extending necessary support:

- Government should provide land to open Carpentry workshop.

- Banks should facilitate to offer liberal loans with low interest or no interest.
- Training and orientation programmes are to be arranged in the to use new technologies and machinary.
- Government should give old age pensions to the workers and provide health cards for free treatment.
- Children of carpenters should be provided free education and hostel facilities.
- Government should extend necessary help to form artisan cooperatives and offer liberal credit flow supply of raw materials and marketing facilities.

Larkuntla Kedari

My name is Larkuntla Kedari. I am 55 years old and my native place is Dharmasagar Mandal, Devunoor village of Warangal District. 40 years back I came to Hanamkonda for my livelihood. I learnt carpentry work from my father. I studied up 5th class and discontinued due to financial problems.

We are five members in my family. My wife aged 50 years illiterate, she does household work. My elder daughter 27 years and undergoing teacher training, not yet married. My son 24 years discontinued Degree course and doing the carpentry work. My younger daughter 21 years old doing the M.Sc organic chemistry course.

Here in Hanamkonda I am living in a rented house. I do not have any agriculture land or other sources of income. My neighbours are members of other castes but we are friendly with each other, help each other, do our own traditional caste work respectively.

I have purchased all the tools required for the trade by spending upto 5000 rupees. But I do not have cutting machines and other required investments. Whenever I need to cut the wood I get it from other workshops. Sometimes it creates some problems. We do the carpentry work with teak wood, neem wood, and other wood. We prepare doors, almarahs, ventilators, window etc which are useful for new houses and also other furniture like benches, stools, tables, chairs etc for use in the house and offices.

Generally we work from morning to evening, either at our home or the house of the customers who place order for their products required. We also carry regularly work in the workshop or certain other allotted places, whenever is concerned.

We get more work on the basis of work orders which we expect during certain seasons and also on the festival days. During the days of construction of new houses, buildings, and apartments, and in Karthika masam we get good works. On some days like gruhapravesham the owners give us gifts like clothes or some amount as rewards.

Generally we earn Rupees 5000 to 6000 per month which is not sufficient for livelihood of a family. In place of wood work now-a-days public is showing a interest to purchase plastic materials as such. Due to this we are loosing our work not able to get good work order. I wish that my children are well educated and marry well educated persons and do not join this profession.

The Issues Include

Traditional occupational work is not recognized by many because of its cost effect and in this connection Government should take necessary steps. We need new instruments and skills and new technologies, need continuous help from government and cooperative societies and bank loan with less interest. Government should take care of the carpentry and provide work in construction sights of government buildings. Help the children of carpenters by providing free education, scholarships, stipends, and hostel facilities etc., Old age pension is to be given for senior citizens.

Velugoju Brahma Chary

My name is Velgoju Brahma Chary, 35 years old. My native place is Laknepally, Narsampet Mandal of Warangal District in Telangana State. I studied up to 10th class and discontinued. I learnt carpentry work from my father and Brother-in-law and I am doing this carpentry work since last 10 years.

My family members include my wife, aged 28 years. She is a housewife and also does some tailoring work. She studied up to 10th class. My elder son is 5 years of age and studying L.K.G and my second son is 2 years old. I want to give them good education and do not want to see them in this profession.

I own a thatched house. I don't have any other property and the required facilities in the house. I am having electricity, Gas connection, and a T.V. We collect water from Gram Panchayath Public Water tank. My neighbors belongs to other castes but are friendly and help each other. I am only the person working in my family.

I prepare agricultural tools required by the agriculturists I also produce tables, chairs, windows, doors and other equipment used in the house and also those useful for shops like Almarah and Counters etc.

The customers come to us to place orders to prepare the articles and they pay some amount in advance and after the articles are prepared they take the articles and pay the balance amount. But in case the advance is not given, I need to borrow money from a money lender and pay interest to purchase the raw material which is becoming difficult for me. Daily I work for 8 hours since morning 9 am to 5 pm and also entire time on seasonal days like marriages and festivals. In some months like ashadam, we don't have any work which causes some difficulty to meet the family expenditure.

My wife is a DWAKRA group member and she took Rs. 30,000 loan from DWAKRA Group we used it as an investment. I had spent Rs. 10,000 towards tools and as a standby I spared a Rs. 20,000 towards purchase of wood. I tried for a bank loan but I could not get it. I did not get any help from the government. I purchase various types of wood like Teak, Wood, Neem wood etc and prepare the articles. I do not have any worker to assist me in my work. I myself work for 8 hours daily and sometime take additional time. In marriage and festival seasons I get maximum work and produce the articles required for the customers.

I get nearly a monthly income of Rs. 5000/- which is meagre and insufficient to meet my family expenditure. Now a days imported Chinese furniture is invading all local markets. Further due to development of new technologies and Big Factories undertaking production, attractive wood furniture is dumped in the market now-a-days and customers prefer most readymade items like sofa sets and other materials for household furniture and other materials for interior decorations. Some businessmen are getting the prepared articles from other states and selling them in our cities. As a result there has been lot of competition over the years. Though not durable, public is more interested in purchasing them and there is no demand for our wood furniture. Further other caste members are also doing the carpentry work and as such, we are loosing our traditional work. I need to earn more to provide good education to my children.

In view of the emerging problems we need help from government:

1. Government should provide modern tools and instruments. Give Training in modern technology and help us open workshops.

2. We Need bank Loans to open a shop
3. Need free education to the children and medical assistance.
4. We also need old age pensions.

For this purpose government should evolve a suitable policy exclusively meant for artisans and their development.

11

Chakali- *The Dhobi Or Washerman*

Chakali or Dhobi is a caste group are said to be specialised in washing clothes. A Chakali is likely to be of many different origins, with those whose ancestors took the occupation of washing clothes follow the customs and traditions of the region they live. The Chakalis or Dhobis in North India rank themselves highest among the scheduled castes. In south India they are grouped under OBCs or BCs.

Chakalis are an occupational caste grouping and usually operate from door to door collecting dirty linen from households. After a day or two, they return the linen washed, sometimes starched and ironed. Chakalis were the forerunners on the Indian subcontinent to modern professional dry cleaners. Since the Chakalis charge are much less than those dry cleaners, they are popular with most households. Each Chakalis marks a unique symbol or character on garments belonging to a particular household. This is marked in black indelible ink to prevent it from being washed off. Chakalis wash the clothes themselves or outsource it to dhobis who only wash clothes. In Telugu speaking states of Telangana and Andhra Pradesh they make up 12% of the Andhra Pradesh population. There are Muslim Dhobis in Karnataka, they are known as Agasar, Parit also, they speak Urdu and Kannada and the Hindu Dhobis are known as Madivala in Karnataka and have Other Backward Class status, while most Dhobis in North India have scheduled caste status. Chakali community is evenly spread across Andhra Pradesh and Telangana.

In addition to working as launderers, some are engaged in cultivation and other subsidiary occupations like animal husbandry, business and skilled and unskilled labour. Literacy levels among the Dhobi are low and child labour exists among them.

Women have a low status in the community and have no right over ancestral property, while male children are given equal rights. Women take active part in the traditional occupation of washing and ironing of clothes but are subservient to their men in all family matters. Their role in society is minimal at best. In this background field work is undertaken to study in detail the socio-economic and work situation of Chakali community.

Sample and Size of Family

Table-1 indicates the details relating to the sample size, number of members in the sample families, the nativity and age group of respondents chosen for the study. Out of 276 Chakali respondents chosen for the study, 43.48% (120) belong to urban areas and the remaining 56.52% (156) belong to rural areas. The age particulars of the respondents indicate that 25.48% (76) belong to 56-65 age group, 23.92% (66) each belong to 46-55 age-group and 36-45 age groups respectively and 21.74% (60) belong to the age-group of 26-35. Respondents 'above 66' was 4.35% (12). All the respondents 'above 66 years' of age belong to rural areas. As per the size of the family, it may be seen that 39.13% of families had four members, 17.39% each had five members and six members respectively in their families. 4.35% are found to be drawn from single-member families, two-member families constitute 8.70% of respondents and 13.04% constitute three members families. In all the nature of respondents indicate that the Chakali respondents are middle aged, rural and mostly drawn from four or five member families.

Education

It may be observed that there were in all 1122 members in the 276 Chakali families chosen for the study. For the purpose of the study, a count of number of members has been taken only from those who stay with the respondents and those who stay outside the respondents 'house have not been taken into consideration. Out of 1122 members, in all 33.16% of the members were illiterate. Further analysis indicates that 21.93% seen to have studied between 1-5th classes, 25.67% between 6-10 classes and 9.63% studied upto intermediate level of education. It may be significantly found that 5.88% of the sample families had graduated. While 2.20% had completed ITI and other courses. It is significant to observe that half of the respondents were illiterate, while 8.70% of their sons and 4.65% daughters were also found as illiterates. Amongst the respondents 41.81% had studied in between 1-10 class, while 8.69% had completed intermediate education.

Thus the table indicates that Chakali community is still far away from obtaining modern education. As the most backward community (despite 68 years of independence) it did not receive government's attention and as a result education is still inaccessible to them. The presence of a large number of illiterates in the families and those completed inter or technical courses, continue to adopt the traditional occupation indicate the social backwardness of the community.

Table 11.1
Size of Family

Sl. No	Age	Place	Single	Two Members	Three Members	Four Members	Five Members	Six Members & Above	Total
01.	Up to 25	Urban	-	-	-	-	-	-	-
		Rural	-	-	-	-	-	-	-
02.	26-35	Rural	-	-	-	24 (66.67) (22.22)	-	12 (33.33) (25)	**36 (100) (13.04)**
		Urban	-	-	6 (25) (16.67)	18 (75) (16.67)	-	-	**24 (100) (8.70)**
03.	36-45	Rural	-	-	6 (25) (16.67)	6 (25) (5.56)	6 (25) (12.5)	6 (25) (12.5)	**24 (100) (8.70)**
		Urban	-	-	-	30 (71.43) (27.78)	12 (28.57) (25)	-	**42 (100) (15.22)**
04.	46-55	Rural	-	12 (28.57) (50)	-	12 (28.57) (11.11)	12 (28.57) (25)	6 (14.29) (12.5)	**42 (100) (15.21)**
		Urban	-	-	-	12 (50) (11.11)	12 (50) (25)	-	**24 (100) (8.70)**
05.	56-65	Rural	6 (14.28) (50)	6 (14.28) (25)	12 (28.58) (33.33)	-	6 (14.28) (12.5)	12 (28.58) (25)	**42 (100) (15.21)**
		Urban	-	-	12 (40) (33.33)	6 (20) (5.55)	-	12 (40) (25)	**30 (100) (10.27)**
06.	66 & Above	Rural	6 (50) (50)	6 (50) (25)	-	-	-	-	**12 (100) (4.35)**
		Urban	-	-	-	-	-	-	
Total			**12 (4.35) (100)**	**24 (8.70) (100)**	**36 (13.04) (100)**	**108 (39.13) (100)**	**48 (17.39) (100)**	**48 (17.39) (100)**	**276 (100%) (100%)**

Table 11.2
Education of Family Members

Sl. No	Relationship with the Respondent	Illiterate	0-5 Classes	6-10 Classes	Inter	Degree	ITI/Other Technical Courses	Others	Total
01.	Respondent	138 (50) (37.10)	30 (10.87) (12.20)	84 (30.94) (29.17)	24 (8.69) (4.05)	-	-	-	276 (100) (24.60)
02.	Father	-	6 (100) (2.44)	-	-	-	-	-	6 (100) (0.53)
03.	Mother	30 (100) (8.06)	-	-	-	-	-	-	30 (100) (2.68)
04.	Elder Sister	-	-	-	-	6 (100) (9.09)	-	-	6 (100) (0.53)
05.	Younger Sister	-	-	-	6 (100) (5.26)	-	-	-	6 (100) (0.53)
06.	Sons	24 (8.70) (6.45)	72 (26.09) (29.27)	96 (34.78) (33.33)	30 (10.87) (26.31)	48 (17.40) (72.73)	6 (2.17) (50)	-	276 (100) (24.60)
07.	Daughters	12 (4.65) (3.23)	90 (34.89) (36.59)	78 (30.23) (27.09)	42 (16.28) (36.84)	12 (4.65) (18.18)	6 (2.33) (50)	18 (6.98) (75)	258 (100) (23)
08.	Wife	150 (73.53) (40.32)	18 (8.83) (7.31)	24 (11.76) (8.33)	6 (2.94) (5.26)	-	-	6 (2.94) (25)	204 (100) (18.18)
09.	Others	18 (30) (4.84)	30 (50) (12.19)	6 (10) (2.08)	6 (10) (5.26)	-	-	-	60 (100) (5.35)
	Total	372 (33.16) (100)	246 (21.93) (100)	288 (25.67) (100)	114 (10.16) (100)	66 (5.88) (100)	12(1.07) (0.70)	24 (2.13) (3.55)	1122 (100%) (100%)

Occupation of Family Members

Table 11.3 indicates the occupational background of the forefathers of the respondents. It indicates that the respondent, his father, grandfather and great grandfather etc, all found to be in the same traditional occupation for four generations. However when it comes to the respondent's son level, 16.77% had adopted the same traditional profession, while 3.73% joined other traditional occupation, another 3.73% joined some modern occupation and 5.59% had joined some Government job. 70.19% are found in the studies. It has been said by the respondents that they do not want to see their children in the hereditary profession. Thus table 11-3 indicates that the earlier four or more generations of the respondents continue to adopt the same hereditary traditional occupation as their forefathers, but only the present generation (respondent's son generation) began to change their occupation. Around 80% of the families found to have witnessed such a change as they might have already shifted to some occupation or continuing in studies to join a modern occupation.

Table 11.3

Occupation of the Family Members

Sl. No		Same Occupation	Other Traditional Occupation	Modern Occupation	Govt. Job	Studies	Total
01.	Respondent	276 (100)	-	-	-	-	**276 (100)**
02.	Respondent's Father	276 (100)	-	-	-	-	**276 (100)**
03.	Respondent's Grand Father	276 (100)	-	-	-	-	**276 (100)**
04.	Respondent's Grand Father's Father	276 (100)	-	-	-	-	**276 (100)**
05.	Respondent's Son	54 (16.77) (100)	12 (3.73) (100)	12 (3.73) (100)	18 (5.59) (100)	226 (70.19) (100.0)	**322 (100) (100)**

Education and Length of Occupation

Table 11.4 indicates that more than 90% of respondents had more than 10 years of experience in the occupation. A large number of them were found to be either illiterates or had relatively lower educational levels. Those who had some early education seem to have dropped out at the school education level. Significantly during the recent years we may find some intermediate degree or graduates joining the occupation. It has been found that for a stop-gap arrangement, the respondents seem to have taken their traditional job for want of joining a suitable job later. An analysis of the emerging situation indicates that a large number of respondents after dropping out from education stick on to the hereditary traditional occupation with no other alternative available to them.

Table 11.4

Educations and Length of Occupation

Sl. No	Education	1-5 years	6-10	11-20	21-30	31-40	41-50	51 & above	Total
01.	Illiterate	-	-	18 (13.04) (25)	36 (26.09) (54.55)	42 (30.44) (58.33)	30 (21.74) (83.33)	12 (8.69) (100)	**138 (100) (50)**
02.	1-5 Classes	-	6 (20) (100)	18 (60) (25)	-	6 (20) (8.33)	-	-	**30 (100) (10.86)**
03.	6-10 Classes	06 (7.14) (33.33)	-	24 (28.57) (33.33)	30 (35.72) (45.45)	24 (28.57) (33.34)	-	-	**84 (100) (30.43)**
04.	Inter	06 (33.54) (33.33)	-	12 (66.66) (16.67)	-	-	-	-	**18 (100) (6.53)**
05.	Degree	06 (100) (33.33)	-	-	-	-	-	-	**6 (100) (2.18)**
Total		**18 (6.52) (100.0)**	**6 (2.18) (100)**	**72 (26.08) (100)**	**66 (23.91) (100)**	**72 (26.08) (100)**	**30 (10.86) (100)**	**12 (4.35) (100)**	**276 (100) (100)**

Stated Occupation of Children

Table 11.5 indicates that as many as 54 children (56.25%) of the respondents (those who are doing some or the other job except those continuing in education) had joined the same occupation as their forefathers used to do. These children who joined the traditional job, 75% were drawn from rural areas only. It has to be seen whether those children of the respondents, who are in large number persuing education join what kind of job in future and how does they make any difference in the socio-economic life styles of Chakali community. All this indicates that education does make a difference and those who pursue education has greater opportunities outside and may not prefer to join their traditional occupation.

Table 11.5

Stated Occupation of Children

Sl. No	Place		Same Occupation	Other Traditional Occupation	Modem Occupation	Govt. Job	Other	Total
01.	Urban	Migrant						
		Local/ Non-Migrant	12 (32.43) (22.22)	04 (10.8)	09 (24.32) (75.0)	12 (32.43) (66.33)	-	**37 (100) (38.54)**
02.	Rural	Migrant	-	-	03 (100.0) (25.0)	-	-	**03 (100) (3.12)**
		Local/ Non-Migrant	42 (75.0) (77.78)	08 (14.28)	-	06 (10.71) (33.33)		**56 (100) (58.33)**
	Total		**54 (56.25) (100)**	**12 (12.5) (100)**	**12 (12.5) (100)**	**18 (32.14) (100)**		**96 (100) (100)**

Occupation of Women in the Families

In Chakali community both men and women participate in their traditional occupation. They do it right from their childhood and due to this 95.93% of women are found involved in the traditional occupation. While the remaining doing the some other job in unorganized sector. No women in the family keep her idle. This is the community in which invariably all the members of the family irrespective of age and gender participate in the occupation. Further, no one requires any separate training in the job as all the members learn it, while doing the job. Even those members who were found exclusively doing the job also learn the skills of the trade by observation and doing the things.

Assets Position

The vital data collected from the respondents indicate that 17.39% families from the sample families possess agricultural land, while other had no assets. 28.26% of respondents had RCC house while 45.65% live in Kacha houses. 26.09% families do not possess their own house and live in rented accommodation. Around 90% possess some cattle, fowls, birds etc., 17.39% had a scooter and 31.78% had a bicycle to their credit. As far as the daily useful amenities are concerned around 40% had no drinking water facility, 18.70% no bathroom facility, 27.22% had no latrines at homes. They depend on outside sources in this regard. 90% had electricity, 73% gas facility, 84.78% had TV in their homes, while only 4.34% possess Radios.

Table 11.6

Occupation of Women in the Family

Sl. No	Age	Involved in Occupation	Doing other work	Idle/unmarried/ Housewife	Total
01.	Up to 25	48 (100) (14.03)	-	-	**48 (100) (12.90)**
02.	26-35	96 (80) (28.08)	24 (20) (80)	-	**120 (100) (32.26)**
03.	36-45	96 (94.11) (28.08)	36 (5.89) (20)	-	**102 (100) (27.42)**
04.	46-55	36 (100) (10.52)	-	-	**36 (100) (9.68)**
05.	56-65	54 (100) (15.79)	-	-	**54 (100) (14.52)**
06.	66 and above	12 (100) (3.50)	-	-	**12 (100) (3.22)**
Total		**342 (91.93) (100)**	**30 (8.07) (100)**		**372 (100%) (100%**

Occupational Priorities

Chakali community members generally involve themselves in their traditional profession as their primary activity but those who have agricultural land also does various activities relating to agriculture. Those who do not possess any agricultural land, also go for participating in other agriculture farms for wage labour. Some of the family members also work in laundries owned by others. All those doing their traditional job are found self-employed and those who does other jobs also involve themselves in the work whenever they get time or whenever the family work demands. Chakali community faces severe problems of lack of availability of Dhobi ghats in their nearby places and had to travel long distances to find water source for washing the clothes. Some have facility of public Ghats and some certain common places where they wash the clothes.

Investment Details

Chakali community need investment to setup a separate laundry shop or facility at their homes. Further they need to purchase furniture, iron boxes and others which require reasonable investment. It has been observed that only 48.00 parent of respondents had 'ironing facility including some kind of open space laundry' and others do not have it. Out of those who had such a facility, 97.36% had spent upto Rs. 5000/-, 17.39% had invested upto Rs. 10,000/- on various items. Only around 2.64% had to spend between Rs. 25001-50000. Though not much investment needed to establish a 'laundry shop' these families cannot afford every such an investment.

Apart from the non-availability of Dhobighats, a large number of respondents had complained that the 'coal' needed for the iron box is not easily available to them due to controls imposed by government. Whatever available in the open market seems to be more expensive? Non-availability of subsidized or government coal has been a major problem faced by this community. The other required for washing the clothes such as washing powder, soaps, bleaching powder etc. are purchased at local markets.

Source of Investment

The investment required for opening of a laundry or purchase of equipment required has been mainly met from the personal savings of the families and other sources. The trend is almost identical in both urban and rural areas. Only

2.17% of respondents could get Bank loans for this purpose. Banks are not accessible to a large percentage of Chakali families. In the absence of loans, the facility available for getting margin money or subsidy has been lost. Moreover many families had to depend upon even moneylenders or private chit fund companies for this purpose. These families need to pay exorbitant rates of interest. There was no other alternative left to these families except to depend on private sources.

Work & Employment Details

It may found that Chakali families in both rural and urban areas work in houses generations together. This is more in case of rural areas. The whole village households, are shared by the Chakali families available in the villages concerned. They continue to serve the 'identified or shared families' which have been informally assigned to them by the community and serve them uninterruptedly. They get monthly or annual wage for the work done to the families. In most villages women collect the clothes from the homes of the families and carry it to the water ponds, in case available in the villages. Most of the times especially in urban areas, they wash the clothes at the homes from where the clothes are collected. In urban areas, Chakali families serve their host families on monthly payment basis. In laundry shops the work is done on piece rate basis. The rates are generally fixed by the Community Association in urban areas and all laundry shops are informed to follow them. In 24 % of cases it is found that the Chakali families attached to the houses also work as domestic servant on additional payments either on part time basis or full time basis. For Chakali women 'domestic service' has become a major source of income generation and occupational activity.

Ceremonial Jobs

In Hindu families whenever marriages, births and deaths or other family celebrations are held, the Chakali families are supposed to carry some special ceremonial duties, for which they are paid separately. In villages such tradition are followed more rigorously than the urban areas. But it is generally considered on all auspicious days Chakali community families are invariably involved. Such 'rituals' are followed in urban areas also where some families however started not believing them in practice.

Government Schemes

No specific schemes are available to the welfare of Chakali community. The general welfare schemes or Anti poverty or rural/urban development programmes meant for poor are made applicable to these families but they hardly reach them. The Government officials concerned either ignore these communities or found indifferent. Table 11.7 indicates that the Artisan Credit Card Scheme, Aadharana Scheme, Occupational pension, etc., did not benefit a single family in the sample. Government pensions reached only 2.18% of the families. Bank loans reached only 2.18% of the sample households. As part of Government schemes specially meant for Chakali community, Dhobighats could cover only 4.36% of the sample. It has been said that in most places the Dhobi Ghats are found to be 'unless' as no water facility is available or found to have set up far off from villages. Thus Government either lacking any policy or evolved any programme, separately meant for the welfare of this community. Thus the Government general programmes evolved so far had little effect on the Chakali families.

Table 11.7
Government Schemes

Sl. No	Government Schemes	Available	Not Available	Total
01.	Artisan Credit Card	-	276 (100)	276 (100)
02.	Aadarana Scheme	-	276 (100)	276 (100)
03.	Bank Loans	6 (2.18)	270 (100)	276 (100)
04.	Government old age Pensions	6 (2.18)	270 (97.82)	276 (100)
05.	Dhobighats	12 (4.36)	258 (95.64)	276 (100)
06.	Others	-	276 (100)	276 (100)

Role of Associations

It has been observed that a large number of Associations functioning right from the locality, ward/ division to villages and towns and cities. These association generally interested in socio-cultural issues of these communities. In some case these associations were also found articulating 'economic demands' of these communities. They fix the payment to be made towards all piece works and ceremonial operations. They sometimes represent the government various issues and demands. Since the Chakali community has been numerically strong and found in every village and towns they can play a very significant role. Though they are numerically strong and found in all areas, politically they are weak as they lack unity and conscious articulation of political demands.

These Associations have also failed to establish cooperative primary societies and even were not successful in making the Government to offer government works, such as hospitals, residential schools, factories etc., but beyond any body's expectation the leadership of the Associations of these communities found to have failed to represent the matters making things more worse. It may be significant to observe women in these families join various DWAKRA/ SHGs, to which helped them gain access to Government welfare programmes, institutional finance and subsidies. The financial assistance they received helped these families to some extent resolving certain minor problems. There are however helpful to 24.0% families, while the remaining did not cover under the programme.

Main Problems

Like any other OBC service community, Chakali community also faces a number of social, cultural and economic problems. Lack of education is the major problem as most of the families still not able to send their children to schools. During the past, the children were not sent to schools and even where they were sent, large percentage of them had found to have dropped out invariably. Chakali community face social and cultural discrimination and their jobs have been treated as impure and inferior. This has made these families suffer from social discrimination, lack of availability of Tanks and water ponds, lack of dhobi ghats, falling income rates due to heavy competition from organized sector, non-availability of coal in the open market are found to be the major problems of Chakali community.

Demands and Solutions

Provision for free and compulsory residential education to the children in the family is considered to be the major demand of this community as it is still a backward in community education. As per the government scheme, construction of Dhobi Ghats in all major localities/wards, free supply of water, electricity etc., supply of iron boxes, laundry shops with the power connection, Free pensions, loans, occupational pensions, old age pensions, loans, subsidies and margin money to start a laundry, issue of government orders facilitating to wash the uniforms and other clothes material in Government hospitals, residential schools and other places, starting of cooperatives, land allotment, housing facility, supply of coal, starting of cooperatives etc., have been demanded by the respondents. Several of the respondents also pointed out to impose ban on 'corporate agencies' entering into 'cloth washing and ironing' trade as it affects the 'livelihood' of several lakhs of people belonging to Chakali Community.

A large number of respondents were 'skeptical' about their future as successive government failed to extend necessary support to these communities. In view of this government should evolve a suitable policy framework based on above, and show in implementing the welfare programmes.

Profiles and Case Studies of Select member of Chakali Community

Chaparthi Kala

My name is Chaparthi Kala aged 58 years. My native place is Ganagadevipally, a model village in Warangal District. We wash clothes and iron them which is my family occupation and I am doing it since 40 years. I learnt it from my parents. I do not have any education. My father and mother are also illiterates.

There are 10 members in my family. My husband 60 years old illiterate and washes clothes and do some agriculture labour. My elder son aged 36 years passed 10th class, discontinued his studies to join the traditional occupation. My elder daughter-in-law aged 29 years illiterate also washes clothes in some houses. My elder granddaughter aged 7 years studying 2nd class and third granddaughter 5 years old just entered into the school. My second son aged 35 years passed 7th class and working as a agriculture labour on daily wage. My third daughter is aged 25 years, studied upto 3rd class wash clothes in some houses regularly and also works as a domestic servant in those houses. My second son 33 years physically handicapped opened a laundry shop to iron the clothes.

We constructed a small RCC house of our own and having minimum facilities like drinking water, sanitation, gas connection and T.V and current facility. We are living in the village since 45 years after my marriage and we are having friends in the neighborhood from other castes. There are only two Rajaka families in the village and the two families share the work available in the village.

We did not get any Bank loan. My son earns nearly 4000/- out of washing and ironing in the laundary. Daily we wash several pairs of dresses and for ironing each pair, we charge 10 rupees. We purchased an iron box for Rs. 800/-

and purchase coal @ Rs 28/- a Bag. Coal is not available openly and sometimes we face difficulties in getting coal.

We have caste societies and committees who will help us in resolving family disputes. We do our work from 8 am to evening 5 pm. We did not get any help or loan from the government or subsidy for any material from government.

We have agricultural land of 2 acres. My son works in the field other members help him in agriculture. Ours is a big family and whatever we earn which is not sufficient to make our livelihood. We are presently facing severe financial crisis as the expenditure for maintenance of family, medical expenses etc., have become more. We have to give good education to our grand children and better employment and we are now bothered only about that.

Apart from washing clothes we also have some traditional occupational works such as looking after delivery cases in some families. On the day of marriage we do some ceremonial works and on the occasion of deaths also we have something to do as per the tradition and the families where we work will pay us in the shape of kind or cash. We need assistance like educational facilities to our children and medical aid to our family members. We need old age pensions to our elders.

We hope that in future the

1. Government provides us residential houses.
2. Help us purchase iron box and other materials on subsidized rates.
3. Senior citizen pension scheme.
4. Free medical and educational facilities.
5. Show us separate places in the market area or main roads for open laundry itself.
6. Create cooperative societies to extend needed financial assistance whenever necessary.

Radandi Komuraiah

My name is Radandi Komuraiah aged 46 years studied up to 3rd class. My native place is Kanagarthy village of Karimnagar District in Telangana State. My family profession is washing clothes. We wash the clothes and iron them. I learnt it from my parents. I did not go to school. I am doing this work since 30 years.

We are five members in our family. My wife aged 42 years illiterate do household work and our professional work. My elder son aged 25 years studied upto 10th class doing the same profession. My younger son aged 22 years doing B.A Final year. My daughter 18 years good in studies doing B.Tech 1st year.

I have my own RCC building constructed by me. I have minimum facilities in my house such as drinking water. Toilets, current and a T.V. I have a Bicycle, but I don't have any pet animals like cow etc. Sometimes I borrow news paper from others to read. Since birth I am staying in the same village street. In our village ours street is known as Washermen Street or Chakaliwada.

In our village every year the caste elders will distribute the houses and work amongst us and we have to work with the families allotted to us. There is a village pond as known as 'Chaki Revue' where we wash the clothes. Every day at 7:00 am we go to chakirevue by bike. We boil the clothes, wash them, dry them and will come back to home at 5:00 pm. We distribute the clothes to the owners and get some meal or other food from them.

My wife and my elder son will assist me in my work. To wash the clothes we need soaps, soap powder which costs about 250-300/- rupees per month. Some household members will pay the monthly amount towards the work done by us and some others will give the food grains after getting the crops.

We did not get any Bank Loan. We purchase the material required for washing the clothes from outside. We settle our disputes through our community elders. In our village every three months we hold a meeting of all our caste members and settle disputes of any with the elders of our caste or sometimes by village Sarpanch.

We get money some additional payment in cash or kind from the houses where we work on the festival days, marriage ceremonies and on crop cutting days. The amount which we earn is not sufficient to lead out livelihood. In our caste there is a lot of change now-a-days when we compare it to olden days. No boy used to go school, earlier even if going to school elders used to ask him to discontinue and do the caste profession. Now every family wants their children to get education and get government employment. The elders also damaged their opinion now and encouraging children to go to school. In addition to our caste occupation of washing the clothes, we also work as paid labourers in carrying lights in marriages and in Temple ceremonies, and even in death days. In peak seasons we also go for agriculture work.

We do all kinds of traditional and ceremonial works in the families on the days of marriage and on the day of delivery and used to get good amount of money and other materials. We also used to assist the families in various works and get remuneration in the shape of kind or cash. But things are changed now and such ceremonial works are not available as in most cases they have stopped doing such things by involving us.

Our Problems Include:

1. We don't have any assistance from the government.
2. No old age pensions.
3. No medical aid.
4. No subsidy for purchase of raw material like coal etc as required.

5. No training facility in new methods of dry cleaning and use of washing machines.
6. Government is not appointing us as washer men in hospitals, in industries or in police Department where we are required and but giving it to contractors and others, other than washer men.

We have submitted many representations to government to readdress the above grievances but so far no action has been taken. We sincerely hope that at least in future government will come to our rescue and help us resolve our problems.

Gummadi Swaroopa

I am Gummadi Swaroopa, 46 years old, washer women living at Warangal of Telangana State. I have been in the hereditary occupation since 26 years, i.e., washing and ironing clothes. While observing parents doing the work I learnt it from them. As they were illiterates and poor they could not send me to school for education.

Actually I married at the age of 13 years, but my husband could not survive due to bad health. Now I am a widow maintaining by family of 5 members. My elder son Devender aged 19 years, while dropping out from school joined this profession. Devender's wife aged 18 years old studied upto 10th class helping me in our occupational and household work. She had a son of 3 months old. My younger son 16 years studying his senior intermediate. Following his elders he also does the work while persuing studies.

I have been living in a rented Kacha house, paying Rs.1000.00 per month, does not have domestic animals and others. We have minimum facilities in the rented house.

As I has been in this profession since 26 years, I had go to Chakirevu (place of washing clothes known as Dhobi Ghat) regularly. Now a day's Dhobighats are not sufficient for all the washermen. Due to insufficient water Dhobighats have become useless. There is hike in prices of soap powder. soaps, soda, Blue and Starch powders etc, and it costs us more I have to face many problems and I had to spend at least a minimum Rs.1500/- per year expenditure on these items earlier. We have starting washing clothes at the employers house itself. I work in the residencies of 10 families with the help of my daughter -in-law, and sons. I do not get sufficient income and due to this not able to fulfill the needs of the family. Further due to rise in coal prices, shed rents whatever we get for ironing the clothes also remains marginal. Somehow we are managing ourselves and meet the expenditure of our family.

I attend to various ceremonial functions during the weddings, cradle ceremonies, etc., on such occasions they give new clothes, rice, called as Talambralu (mylapopu) and money for doing the ceremonial functions. I also used to participate in temple festivals to carry lanterns, Pallakies of idols and get some money out of it. But despite all these we are facing caste discrimination in the society and being treated as low and unclean. The paradox is that we clean the clothes of others and make their houses clean and keep them clean and fresh but they call us 'unclean'.

Like in all other castes, we also have our Panchayat and it would settle disputes between the members of the community. Because of washing machines, and also not encouraging the washer women to wash the clothes at the tanks and canal sights our caste people are loosing their income. We have represented many a time to the government to look into our problems and extend necessary support especially for arranging working sheds, bank loans, and the pensions to our old aged, widows, physically handicapped, etc., but Government has hardly come forward to help our community. Government should provide us free residential education to the children of our families and help them gain access to government employment. Unless government extends necessary help we are not sure of our survival.

Mukku Komataiah

My name is Mukku Komataiah, aged 55 years. My native place is Laknepally Village District Warangal, Telangana State. Our profession is washing clothes and ironing clothes. My forefathers did the same profession. I learnt this profession watching my father doing the work. My parents are illiterates and due to financial problems my parents did not send me to school. I have been doing this profession since 43 years. At present all my family members do the same work. My wife 50 years old is illiterate. My son 30 years old studied upto 10th class and does our profession reluctantly and go for other work, wherever he finds it. My daughter-in-law aged 25 years work as domestic servant and also wash clothes. My eldest granddaughter aged studying 3rd class, granddaughter 5 years studying 1st class.

I have been living in this village since my birth. In Laknepally village we have our own house. It is a Katcha House built by me. We don't have any cattle or other domestic animals. We don't have sanitation facility. We have current facility. We have good relationships with neighbours. All the people cooperate with us in our profession. We used to wash clothes in a "Dhobi Ghat". Once upon a time, we carry all the clothes to be washed along with materials like soap, blue colour, bleaching powder, soda etc., at morning 7o' clock to a nearby tank. We wash clothes till evening and after washing them we distribute the clothes to respective people. In the evening the employer gives us some food and curries. We also wash clothes at some employer's houses. We don't have Iron Box and hence don't do iron the clothes.

We used to spend money upto Rs.1000/- to 1500/- per year on soda, surf, bleaching powder and blue colour during the past. But now we don't spend any amount because we ask the employer to pay for it or we undertake washing of clothes at owner's house. Owners bear all the expenditure. Till today I haven't taken any loan from any Bank as they don't give us. We don't have any other source. We somehow manage ourselves.

We earn around 3000/- to 4000/- for a month. It is not sufficient for my family needs. I have 1 acre of agricultural land. My son and I also do agriculture work. We get nearly 20,000/- to 25,000/- income per year on agriculture. To do agriculture we need investment, which we get from money lender or Asami and we clear the loan after the crop.

When I stared this work we used to get money as well as food and the employers had some regard but many changes have come over the years. My son studied 10th class and not interested to do this work and doing as a daily wage worker in the market. Now a days in our village most of the people are washing their clothes on their own and we loose employment and get less income due to this.

We used to get some additional payment whenever certain ceremonial functions are held. Especially we get money and new clothes for the work we do in the houses where new child is born and a 21st day function is arranged. During the ceremonies we clean their clothes which are not supposed to be touched by others. At the time of celebration of marriages, we used to distribute invitation cards to their relatives; we have honour and regard in the society due to these ceremonies and the role play in it. People think it is good men for them if we work. We also used to do painting the walls of temples and participate in temple celebrations. We used to carry lights during the ceremonial procession. It has been done as a hereditary custom. In marriages we perform the decoration of dais, with rice, flowers and others. We were very happy with the honour given during those days. We also perform all Karma Kanda work and cleaning work when some death takes place in the house of the master. We get money and rice also for doing this work.

But now, we have no honour in the society. Only for important works we are being called and on other occasions we are being ignored. Government did not extend any help to build Dhobi Ghats and provide freely water facility at the Ghats. We are forced to take loans from money lenders. The Federation created for us has not been helpful to our Community. Our children should get free education, mid day meal and health facility. Free hostels and good education must be provided by Government. In view of this Government should evolve a suitable policy for development of our Community.

Nagavelli Sadanandam

My name is Nagavelli Sadanadam, age 48 years, native Village Kothagudem District Khammam-Telangana State. I came to Hanamkonda 2 years back due to lack of availability of proper work there. Our traditional caste occupation is washing clothes and ironing dresses. It's a hereditary profession. I watched it myself, while my father and mother doing the work and learnt it from them. I have studied only upto 3rd class and dropped out due to financial problems. I could not go for further studies. I have been doing this profession for the last 34 years.

At present we are five members in the family. My wife aged 42 years also does our traditional occupational work, apart from the household work. She is an illiterate. She also works as domestic worker in some nearby houses. My eldest daughter Sindu studying degree second year and was married. My second daughter 17 years studying 10th class also helps us in our work. My son aged 14 years studying 9th class. He also helps me in my work.

We don't have any cattle or other domestic animals. I have my own house at Kothagudem, my native place. I get Rs. 300/- rent to it. We have taken a rented house here and staying at Hanamkonda. I pay Rs.1000/- rent to it. It's a RCC roof house. It has drinking water tap, lavatories and bathrooms facility. We have a TV and a gas stove.

We have been living here for the last two years. A part from washing cloths and ironing dresses, I also work as a watchman at an Apartment. I also do whatever work is available on extra payment.

Our neighbours belong to different castes and they do their work and they are very cooperative with us. In our native place we used to collect clothes for every two days and wash them at a "Dhobi Ghat", but now in the city we wash clothes here in Hanamkonda at owner's houses. Owners bear all expenses of Soda, Surf, and Blue Colour etc. I purchased an iron box to iron clothes. We purchase the coal from nearby places by making payment of Rs. 50/- per kg. All family members help me in washing and ironing clothes.

We haven't taken any loan from any bank or private finance company. In urban areas other caste people such as "Muslim Dhobis" "Thuruka Chakali" etc are entering the occupation. But in villages other caste people are not allowed to do our work. Every morning at 7'o clock to 10'o clock we wash clothes and clean bowls in the specified houses. We iron clothes for every two days. We get Rs. 8/- per a pair of clothes. But outside they take 10 to 12 rupees per pair of clothes. We iron 30 or 40 pairs a day.

In the overall sense we get 5000/- to 6000/- income every month. It is not actually sufficient to meet the family needs. Since we wash clothes for long hours we suffer from back pain, neck pain and nerves problems in forties and fifties of our age and we do not get proper medical attention. We haven't got any help from our caste societies in any form in this regard.

Most of our community members are facing severe financial problems. Our income is not sufficient to meet the present day increased daily expenses. There has been lot of competition from laundry shops and even other washing companies. Most people are also using washing machines at home and they do not need our assistance. Due to this we were reduced to the status of only domestic servants. As I have not studied and did not have any other alternate employment. I do not want my children to follow me like myself following my forefathers. Hence I want to educate my children. We are prepared to do hard work, but unable to get suitable work that fetches regular income and due to this we are afraid that we may not be able to send our children to higher education.

We used to get very less income earlier in Kothagudem our native place. But in Hanamkonda our income is relatively better than Kothagudem. But things are not sufficient. Infact, Government and private hospitals, industries and hostels need our services on regular basis but Government is not considering our services. Instead they prefer private companies to do our jobs.

Traditionally, (especially in villages) whenever there is a marriage in the families where we work, Our services are saught for helping them. In the past we used to distribute marriage invitation cards during "Shubhakaryas". We were involved in various ceremonial and rituals. We used to assist women during the pregnancy and both before and after the delivery of the baby. We used to undertake especially wash of clothes of mother and child upto 21 days. We also used to decorate wedding dias and carry 'lights' in the marriage profession. Our services are sought even for various works relating to Karma Kanda and cleaning house and washing all people's clothes and other works during the ceremonies. We used to get lot of money for all these works. But such things are not practiced and due to this we lost out traditional income source.

Even today in some villages, the hereditary work of white washing temples, carrying lights in the (shava procession carrying the tools of Gods) or Rathayatras. But most of these things have been found disappeared now a days and no one is calling us for any ceremonial works. In that way also we have lost our traditional income source. As the occupation has been facing lot of competition from others including professional companies with high investment and technologies and the traditional ceremonial work also getting disappeared most of our community people had lost their source of employment and income. Since most of us had no education, we were also unfit for modern jobs. Due to this, there has been lot of migration, amongst the washermen community, being displaced from their native places as well as occupations, had to go for physical labour to earn some livelihood. During the recent years several atrocities have also been committed on our women. They abuse us simply for no reason even by taking our 'caste name' whenever we demand higher wages for our work or better treatment as humans. There were social boycott calls in some places where 'upper castes landlords' found committing social crimes against us. We cannot ask for hike in wage and if we does, they go to the extent of boycotting us.

In view of this precarious situation we began requesting the government through our Associations seeking the allotment of cleaning and washing works from Government hospitals, school and college hostels, industries, transport undertaking etc., so that we get regular work. This may provide us full employment and required income and also may some social respect. But there was no positive response from government. We have been also requesting the government for allotment of housing accommodation, shop accommodation, raw materials, and support for purchasing iron boxes and arrangement of loans and subsidies for setting shops. We have submitted many representations to provide residential English medium education to our children and extend necessary help in their higher education. But there was no response due to lack of assets and also money we are not found in business or industry, or modern occupations. Our community is still a most backward community. They are socially weak and economically highly disadvantage Community. Unless Government comes forward with necessary support we cannot survive and lead a respectable life.

12

Kamsali- *The Gold Smith*

The Kamsalis are Gold and Silversmith. They make jewelry and ornaments that are elaborately designed and inlaid with precious and semi-precious stones. Some Kamsalis even cut and polish Diamonds, while others engrave deities on pendants and Gold and Silver plates. Nuclear families are most common among the Kamsali, though joint families also exist. The status of women is secondary to that of men though they participate actively in ritual, religious and social activities. Sometimes they help their men by cleaning the ornaments.

The Vishwakarma (or Visvakarma) community, known within the group as the Vishwabrahmin, is a group that is sometimes referred to as a caste and which comprises five sub-groups: carpenters, blacksmiths, bell metal workers, gold smiths and stonemasons who describe themselves as descendants of the Hindu god Vishwakarma. They worship various forms of the deity and follow five Vedas: Rigveda, Yajurveda, Samaveda, Atharvaveda and Pranava Veda. The Communal name of Vishwakarma is of fairly recent usage. Among the changes that occurred during this period, the census administrator J.E. Hutton recorded in 1931 a caste called the Vishwakarma, which was an administrative creation defined as a community of artisans who were geographically found distributed but shared fairly similar occupations.

The community prefers the new name, which has evidential support in 12th century inscriptions that refer to smiths and sculptors belonging to the Vishwakarma kula, although Vijaya Ramaswamy notes that "....the Vishwakarma community is obviously cutting across caste lines and ....comprises few socially and economically differentiated jatis". Prior to the Raj period, these communities were referred to names such as Kammalar in present-day Tamil Nadu and Kerela, Panchalar in Karnataka and Panchanamuvaru in Andhra Oradesh, while there are also medival inscriptions that refer to them as the Rathakarar and Kammala-Rathakarar.

The God Vishwakarma is considered by followers of the Hindu faith to be the divine architect or engineer of the universe. He had five children-Manu, Maya, Tvastar, Shilipi and Visvajna-and these are believed by the Vishwakarma community to have been the forebears of their five sub-groups, being respectively the gotras (clans) of blacksmiths, carpenters, bell metal workers (metal casters), stone masons and goldsmiths. It is not known whether these five sub groups historically practiced endogamy, which is a frequently-found feature of the Indian caste system.

Ramaswamy notes that the socio-economic and geographic stability of a medivel village-based maker of ploughs differed considerable from that of the various people who banded together as Vishwakarma and lived a relatively itinerant lifestyle that was dependent on the "temple economy" that waxed and waned as dynasties such as the Vijayanagar empire were formed and disintegrated.

They have claimed a status as Brahmins or some equivalent for many years and believe that the trades which they traditionally follow are superior to the work of a manual labourer because they require artistic and scientific skills as well as those of the hand. Somanathan argues that the artisanal groups were a part of the Indus Valley Civilization, found even before the arrival of Brahmins and their caste based division of society. He claims remarkable achievements are evidenced in both the arts and sciences during that egalitarian pre-Brahmin era, including the construction of aeroplanes.

The Vishwakarmas are largely found in the South of India: Kerela, Tamil Nadu, Karnataka, Andhra Pradesh, Goa and Konkan. In Rajasthan, Uttar Pradesh, Madhya Pradesh and Gujarath. Other Indian Vishwakarma populations are in: Madhya Pradesh, Maharashtra, Bengal, Delhi, Haryana, Bihar and Orissa.

Some of these castes attempted to dwija-ize themselves by allowing their men to wear the sacred thread across their body, their women to cook food while enwrapped in a wet piece of cloth, and so on. The artisan castes have built and developed enormous knowledge of engineering in several fields.

The process of ornament making has been exclusively practiced by the gold and silversmiths of India. They are known as Ausulas or Kamsalis in the Telugu region. The gold smiths operation in India expressed one of the finest engineering skills of the people involved in the process.

In the most traditional form of ornament-making, a village goldsmith sets the gold in a small crucible and keeps it in a small coal hearth that he exclusively arranges for the purpose in his own house. He uses a mouth pipe to blow air into the hearth by straining his lungs and keeps on blowing till the gold melts in the crucible. Sometimes, the blowing process takes several hours. This is one of the reasons why several goldsmiths die of lung-related diseases. The smith, then, stretches the melted gold into threads and weaves and moulds that gold into threads of all kinds of ornaments that the Indian people wear on their bodies with pride. Similarly, the smiths also make next stage; the smith uses several tools like pliers for cutting and hammers of various sizes to make gold and silver threads. He weaves and bends these threads into beautiful ornaments. In some models of ornaments making, gold and silver are shaped into rods. The way a rod is moulded to make an ornament shows the skill of our Goldsmiths and Silversmiths.

The ornament making process is quite complicated and requires sophisticated engineering skills. The smith of India learnt these skills in a long drawn out process of self training. Once the basic training was acquired through regular practice and struggle in the process of work, they learnt many intricacies of ornament-making. Once the knowledge of smithing was perfected by the parent in most cases by the father (through there have been women smiths in the villages who also acquired smithing skills) the sons were trained in the profession with great care.

There are several community associations for the Kamsali community at a local, regional and national level. These regulate social control, settle disputes and initiate welfare activities. The Kamsali celebrate all Hindu festivals like Dussehra, Diwali, Holi, Janamashtami, Navratri.

In this background an attempt has been made to collect primary field data from a select sample of Kamsali Community living in both rural and urban areas. The field data refers to the socio-economic and work situation of the Kamsali community and the changes that are taking place over the years.

Size of Family in relation to Age & Nativity

Table-1 indicates the size of the family of respondents chosen for the study. Out of the sample of 120 Goldsmith respondents chosen, around 60% were drawn from urban areas and the remaining from rural areas. About 60% of all are in the age-group- of '36 and above'. 40% belong to the age-group of 'upto 35'. It is significant to observe that about 47.5% of respondents had more than five members in their families, while 7% each had upto two members and upto three members each respectively. Thus relatively speaking the Kamsali community had more members in their families than others artisan groups.

Table 12.1

Size of Family in Relation to Age & Nativity

Sl. No	Age	Place	Single	Two Members	Three Members	Four Members	Five Members	Six Members & Above	Total
01.	Upto 25	Rural	-	3 (100) (33.33)	-	-	-	-	3 (100) (2.5)
		Urban	-	-	3 (50) (33.33)	-	3 (50) (7.14)	-	6 (100) (5)
02.	26-35	Rural	-	-	-	3 (100) (6.67)	-	-	3 (100) (2.5)
		Urban	-	3 (7.70) (33.33)	6 (15.38) (66.67)	18 (46.16) (40)	6 (15.38) (14.28)	6 (15.38) (40)	39 (100) (32.5)
03.	36-45	Rural	-	-	-	-	12 (100) (28.58)	-	12 (100) (10)
		Urban	-	-	-	3 (33.33) (20)	15 (55.56) (35.72)	3 (11.11) (20)	27 (100) (22.5)
04.	46-55	Rural	-	3 (12.5) (33.34)	-	12 (50) (26.67)	6 (25) (14.28)	3 (12.5) (20)	24 (100) (20)
		Urban	-	-	-	-	-	3 (100) (20)	3 (100) (2.5)
05.	56-65	Rural	-	-	-	3 (100) (6.66)	-	-	3 (100) (2.5)
		Urban	-	-	-	-	-	-	-
06.	66 & Above	Rural	-	-	-	-	-	-	-
		Urban	-	-	-	-	-	-	-
Total				9 (7.5) (100)	9 (7.5) (100)	45 (37.5) (100)	42 (35) (100)	15 (12.5) (100)	120 (100%) (100%)

Education in the Family

Table 12.2 indicates the educational levels of all the members of the families of the total sample respondents. Out of 540 total respondents all younger and elder, around 22% constitute illiterates, while 21% each had education 'upto 5' and 6-10 class respectively. It shows that around 42% of members of the families were found to be having studied upto 10th class and dropped out. 7.78% had after completed a Degree course and the other graduating ITI or technical courses to their credit. Further analysis says that female education is much lower in comparison to male education in the families. The younger generation is found in schools as their parents recognized the importance of education to their children. In the overall analysis it may be observed that the educational attainment of the Kamsali families is lower but the educational opportunities are made use of by the younger generation during the recent years.

Occupation of Family Members

It may be found that the Kamsali traditional occupation is male-oriented and only in some part and except in some cases Kamsali women do not involve themselves in the occupational activities of the Community. It may be found that except the Respondents generation (95%) and the generation of his son 66 (67%), all the earlier three generations had their traditional occupation as primary livelihood occupation. The occupation has been adopted hereditarily as

Table 12.2

Educations of Family Members (Cumulative)

Sl. No	Relationship with the Respondent	Illiterate	0-5 Classes	6-10 Classes	Inter	Degree	ITI/Other Technical Courses	Others	Total
01.	Respondent	6 (5) (5)	12 (10) (10.53)	15 (12.5) (13.16)	66 (55) (59.46)	18 (15) (42.86)	3 (2.5) (7.70)	-	120 (100) (22.22)
02.	Father	21 (77.78) (17.50)	3 (11.11) (2.63)	3 (11.11) (2.63)	-	-	-	-	27 (100) (5)
03.	Mother	42 (93.33) (35)	3 (6.67) (2.630	-	-	-	-	-	45 (100) (8.34)
04.	Elder Brother	3 (33.33) (2.5)	-	-	6 (66.67) (5.40)	-	-	-	9 (100) (1.67)
05.	Younger Brother	-	-	6 (66.67) (5.26)	3 (33.33) (2.71)	-	-	-	9 (100) (1.67)
06.	Younger Sister	-	-	-	-	3 (100) (7.14)	-	-	3 (100) (0.55)
07	Elder Sister	-	-	-	-	3 (100) (7.14)	-	-	3 (100) (0.55)
08.	Sons	-	33 (37.93) (28.95)	15 (17.24) (13.16)	15 (17.24) (13.51)	3 (3.45) (7.14)	21 (24.14) (53.84)	-	87 (100) (16.11)
09.	Daughter	3 (2.70) (2.5)	42 (37..84) (36.84)	24 (21.62) (21.06)	15 (13.51) (13.51)	12 (10.82) (28.58)	15 (13.51) (38.46)	-	111 (100) (20.56)
10.	Wife/Husband	45 (41.66) (37.5)	12 (11.11) (10.52)	45 (41.67) (39.47)	3 (2.78) (2.71)	3 (2.78) (7.14)	-	-	108 (100) (20)
11.	Others	-	9 (50) (7.90)	6 (33.33) (5.26)	3 (16.67) (2.70)	-	-	-	18 (100) (3.33)
Total		120 (22.22) (100)	114 (21.11) (100)	114 (21.11) (100)	111 (20.56) (100)	42 (7.78) (100)	39 (7.22) (100)	-	540 (100%) (100%)

a matter of pride in earlier generations and during the present Respondent generation only 5% had switched over to other occupations that too other traditional occupations, while the next generation (Respondents son) has been found in studies and had plans to go for other modern occupations. The analysis of the data in the table thus indicate that there has been a change in the occupational preferences, which could be experienced only during the present generation and the next. The forefathers of the respondents found to have been restricted themselves confined to their ancestral profession.

Table 12.3

Occupation of the Family Members (Cumulative)

Sl. No		Occupation	Other Traditional Occupation	Modern Occupation	Others/ Study	Total
01.	Respondent	114 (95) (23.46)	6 (5) (100)	-	-	**120 (100) (24.10)**
02.	Respondent's Father	120 (100) (24.69)	-	-	-	**120 (100) (24.10)**
03.	Respondent's Grand Father	120(100) (24.69)	-	-	-	**120 (100) (24.10)**
04.	Respondent's Grand Father's Father	120(100) (24.69)	-	-	-	**120 (100) (24.09)**
05.	Respondent's Son	12 (66.67) (2.47)	-	-	6 (33.33) (100)	**18 (100) (3.61)**
Total		**486 (97.60) (100)**	**6 (1.20) (100)**	**-**	**6 (1.20) (100)**	**498 (100%) (100%)**

Education and Length of occupation

Table-12.3 indicates the general trend relating to the educational achievement and the length of the occupation of respondents. It may be found that during the present generation 'education' did not motivate them to shift their occupation as those who had even completed graduation stick on to the traditional profession over a period ranging from 6 to 30 years. Those who had completed inter studies also found joining the ranks and file of their forefathers and has been found in the occupation 6 to 40 from years. Those who had lesser education continue to be in the profession but as they were dropped out from school. The analysis further indicates that Kamsali families for long have not given any priority to education as most of them cannot afford to send their children to schools. Like other artisan Communities Kamsali school dropouts had also entered their traditional occupations at an early age assisting their fathers and brothers. Girl's education has also been not encouraged for reasons of family taboo and also economic backwardness. Only during the recent years, there has been some change in the mindset of Kamsali families to educate their children despite some odds they face.

Dropout

Table 12.4 indicates the co-relation between the drop out levels of the present generation of the respondents and their parents and their children. It may be found that there is higher dropout rate in the earlier generation in relation to the present generation. Thus in the overall analysis it indicates the dropout rate has been falling as the higher dropout rate of their own fathers did not influence them much, as the modernization impact has been steady and positive.

Table 12.4

Education and Length of Occupation of Respondents

Sl. No	Education	0-5 years	6-10	11-20	21-30	31-40	41-50	51 & above	Total
01.	Illiterate	3 (50) (100)	-	3 (4.76) (50)	-	-	-	-	**6 (100) (5)**
02.	0-5 Classes	-	-	6 (50) (9.52)	3 (25) (12.56)	3 (25) (50)	-	-	**12 (100) (10)**
03.	6-10 Classes	-	6 (40) (2.25)	3 (20) (4.76)	6 (40) (25)	-	-	-	**15 (100) (12.5)**
04.	Inter	-	12(18.18) (50)	45 (68.18) (71.43)	6 (9.09) (25)	3 (4.55) (50)	-	-	**66 (100) (55)**
05.	Degree	-	3 (16.66) (12.5)	6 (33.34) (9.53)	9 (50) (37.5)	-	-	-	**18 (100) (15)**
06.	Others	-	3 (100) (12.5)	-	-	-	-	-	**3 (100) (2.5)**
	Total	**3 (2.5) (100)**	**24 (20) (100)**	**63 (52.5) (100)**	**24 (20) (100)**	**6 (5) (100)**	-	-	**120 (100) (100)**

Stated Occupation of Children

Table 12.5 indicates the occupational preferences of their children in relation to the place of living of families. Out of 120 families, significantly it may found some inter-village migration as 42 (35%) families had migrated from their native villages to other villages. 27.5% had migrated from rural to urban areas and 7.5% are found in reverse-migration from urban to rural areas. Significantly 32.5% each had come back to their native places (either urban or rural). Significantly a large number of those migrated to other areas had opted for other traditional occupations such as vadrangi, shilpi etc., instead of modern occupations. Some of those who went for higher studies from the remaining had settled down for lower traditional occupations. Thus 'migration to other areas' in search of livelihood or education had little impact and they had very little choice in relation to the modernization trends that are taking place widespread in and around.

Table 12.5

Stated Occupation of Children in relation to special background

Sl. No	Place		Same Occupation	Other Traditional Occupation	Modern Occupation	Labour	Others/Study	Total
01.	Urban	Migrant	-	27 (81.82) (32.14)	3 (9.09) (100)	-	3 (9.09) (16.66)	**33 (100) (27.5)**
		Local/Non Migrant	3 (7.69) (25)	30 (76.93) (35.72)	-	-	6 (15.38) (33.34)	**39 (100) (32.5)**
02.	Rural	Migrant	3 (33.33) (25)	3 (33.33) (3.57)	-	-	3 (33.34) (16.66)	**9 (100) (7.5)**
		Local/Non-Migrant	6 (15.38) (50)	24 (61.55) (28.57)	-	3 (7.69) (100)	6 (15.38) (33.34)	**39 (100) (32.5)**
Total			**12 (10) (100)**	**84 (70) (100)**	**3 (2.5) (100)**	**3 (2.5) (100)**	**18 (15) (100)**	**120 (100) (100)**

Occupation of Women in the Families

Table-6 presents the data relating to the occupational preferences of women in relation to their age background. Women in Kamsali community traditionally prefer to stay at home, as they were not being generally involved in the family occupation. Out of 162 adult women in the sample families, it was found that only 1.85% (3) women, whose age-group was 36-45, found doing their traditional activity. Around 5% found in other works, while a large majority women remained as house wives doing domestic activities within the families concerned. Despite the poverty and economic backwardness of the communities, women tend to remain as housewives and hardly go out for outside occupations or does the work relating to their own traditional occupation. Family taboo and tradition has more influence than the 'modernization processes' and changes taking place outside. This trend has been distinctly found in five Vishwa Brahmana or Vishwa Karma communities than the other OBC communities. This has been traditionally self-inflected restrictions on women in the families and where ever there has been some 'shift or change', it was mainly because of 'education' in the families.

Table 12.6

Occupation of Women in the Family

Sl. No	Age	Involved in Occupational work	Doing other work	Idle/unmarried/ Housewife	Total
01.	Up to 25	-	3 (16.66) (33.34)	15 (83.34) (10)	**18 (100) (11.11)**
02.	26-35	-	-	51 (100) (34)	**51 (100) (31.48)**
03.	36-45	3 (6.66) (100)	6 (13.34) (66.66)	36 (80.00) (24)	**45 (100) (27.78)**
04.	46-55	-	-	18 (100) (12)	**18 (100) (11.11)**
05.	56-65	-	-	21 (100) (14)	**21 (100) (12.97)**
06.	66 and above	-	-	9 (100) (6)	**9 (100) (5.55)**
Total		**3 (1.85) (100)**	**9 (5.55) (100)**	**150 (92.60) (100)**	**162 (100%) (100%)**

Education and Occupational Training

Table 12.7 indicates that paradoxically there has been little impact of education on the preferences of all ready those in the profession for undergoing training in their traditional occupations concerned. Since their traditional occupation has been hereditary in nature, male children in the families learn the technique and skills of the profession from their own fathers or elders in the families concerned and hardly receive any formal training. 82.5% of the respondents irrespective of their educational levels had learnt acquired the skills of their trade by 'observation and doing things' under father's guidance. Only 17.5% had undergone Government sponsored institutional training. It is however significant to observe that those who had completed secondary school education and above including graduation had incidentally preferred to undergo institutional training. They seem to have some influence of modernization of tradition as corporate agencies entering 'readymade gold ornamental business', monopolizing and taking over the work of Kamsali communities and affecting their occupational prospects. In view of this educated Kamsali men prefer to be trained in new designing and modeling technologies and getting benefitted out of modernization. But in the overall sense, modernization has a negative effect on these communities ruining their occupational prospects as factory made technology-based designary ornaments are invading the markets, while robbing the work and incomes of Kamsali community.

Table 12.7

Education & Occupational Training

Sl. No	Education	Only Family Training	Institutional Training also	Total
01.	Illiterate	6 (100) (6.06)	-	**6 (100)** **(5)**
02.	SSC	66 (91.66) (66.66)	6 (8.34) (28.57)	**72 (100)** **(60)**
03.	Inter	9 (50) (9.09)	9 (50) (42.85)	**18 (100)** **(15)**
04.	Degree	15 (69.43) (15.15)	6 (28.57) (28.58)	**21 (100)** **(17.5)**
05.	ITI	3 (100) (3.03)	-	**3 (100)** **(2.5)**
Total		**99 (82.5)** **(100)**	**21 (17.5)** **(100)**	**120 (100%)** **(100%)**

Assets

An analysis of Assets including movable and immovable properties of sample Kamsali families indicate that out of 120 only three (2.64%) had agricultural land to their credit. They cultivate it seasonally or give it for lease occasionally. These families were able to get found grains needed for them by cultivating the land available to them.

It is significant to observe that out of 120 sample households, 57.5% had their own houses. (42.5% RCC houses and 15% Kacha houses). The remaining 42.5% live in rented houses. It may be found that only 6 families had cattle or fouls in their household. Almost every sample household and except three all had power and gas connections. Majority of them own TVs and only some of them had Radios and sewing machines. A couple of households had rice cookers and some get news papers. In all more than half of the families had moderate facilities at home. As the women in their families cannot go out from the houses due to religious restrictions, despite the economic backwardness, these households do not consider it essential to have more or higher amenities at home.

Occupational Status

The data collected from the sample communities indicate that all the households had no secondary occupation of any sort as they concentrate on their primary occupation relating to gold and silver ornaments making. All of them are self-employed and do not work in firms owned by others thus all the households had their 'Own Account Family Enterprises'.

Normally both urban and rural sample household produce/make Bangl7es, tops, Necklace, Chains, Lockets,, Mangal Sutras, Rings, Vaddanam and various types of other gold and silver ornaments. They also undertake repair works of various ornaments. 65% of sample respondents had spared a room of their house to create a place for 'workshop or floor area' 'room all-in-one' as their 'production place'. Normally the sample households produce for individual customers, most of them are known to them, and sometimes they also work for shops or ornament dealers while producing various ornaments on order basis. In almost all the cases the customers or shop dealers provide them the 'raw gold or silver required' for making ornaments. Sometimes the sample households in limited number of cases prepare items popularly used 'by all' and keep it on display for sale at their shop so that those visiting customers may buy them if required. Only 18% of cases such things happen, while all other make ornaments on the basis of orders received. It may be found that during the marriage and festival seasons, they get more work and during those times they work for 'day in and day out' based on the quantity of orders and types of designs needed. During the off season repairs and petty works are undertaken and orders for fresh ornaments during those times are limited. There may be occasions they don't get any work at all and sit idle.

Investment Details

The field data on the cumulative investment details of the sample Kamsali communities indicate that 63.05% of sample respondents had invested only upto Rs. 10000/- on floor area, raw material (minus gold) tools and work instruments and others. 14.67% invested upto Rs. 25,000/-, 15.22% upto Rs. 50,000/- and 3.80% ranging upto one lakh rupees. About 1.6% each had spent between 1 to 2 lakhs and 2 lakhs and above each respectively. Only one household in the later category had spent Rs. 2.5 lakhs towards various items as indicated earlier. The cumulative response as calculated in table-8 indicates the marginal investment required for the job except those who use cutting machines, designing machines etc, the general investments are not much. Some of them made investment to have 'show-room-cum-floor-area', but such things are rare as found in the sample. Those who run 'gold business' with show room facilities were not covered in the sample as most of them with minor exception are run by other than Kamsali communities. It may be observed that once upon a time till fifties and sixties almost all gold shops or ornament shops or workshops were exclusively owned by Kamsali community. But by the entry of outside capital and growing corporate gold business, they started monopolizing the whole 'ornamental production' or businesses and Kamsali families had been forcibly displaced from the trade. Those who attempted to expand the business or tried to modernize their business could face 'stiff competition' from the corporate world and in the process some even had lost grip on the trade. Several of the families could not survive the competition and left the field to seek outside occupations or simple confined them to a small or medium production-cum-business activity.

Source of Investment

Table 12.8 indicates the details relating to the sources of investment made. 60% of the sample households had used their own sources to invest the money. Only 7.50% had the opportunity to get a bank loan for investment. 32.5% depended on financing institution or money lenders (mostly gold business dealers). It may be observed that those who are drawn from urban areas had to approach money lenders and took loans for investing the same in their occupation. As it may be seen that Banks as usual for various reasons fail to provide loans to these artisan communities and as a result these people have to invariably depend on financing agencies or gold-businessmen-cum-money lenders while paying interest rates. It has been observed that many of the families also found taking consumption loans due to non-availability of work during the lean seasons. It has been witnessed over the years that several of the families had become indebted and failure to clear the loans even in resulted suicides. Suicides have become rampant in Telangana region from amongst the Kamsali Communities due to non-availability of alternate livelihood opportunities and growing indebtedness or failure to clear the loans taken.

Almost all the sample households said that they generally depend upon the local orders, especially from the known people. Since gold has become a costly commodity and apprehension of adulteration or other kinds of cheating, work is not given to a stranger. Hence only known customers with faith on the 'makers' approach for ornaments. These problems do not arise with 'the Business or corporate showrooms', since they provide standard warranty certification. Such a competition and warranty facilities made the customers prefer corporate show rooms, instead of even known Kamsali community households. These developments had forced a large number of Kamsali households either to leave the occupation or found as paid workers or gumasthas in the 'big business Gold shops or corporate companies' loosing self-employment or closing down their own account enterprises.

As per the religious belief the traditional Hindu families prefer only Kamsali community persons to supply certain ceremonial ornaments on the occasion of engagements, marriages, birthday ceremonies and others. During these occasions Kamsali people get additional gifts and payments for the work done or visits made. For a long time such practices have observed in many Hindu families and it provided additional income and respectable social status to these communities, but during the recent years such things have become rare as in the name of modernization, people

Table 12.8

Source of Investment

Sl. No	Source	Urban	Rural	Total
01.	Own	30 (41.67) (41.66)	42 (58.33) (87.5)	**72 (100) (60)**
02.	Bank	9 (100) (12.5)	-	**9 (100) (7.50)**
03.	Society	-	-	-
04.	Finance/Money Lender	33 (84.62) (45.84)	6 (15.38) (12.5)	**39 (100) (32.5)**
Total		**72 (60) (100)**	**48 (40) (100)**	**120 (100%) (100%)**

are avoiding such ceremonial practices. Thus 'corporatization and modernization' has effected these comminutes very badly both economically and socially.

Government Schemes

Government schemes generally proposed to meet the requirements of general poor families all artisan families which did not reach or benefit the Kamsali Sample communities at all. Table-12.9 clearly indicates that the Artisan credit card scheme, Aadharana scheme, Government pensions etc., had not benefitted these communities at all. Only 7.5% of the sample communities could get Bank loans. As a result a large number of people drawn from Kamsali communities are kept outside the preview of the government schemes, not being beneficial to these communities.

Table 12.9
Government Schemes

Sl. No	Government Schemes	Available	Not Available	Total
01.	Artisan Credit Card	-	120(100) (25.48)	**120 (100) (25)**
02.	Aadarana Scheme	-	120(100) (25.48)	**120 (100) (25)**
03.	Bank Loans	9 (7.5) (100)	111 (92.5) (23.56)	**120 (100) (25)**
04.	Govt. Pensions	-	120(100) (25.48)	**120 (100) (25)**
Total		**9 (1.88) (100)**	**471 (98.12) (100)**	**480 (100%) (100%)**

Associations

There are a number of Artisan Community Associations working in the field but their role has become very much limited. This is also same in the case Kamsali community Association as they were hardly useful to represent the problems of the community. They have even failed to exert pressure on the government to seek favours. Due to this, government has not evolved any specific policy to meet the problems of these people and not evolved any popular programmes to rehabilitate them.

Migration

Kamsali community families over the years are found migrating to other places for work for maintaining their self respect. About 32.5% of respondents (during their generation) had to migrate to other areas along with their families. Table 12.10 indicates that their parents and grandparents also found moving to other areas for work especially to towns and cities in their life time. Most of the respondents had said that although much work is not assured but they go to places where their relatives or acquaintance are found and found always a lookout for better survival.

Table 12.10

Migration Trends (Cumulative)

Sl. No	Migrated to other Village	Migrated to Town/City	Not Migrated	Total
01.	Respondent Alone			
02.	Respondent with Family	39 (32.5) (100)	81 (67.5) (25.24)	120 (100) (33.33)
03.	Respondent Parents		120 (100) (37.38)	120 (100) (33.33)
04.	Father/Grand Father and other Relation of Respondents Family		120 (100) (37.38)	120 (100) (33.34)
Total		39 (10.84) (100)	321 (89.16) (100)	360 (100%) (100%)

General Development of the Families

Respondents were asked to comment in general about the 'development' of family in relation to their education, economic, social and occupational status. Although the 'term' used to measure 'general development' has not been defined in specific terms here, it would only be able to provide only a general assessment of what has been happened over the years. It may be found in Table 12.11 that 67.5% of respondents had categorically said that educationally speaking their families had not been developed. 95% said 'economically' not developed, 97.5% said that socially 'not developed' and 'occupationally' the opinion was unanimous as they said that they have not developed' at all. 27.5% however said that there was 'development with regards educational status only to some extent', while 5% said that educationally they have 'developed' to the extent they desired only 2.5% said that economically they had witnessed 'satisfactory development' during their lifetime. The data and the opinions expressed by the respondents indicates the 'precarious situation' of the community as educationally, economically, socially and occupationally not much development' has taken place but in other words their educational, social, and occupational situation and conditions seem to have been deteriorated over the years.

Table 12.11

General Development

Sl. No	Nature of Development	Developed	Not Developed	To Some Extent	Total
01.	Educational	06 (5.0)	81 (67.5)	33 (27.5)	120 (100) (25)
02.	Economical	3 (2.5)	114 (95.0)	3 (2.5)	120 (100) (25)
03.	Social		117 (97.5)	03 (2.5)	120 (100) (25)
04.	Occupational		120 (100)		120 (100) (25)
	Total	09 (1.8)	432 (90.0)	39 (8.12)	480 (100%) (100%)

Occupational Problems

An analysis of available data based on the opinion of sample Kamsali households indicate that Non-availability capital, margin money, subsidies from the side of Government, negative attitude of bankers in extending loans, raising market competition or outsiders penetration into the trade and business, availability of modern products or designer ornaments on large scale, quality assurance problems and police harassement etc., are considered to be the major problems faced by these communities. It has been observed that police people harass these communities whenever some theft of gold ornaments takes place in their vicinity. Police people always have suspicious attitude towards these people and extort money for nothing of their fault. Due to continuing police harassment some of the families had left the profession and even migrated to other places. The community association could not do much and other backward class organizations only express sympathy but nothing concrete has been done by them. General public including their own customers are indifferent about it. Though during the festivals and auspicious occasions, these occupational communities were treated well and with high esteem but normal times people are indifferent. Many of the respondents are reported that they also face various health problems due to the gold work such as they use chemicals/tejab etc., and get eye-diseases, neck problems, back pain, nervous problems etc., No one seems to taken any health insurance for the same.

Solutions to Problems

Table-12.12 presents the cumulative responses of the sample households in relation to other occupational issues and problems. 43.37% of respondents wanted that police harassment be stopped forthwith, 21% said that they should be provided 'subsidy', margin money along with bank loans to set up their workshop. 17% said that there should be some law to stop the Non-Kamsali Bengali workers influx into the trade, 16% said that 'corporate business' should be restricted not to enter into small ornaments making and its trade, law should also be made to stop big jewelers entering into all sorts of ornament making etc., Others said supply of cutting machines, allotment of work sheds and housing, creation of separate special economic zones, free and compulsory residential education to their children and counseling and guidance to those who attempt to commit suicide etc., some of these are 'stray suggestions' made by them during the discussion. As the successive government fail to bother about their growing problems, they became skeptical and not in a position to suggest concrete strategies and solutions to resolve their problems. However they still consider that their problems are many and complex and they have confidence that their problems will be resolved soon.

Table 12.12
Solutions to Problems (Cumulative)

Sl. No	Respondent	Rural	Urban	Total
01.	Stop encroachment other communities in their work	9 (14.28)	54 (85.72)	**63 (100) (17.65)**
02.	Restrict corporate business to some segments of gold ornaments	15 (26.31)	42 (73.69)	**57 (100) (15.97)**
03.	Prevent big jewelers monopolizing the trade	42 (100)	-	**42 (100) (11.77)**
04.	Provision for free Supply of Cutting Machines	3 (33.34)	6 (66.66)	**9 (100) (2.52)**
05.	Liberal Bank Loans/technical advice and training facilities	27 (36)	48 (64)	**75 (100) (21)**
06.	Houses and worksheds in separate SEZ.	3 (50)	3 (50)	**6 (100) (1.68)**
07.	Subsidies / Margin Money	18 (24)	57 (76)	**75 (100) (21)**
08.	Law to prevent police harassment.	27 (36)	48 (64)	**75 (100)**

Future Perspective

To windup the discussion, the respondents were asked to comment about their 'future perspective'. Most of the respondents had skeptical about their future but had unanimous in their opinion that 'future is not hopeful' as they had bad experiences in their 'occupational life'. 55% respondents had categorically said that the future is 'not hopeful and dark' and the remaining 45% said 'future is uncertain'. They said that they had no or a very little option or opportunities available outside their trade and despite the 'bad experiences' they have, they had to pull on with the profession. They were also unanimous in their decision that they do not want their children to carry on the profession. They said categorically that government should come forward to provide 'free and compulsory residential education to their children and relieve them from the 'uncertain future'.

Profiles and Case Studies of Select Kamsali Respondents

Sunkum Vinod

My name is Sunkum Vinod, aged 28 years. My native place is Tadapakala Village in Karimnagar District. Due to unemployment I came to Korutla 20 years back and here I am doing my professional work. i.e., Gold Smithy. I prepare Gold Ornaments which I learnt it from my grandfather. My father died when I am in 5th class. I started doing this Gold work when I was only 12 years old. I stopped my studies after V class. My mother and wife apart from household work. Due to poverty and family problems, I have stopped my studies. My brother had studied B.Sc., and working as a teacher in a private school and his wife also earns some additional money by stitching dresses.

I have one small RCC building. Water facilities and sanitary facilities are available at home. We do not have any pet animals. Here we are living since 20 years. The other caste members as neighbours are friendly with us and helpful.

Now I am the only person doing the work in my workshop. Previously I used to work in other workshop owned by a relative for three years. Presently I have opened my own workshop in my home itself and doing the work independently for the last 15 years. I use cutting machine which I had purchased for Rs. 10,000/-. We don't have other machines such as I cannot afford to purchase the same due to investment problems. I purchase Gold from Warangal and also from Hyderabad. Every month I spend an amount of Rs.25000 to 30000 towards purchase of raw gold to prepare small items which I can sold to customers.

The customers give us Gold for preparation of ornaments, in such cases we have no problem of investment. I can prepare ornaments and hand it over to the customers on time. Sometimes we don't have any work. This occupation depends on the belief of the customers. Mostly known people will come to my shop and place orders for preparation of ornaments. Previously the price for 10 Gram gold was between Rs. 15 to 20 thousand, but now it is very high because of high rate of gold. Now-a-days not many people are coming forward to purchase gold for preparing ornaments. Consumers however purchase Gold at the time of marriages, festival season and on Dhana Trayodashi day.

The Vyshyas in our town sell the readymade jewellary in their shops and many more such shops have come up during the recent years. As many jewellary shops have come up many customers now prefer readymade ornaments and due to this we lost our traditional work. I used to work daily from 8 am to 8 pm and nearly I used to get an amount of Rs. 20,000/- per month during seasonal days. I also do silver work but occasionally and income for doing silver work has been not much. In any case there has been fall of income and lack of sufficient work. Due to competition from readymade shops and also corporate gold business houses the gold smith entrepreneurs had lost their traditional occupational work and their livelihood.

Most of the big jewellary shops give advertisements in news papers and also Televisions and public are attracted to the discount sale of ornaments or other incentives offered. This has affected all. Apart from loosing work orders, we face problems with the police. When I was in 8th class, police took my grandfather into police custody that he has in his processions of stolen gold. It was a great insult to our family, my grandfather was a honest man and he could not bear the insult and Committed suicide later. Due to these conditions most of our families and relatives now feeling insecure and leaving the profession. Many of our Community members had such bad experiences and due to this many had stopped the work and began sitting idle at home. Many such cases are reported where they have committed suicide and because of the mistake identity of the police. In view of this government should extend necessary help to resolve our problems and create conditions in which our community members will be able to carry on their occupation smoothly? Government should also extend loan facilities to those who setup shops and provide necessary support. It should offer free residential education to the children of these families to the college level that this community also becomes educationally strong.

Madipadi Venkateshwarlu

My name is Madipadi Venkateshwarlu aged 42 years. My native place is Husnabad village of Karimnagar District in Telangana State. I came to Warangal 22 years back in search of employment and I started doing my traditional occupational work. I did Intermediate 1st year at Husnabad and discontinued studies due to financial problems. I am in this profession since 20 years.

My wife is 39 years old illiterate housewife, doing household work. I am having one son aged 14 years studying 9th class. My elder daughter 17 years studying intermediate II year, younger daughter 16 years studying 10th class. I am only the earning member in the family and I do not allow any of my family members to help me in my work. I do not want my son should learn this work. I want him to be educated and get government job. I also do not want my daughters get good education. I do not want to marry them a goldsmith doing the traditional occupation but instead prefer a goldsmith government servant. I used to have my own house and but due to debts I have sold my house and living in a rented house by paying Rs. 2000/- rent per month. I have setup my own workshop to prepare gold ornaments and sell.

My neighbors belong to other castes such as Vysya, Sri Vyshnavas, Padmashali and all of them are friendly and they are having their own traditional occupations to do.

I use different tools like cutting player, current stone, gas cylinder, wax, copper, bronze and other to do my work. Mostly middle class and lower middle class customers approach us for preparation of gold ornaments and they need light weight and less expensive ornaments. If customers give me Gold to prepare the ornaments required, I prepare and give them the finished product as per their specifications. Previously the gold rate was less and many people used to come to us for preparation of gold ornaments but now-a-days the gold rate is high so we are not getting sufficient orders for preparing the ornaments.

I took a Bank loan of Rs. 50,000/- and used it as an investment to setup the shop. Two years back I took gold under PMRY scheme and paid the price on installment basis. I purchase raw gold from Warangal or sometimes from Hyderabad, whenever the customers place orders for ornaments.

Now-a-days we find a number of big jewellery shops in the market and who are giving advertisements attracting consumers to purchase ornaments. Due to this we are unable to get many orders to prepare the ornaments. Moreover one gram gold readymade ornaments are now a day's available in the market and most of the customers prefer it as these ornaments look like pure gold. Due to all this we are not able to get sufficient orders and full work. As a result we could not earn required amount per month which is not sufficient to pay the bills and also fulfill the needs of my family.

We work from 8:00 am to 5:00 pm and when the work is more we work for more number of hours. We are now getting Rs. 10,000/- to 15,000/- per month. Customers are also now finding it as prestigious to go to big Jewellery shops. We can prepare ear rings, Chains, Necklace, Braclets and all other articles as available in big shops but the customer are not giving preference to us. Jewellery shops sell the KDM gold which we cannot afford. Due to non availability of sufficient work and falling incomes, several of us are unable to repay the debts taken and in my own relations some have committed suicide.

Government should extend a helping hand to the families which committed suicide and assist them. It should provide interest free loans to the workers. As things are getting worsened, we have left with no other alternative except either to shift from the profession and go for physical labour or commit suicide.

Kunelapaka Venkateshwarlu

Kunelapaka Venkateshwarlu, aged 48 years belongs to Kanagarti village of Odela Mandal in Karimnagar district, Telangana State. I am a Goldsmith by birth I learnt the art of making Jewellary at Ramakrishnapuram of Adilabad with my uncle. I studied upto 10th class and due to economical problems I did not go for higher education.

I had 4 members in my family, wife aged 45 years stopped education at primary level, does tailoring and household work, son 22 years living in Hanamkonda doing B.Tech and daughter aged 20 years doing Pharmacy at Karimnagar. I had a Kucha house with no facilities like drinking water and sanitation facilities. We have a sewing machine. Since my birth I am residing in this house only. A number of families live in surroundings place like Blacksmiths, Washermen and others. We have good relations with all these caste people.

For making Gold Jewellery we need different tools such as cutting plates, small cutting machine, cutting players, Tejab (Sulfuric Acid), Coal, manual stove Gas stove, weighing machine, wire cutting machine etc, and most of these are traditional instruments which we own. Now a day's modern tools are available but which are expensive and we cannot afford to have them.

Customers purchase readymade gold and jewellary according to their wish. We take time to make the jewellery.

Here satisfaction of customers is our motto. Our profession is dependent upon customer's faith on us and their order to make ornaments. I am the only person in this family making gold ornaments. Nowadays so many readymade jewellery shops appeared in the market. The middle class families do not prefer handmade ornaments because it relatively need more gold. Readymade ornaments are light weight and most people prefer it because its price-flexibility. We cannot produce such light weight ornaments as they could be made only by using modern machines. I did not take any loans from any bank or any financial Agency. I had to invest some capital on gold out of my savings. I get raw gold from nearby cities. I work at home and receive orders from customers. During the seasons such as Marriages, Diwali, Dhana Trayodashi, Akshya thrutiya and Sravana Pournima more work orders we get from various customers. I need to work for more hours based on the orders which I receive. In general I work from 8.00 a.m. to 6.00 p.m.

Nowadays women are interested in one gram gold ornaments and this is affecting our work. Due to non-availability of sufficient work many of our gold smiths had left the profession during the recent years and settled as agriculture labour. My brother is best examples for this being educated upto intermediate my brother is working as a worker in a market to fulfill the household needs. For this reason he is not getting matches for marriage of his daughter and another member of family has been working as postal courier, but more are found in agriculture. Many Bengali families are migrating to this state and they make designer jewellary which are more attractive. As there is no sufficient work in this field, many families now started migrating to other places to take up other jobs.

As I am getting a monthly income of Rs.6000/- to Rs.8000/- during the season and it will not be enough to fulfill our family needs and during off season there will be loss or no work and no income. We have not received any help from Government or any other organization. I feel that Government should extend necessary support to our families and help us show alternate employment or protect us from corporate jewellary shops which had ruined our employment prospects.

Guggili Rajeshwar Rao

My name is Guggili Rajeshwar Rao aged 44 years. My native place is Venkatapoor village of Mulugu Mandal Warangal District in Telangana State. I came to Warangal 20 years back as I do not have work at Venkatapoor Village. My job is preparation of gold ornaments. After my completion of Intermediate I got married and due to family problems I could not continue my further studies. As I could not get any other employment I had joined my traditional occupation as there was no other alternative.

I have altogether five members in the family, my mother who is 80 years old, my wife 40 and my son and daughter. My mother and my wife did not go to school. My daughter now studying B.Tech III year and my son B.Tech II year. As I have decided not to see my children in Gold Smith occupation, somehow I had managed to send them to college and get higher technical education.

I have got one R.C.C building at Warangal. I own scooter, water tap and other facilities at home. My neighbors belong to my own caste and they are helpful. There are also other backward caste members also living in the neighbourhood also help each other.

I have started my own workshop in one of the rooms of my house and I am the only person in my family presently doing the Gold Smith work. I spent 50,000/- to open the workshop. Initially I took a Bank Loan of Rs. 50,000/- to purchase tools and materials and I repaid the amount later.

Previously customers used to purchase gold and come to us for getting their ornaments prepared. I worked for 20 years in the profession. Customers have good belief in me and I used to get good number of orders for preparation of ornaments. Previously the gold rate was low but now it has high rate and due to this public is unable to purchase. Only on festivals days like Dussehra, Deepavali, Akshaya Trayodasi, and Public generally purchase gold and come to us for preparation of ornaments. But now a days not many people are venturing to purchase gold regularly and as a result there has been gradual decrease in the number of people who come to me for getting gold ornaments prepared.

Most of the public now-a-days are going for the purchase of one gram gold ornaments in Jewellery shops and this has also contributed to loss of our work. I used to get monthly an amount of Rs 10-15/- thousand previously but now it has become difficult to get such an amount as I do not have sufficient work to do. We have our own professional Community organization which is now organizing meetings to exert pressure on government to extend necessary facilities.

Big Jewellary shops are giving advertisements in newspapers, and T.Vs and public are attracted towards it. As such we are not selling sufficient work now and we are witnessing fall of our incomes and deterioration of our conditions.

Due to non availability of work most of the community members of this profession are shifting to other occupations or works whatever is available to them. Due to this their families are facing a number of problems. I feel that Government should come forward to rescue us from the bad state of affairs. Otherwise there is no better future for us.

13

Kummari- *The Potter*

The Kummara or Kumhar are potters who make earthen vessels, water pots, decorative home wares, toys and idols of gods and goddesses. The name Kumhar denotes a maker of pots and pitchers or someone who creates. They are an integral part of Indian society because their creations are an integral part of an Indian's daily life rituals.

They make idols, statues of famous people and folk deities and animals. They can be found at local markets selling their wares on most days. They have started using terracotta instead of red clay as it can be painted and is less fragile.

One of the largest castes, they are reportedly spread across 212 districts of India, predominantly in the states of Punjab, Haryana, Rajasthan, Uttar Pradesh, Bihar, West Bengal, Gujarat, Maharashtra, parts of Karnataka, Telangana and Andhra Pradesh. They are known by different names in each state. In Madhya Pradesh & Uttar Pradesh, they are listed as a scheduled caste (previously called untouchables.) They themselves do not consider themselves as such.

The Kummara are a landless community who continue in their traditional occupation as potters, with some engaged in animal husbandry and crop farming on a share-cropping basis. Some work as masons and manual labour for a daily wage.

When we compare the accounts of 19th and early 20th century ethnographers, we can see that the Kummaras traditional occupation has diversified considerably. In addition, there has been a devolving of subgroups and an increasing identity-consciousness across states.

The literacy rate is very low and child labour is common. Response to developmental aid is mixed – they are encouraged to educate their children, but boys are favored over girls and the dropout rate is high due to social and economic reasons.

The Kummaris are predominantly Hindu. Although quite low in the Hindu caste hierarchy, they have access to all the sacred shrines of pilgrimage for Hindus. Families may choose to give importance to a deity. All Hindu workmen, including the Kummara, regard the tools of their trade as the cause of their prosperity and worship them as such.

India was home to some of the earliest knowledge of pot making in the world. Pot making was well- advanced by the time of the Indus Valley Civilization, which existed much before the Aryans invaded India. Who developed that knowledge of pot making? As of now, there are castes and communities which possess very advanced knowledge of pot making in the Indian villages. Such possessors of pot making technology are known as the Kummaris in Telugu region. Similar castes exist in all other states.

The pot making process on the wheel involves several stages. The first stage is that of converting the soil into clay by mixing in proper ratios of soft soil, ash or saw dust and soft sand. This mixture is worked out by adding the necessary amount of water as the mixture is crushed under human feet. Once the clay is ready, the pot maker places it on the wheel specifically constructed with the combined knowledge system of the potter, the ironsmith and the carpenter. This wheel stands on a wooden (in Telugu region they use Sandra wood to make the support of the wheel) rotator fixed on a marble stone which has a round whole. The potter keeps on applying greasy oil on the wooden support that keeps the movement of the wheel smooth.

The clay placed on such fast-running wheel gets pressed with the finger tips into an initial shape called the niluvu. At this stage, the artful operation of the fingers and nails of the potter plays a crucial role. The potter also uses a wet cloth as an instrument to work out a well-designed mouth of the pot. Even to carve out the curls and chains at the mouth of the pot, the potter only uses his nails.

This hand work involves skillful handling of the wooden slate, a round stone and dry ash. From this stage, women too enter the process of shaping the pot. There are many women who are experts in this operation. Depending on the size of pot that a given niluvu can produce, the potter uses slate, stone and ash to blow up its middle part and shape up its base.

The third stage is that of burning all the dry pots in a specific place called the Kummari vaamu (in Telugu region), which accommodates hundreds of pots. After the pots are arranged, the vaamu is covered with mud so that the heat generated by creating a huge fire in hearth at the bottom of the vaamu is absorbed into the pots. After the pots get burnt to a particular level of heat, the vaamu is allowed to cool down gradually so that the pot becomes stronger and stable and can be used for all kinds of purposes-cooking, preserving water, oil, grain, and so on.

Thus the products produced by the potter has always been near and dear to the daily life of the rural as well as urban people. To examine more details the present study makes an attempt to conduct a field study to collect information relating to the socio-economic and work situation of the potters and analyze the process their transformation over the years.

Sample and Size of Family of Respondents

Table 1 gives clear information about the sample of respondents chosen, their rural-urban background, age-group and the number of family members. The data clearly indicates that out of 189 respondents chosen for the study, 65.07% (123) belong to urban areas, 34.92% (66) belong to rural areas. The age-group details of urban area respondents indicates that 23.81% belong to 46-55 age group, while 19.05% belong to 56-65 age group, 14.28% belong to 36-45 age group, 4.76% belong to 26-35 age group and 1.58% belong to the age group upto 25 years. The data shows that the majority of the respondents belong to middle and above middle aged category.

Regard to rural background, 15.88% of the respondents belong to 56-65 age group and it was followed by the age groups '66 and above' with 7.94%, 6.35% belong to 46.55 age group, 4.76% were of 26-35 age group and 1.58% each belong to 26 and above and 36-45 age groups respectively.

It may be found in rural and urban areas that the size of 30.16% family members of the respondents comes to four members each, while 20.64% were of two member families, 19.05% of respondents had six and above family members. 12.70% families were of three members each and 1.58% is found to be single member families. Thus predominantly the sample constitute the middle and above middle aged, drawn from both rural and urban areas.

Table 13.1

Size of the Family

Sl. No	Age	Place	Single	Two Members	Three Members	Four Members	Five Members	Six Members & Above	Total
01.	Up to 25	Urban	3 (100) (100)	-	-	-	-	-	3 (1.58) (100)
		Rural	-	-	-	-	-	-	-
02.	26-35	Urban	-	-	-	9 (100) (15.79)	-	-	9 (4.76) (100)
		Rural	-	3 (33.33) (7.70)	-	6 (66.67) (10.52)	-	-	9 (4.76) (100)
03.	36-45	Urban	-	-	3 (11.11) (12.5)	15 (55.56) (26.32)	6 (22.22) (20)	3 (11.11) (8.33)	30 (100) (14.29)
		Rural	-	-	-	3 (100) (5.26)	-	-	3 (100) (1.58)
04.	46-55	Urban	-	-	9 (20) (37.5)	12 (26.67) (21.06)	6 (13.33) (20)	18 (40) (50)	45 (100) (23.81)
		Rural	-	6 (50) (15.39)	-	3 (25) (5.26)	3 (25) (10)	-	12 (100) (6.35)
05.	56-65	Urban	-	9 (25) (23.07)	6 (16.67) (25)	3 (8.33) (5.26)	12 (33.33) (40)	6 (16.67) (16.67)	36 (100) (19.05)
		Rural	-	9 (30) (23.07)	3 (10) (12.5)	6 (20) (10.53)	3 (10) (10)	9 (30) (25)	30 (100) (15.88)
06.	66 & Above	Urban	-	-	-	-	-	-	-
		Rural	-	12 (80) (30.77)	3 (20) (12.5)	-	-	-	15 (100) (7.94)
Total			3 (1.58) (100)	39 (20.64) (100)	24 (12.70) (100)	57 (30.16) (100)	30 (15.87) (100)	36 (19.05) (100)	189 (100%) (100%)

Education of the Family Members

Out of the total 552 members in the families of 189 respondents 35.87% were illiterates, 20.80% of members of the families had education between 6th 10th classes, 10.87% had studied upto 5th class, 7.60% had intermediate, 9.79% of family members of respondents had degree qualification to their credit, while 7.07% were graduates.

Out of the total respondents, 35.87% were illiterates, 28.80% with 6th to 10th class 10.87% studied upto 5th class, while 9.79% had degree level education and 7.07% of respondents have been educated upto post graduation level.

It may be found that several of the respondents and their parents were illiterates but it may be observed that the respondents are found encouraging the girls' education with equal spirit as well of their male children. They wish to give top priority to the education of their children.

Occupation of the Family Members

The table 13.3 focussed its attention on the 5 generations way back of the respondents. It may be found that except the generation of the respondent's son, all his order generation had adopted the same traditional occupation of the family. Only in the present generation, it means (sons of the respondents) 13.95% found to have adopted the community based traditional occupation, while 81.40% are found to have shifted their occupation from their traditional occupation towards other or a modern occupations which are available to them and 2.32% of the sons of the respondents are found to be working as employees in Government sector.

Further examination found that all the family members of the respondents irrespective of whether they adopted the (87.45%) same profession or not, they have learnt the skills of the trade in their early ages from the elders of the family.

Table 13.2

Education of Family Members (Cumulative)

S. N.	Relationship with the Respondent	Illiterate	0-5 Classes	6-10 Classes	Inter	Degree	ITI/P.G	Total
01.	Respondent	3 (50) (1.52)	-	-	3 (50) (7.14)	-	-	**6 (100) (1.08)**
02.	Father	3 (100) (1.52)	-	-	-	-	-	**3 (100) (0.54)**
03.	Mother	9 (100) (4.55)	-	-	-	-	-	**9 (100) (1.64)**
04.	Sons	6 (2.85) (3.03)	15 (7.14) (25)	99 (47.15) (22.64)	36 (17.15) (85.72)	24 (11.43) (44.45)	30 (14.28) (76.92)	**210 (100) (38.05)**
05.	Daughter	-	24 (25) (40)	36 (37.55) (22.64)	3 (3.15) (7.14)	24 (25) (44.45)	9 (9.3) (23.08)	**96 (100) (17.40)**
06.	Wife/Husband	156 (88.14) (78.78)	-	18 (10.17) (11.33)	-	3 (1.69) (5.55)	-	**177 (100) (32.06)**
07.	Others	21 (41.17) (10.60)	21 (41.17) (35)	6 (11.77) (3.77)	-	3 (5.89) (5.55)	-	**51 (100) (9.23)**
	Total	**198 (35.87) (100)**	**60(10.87) (100)**	**159 (28.80) (100)**	**42 (7.60) (100)**	**54 (9.79) (100)**	**39 (7.07) (100)**	**552 (100%) (100%)**

Table 13.3
Occupation

Sl. No		Caste Occupation	Other Traditional Occupation	Modern Occupation	Government Job	Others	Total
01.	Respondent	189 (100) (24.71)	-	-	-	-	**189 (100) (21.36)**
02.	Respondent's Father	189 (100) (24.71)	-	-	-	-	**189 (100) (21.36)**
03.	Respondent's Grand Father	189 (100) (24.71)	-	-	-	-	**189 (100) (21.36)**
04.	Respondent's Grand Father's Father	189 (100) (24.70)	-	-	-	-	**189 (100) (21.36)**
05.	Respondent's Son	9 (6.98) (1.17)	9 (6.98) (100)	105 (81.40) (100)	3 (2.32) (100)	3 (2.32) (100)	**129 (100) (14.56)**

Length of Occupation

Out of the total of 189, 28.58% of the respondents had 31 and above years of experience, 25.40% with 41-50 years of experience, 22.23% with 21 to 30 years of service, 12.70% with 11 to 20 years of experience, 6.34% with 51 and above years of experience, while 3.17% had only 1 to 5 years of experience.

Regarding the education and the length of occupation 34.15% were illiterates and they were doing their traditional based occupation since 26 and above years. 41.66% of respondents with an education between 6th to 10th classes had 11 to 20 years of experience. 40% with an education upto intermediate level are also found working in the profession and put up more than 31 years of experience. Even those respondents who passed Intermediate (7.94% and graduates (1.58%) are also found doing the occupation and put up long years of experience in the profession and continue to do the same.

Thus the data shows that the education is not a criterion to determine their lives. Whether they are educated or not they must depend on their traditional-based occupation for their livelihood as they find no other alternative.

Table 13.4

Education and Length of Occupation

Sl. No	Education	1-5 years	6-10	11-20	21-30	31-40	41-50	51 & above	Total
01.	Illiterate	-	-	6 (4.88) (25)	30 (24.39) (71.42)	36 (29.26) (66.66)	42 (34.15) (87.5)	9 (7.32) (75)	**123 (100) (65.08)**
02.	1-5 Classes	-	-	-		6 (50) (11.11)	3 (25) (6.25)	3 (25) (25)	**12 (100) (6.35)**
03.	6-10 Classes	-	-	15 (41.66) (62.5)	12 (33.34) (28.58)	6 (16.66) (11.11)	3 (8.34) (6.25)	-	**36 (100) (19.05)**
04.	Inter	6 (40) (100)	-	3 (20) (12.5)	-	6 (40) (11.12)	-	-	**15 (100) (7.94)**
05.	Degree	-	3 (100) (100)	-	-	-	-	-	**3 (100) (1.58)**
06.	Others	-	-	-	-	-	-	-	-
	Total	6 (3.17) (100)	3 (1.58) (100)	24 (12.70) (100)	42 (22.23) (100)	54 (28.58) (100)	48 (25.40) (100)	12 (6.34) (100)	189 (100%) (100%)

Stated occupation of respondents children

According to the data, out of the total sample, 6.98% of respondent's sons are stated to be in the same traditional occupation following the footsteps of elders, while 6.98% preferred other traditional occupation other than their own. 81.40% of respondents are found preferring modern occupations, while 2.32% are found already working as government employees and another 2.32% of them are found pursuing their education.

Educational Dropouts children of the respondents

There has been wide-spread dropout earlier from education in the families but in the recent years especially from the parents' generation, the importance of education has been seriously recognized and families began to educate their children. As a result of it unlike in the past there have been only 39.68% of children as found dropouts and 44.44% are found persuing education.

Occupation of Women in the Family of the Respondents

It may be found that all the women in the families of the respondents share the work and 91.01% are found sharing the work of their traditional occupation. Both men and women share the work in the family. It may be found that the age background of the women sharing the work 56.41% are of young, 27.16% are middle aged belonging to 46-55 age group, 17.29% are above middle aged, and 2.46% are belong to 66 and above age group who are all found to be totally involved in their traditional occupational work. While some women in the family has been found doing some other work especially those belong to the age group of below 35 years, all women irrespective of their age and education are found doing the work.

Occupational Training

It may be observed that almost all respondents had taken informal training from their family members by observation and also while doing the work. Significantly even those who are persuing education also participate in 'production activities' during their off-school and college time. Despite the fact that in future they may or may not go for their ancestral occupation but as a 'tradition' they learn the skills and share the family works.

Land holding particulars

It may found that the 76.20% of the respondents do not own any agriculture land and remaining 23.80% seem to own some cultivable land which they cultivate during the rainy season as a secondary occupation.

Other Assets position

Table 13-5 indicates a large majority of respondents 'own' their own house and amongst them 46.04% own RCC buildings two or three rooms and 41.26% own Katcha houses. Out of the remaining (12.70%), 7.14% live in RCC rented houses. Only 14.28% own some cattle, 1.58% Fowls and 28.57% own vehicles such as Bicycle or Motorcycle or Moped. Only 57.14% had drinking water facility at home and others need to procure it every day from outside sources.

95.23% had Bathroom facility, 90.47% Latrine facilities at home, while others had to depend upon 'open sources'. It is significant that every household had electricity at home, 84.13% had cooking gas connection, 79.36% 'cable TV connection'. 4.76% had Radios, 3.17% had sewing machines, while 1.58% had Rice-Cookers. It indicates that a large number of Kummari families had below average assets with not-so-good housing and workshop condition.

Table 13.5

Assets of Facilities

		Yes				**No**	**Total**
Sl. No	**Particulars**	**Own**					
01.	House	RCC 87 (46.04) (6.97)	Kacha 78(41.26) (6.25)	RCC Rent 15 (7.14) (1.20)	Kacha Rent 9(4.76) (0.56)		**189 (100) (6.66)**
02.	Cattle	27 (14.28) (2.16)				162 (85.72) (10.20)	**189 (100) (6.66)**
03.	Fowls	3 (1.58) (0.24)				186 (98.41) (11.73)	**189 (100) (6.66)**
04.	Vehicle	54 (28.57) (2.32)				135 (100%) (6.66)	**189 (100)**
05.	Drinking Water	108 (57.14) (7.86)				189 (100%) (6.66)	**189 (100)**
06.	Bathroom	180 (95.23) (14.43)				9 (4.77) (0.56)	**189 (100) (6.67)**
07.	Latrine	159 (90.47) (13.70)				18 (9.53) (1.13)	**189 (100) (6.67)**
08.	Electricity	189 (100) (15.15)					**189 (100) (6.67)**
09.	Gas	159 (84.13) (12.74)				30 (15.87) (1.89)	**189 (100) (6.67)**
10.	T.V	150 (79.36) (12.02)				39 (20.63) (2.45)	**189 (100) (6.67)**
11.	Radio	9 (4.76) (0.72)				180 (95.14) (11.34)	**189 (100) (6.67)**
12.	Sewing Machine	6 (3.17) (0.48)				183 (96.83) (11.54)	**189 (100) (6.67)**
13.	Rice Cookers	3 (1.58) (0.24)				186 (98.42) (11.73)	**189 (100) (6.67)**
14.	Refrigerator	3 (1.58) (0.24)				186 (98.42) (11.73)	**189 (100) (6.67)**
15.	News Paper	6 (3.17) (0.48)				183 (96.83) (11.54)	**189 (100) (6.67)**
Total		**1248 (44.02) (100)**				**1587 (55.98) (100)**	**2835 (100%) (100%)**

Occupational Priorities

The primary work relating to their occupation mainly revolves around the pot making as 98.42% of respondents focus on their traditional occupation. As far as secondary occupation is concerned, 38.09% preferred agriculture labour work or other works. The data clearly indicates that apart from the primary or traditional work the respondents have given priority to secondary works for supplementing their income. Since the use of 'pots' is fast disappearing, the Kummari occupation is also fast disappearing.

Place of Production

Most of the Kummari families set up their enterprise besides their home. Most of the homes are found in one or the other corners of the village, where they get some open space to 'dry' their products. They also get sometimes the required quantities of 'mud' outside the village or nearby tanks. Those who own the houses inside the village with no sufficient open space, setup separate 'work shed' outside the village and does the work.

Investment Details

Regard to the investment on the objects by the respondents, 49.80% seem to have invested on Shed/Hut/ House and Shop, while 24.70% on raw materials and 23.07% on tools machines etc., Regard to the investment amount, 47.09% of the respondents invested between Rs. 1000 to 10,000 and it was followed 30.08% of respondents who spent 1 lakh and above, Rs. 25,000/- to 50,000/- about 14.99% and 10.12% of the respondents between Rs. 50,000/- to 1 lakhs. This indicates that a large number, through need higher could not spend more due to non availability of funds and only a few families could manage some reasonable amount for investment and most of the investments is incurred on construction of 'shed or shop floor'.

Source Investment

It has been found that in table 13-6 that 96.82% of respondents had their own sources of investment, while the remaining 3.18% had to depend up on a bank. Refer to urban areas a large majority of the respondents (97.82%) had used their own sources while the remaining 2.18% had taken loans from the banks. While in rural areas 94.12% used their own sewing and 5.88% relied on banks. It is significant to observe that those who used their own savings/sources of money. 73.77% were drawn from urban areas and 26.23% from rural areas. It may be observed that majority of respondents made investments by using their own sources while only a small percentage could get loans from Banks. In this context, they are completely deprived of Government help.

Table 13.6

Source of Investment

Sl. No	Source	Urban	Rural	Total
01.	Own	135 (73.77) (97.82)	48 (26.23) (94.12)	**183 (100) (96.82)**
02.	Bank	3 (50) (2.18)	3 (50) (5.88)	**6 (100) (3.18)**
Total		**138 (73.01) (100)**	**51 (26.99) (100)**	**189 (100%) (100%)**

Source of Raw Materials

It may seen from the available data that a large majority of the respondents got the raw materials from sources nearby their residence (73.43%), while 6.06% found collecting from government places, 20.05% from a broker agency and remaining 0.46% from other sources. Among the nearby living place category, majority of the respondents had the raw material such as Grass, Wood, Dust and Dusk and Colours from nearby places. The earthen material however was secured by a large number of respondents from government sources (41.27%), 39.69% from a broker agency and 3.16% of other sources. As far as the sand is also concerned, 70.94% has relied on a broker agency.

Production of Plan

The data clearly indicate the details of how the respondents had planned their regular production activity. Out of the total respondents, 51.26% had produced the material on their own orders, 31.09% by themselves without obtaining from outside on local orders, 17.65% from outside orders respectively.

Family Participation in Production

The data clearly indicates that the among the family members of the respondents, majority of them are found participating in production with 48.39% cases by spouses, was followed by children (41.13%), and (3.23%) parents respectively. Out of the total respondents, 52.42% are participating in production on full time basis and it was followed by 37.10% of family members especially women occasionally participating, while 9.68% are found not participating. Among the parents, majority of them are found participating, while 25% are found not participating, With regard to children majority of them are participating only occasionally. In general, most of the members in the family participate in the production wherever and whenever is required.

Unseasonal activity

As far as the unseasonal activities of the respondents in rural and urban areas majority of the respondents (80.95%) said that they depend on agricultural labour work, or any whatever labour work (15.87%) available. Those who live in urban areas also found going to rural areas to participate in agricultural activity for wage.

Sale of Products

The study also explores the nature of sale of products by the respondents in rural and urban areas. Out of the total sample about 86.36% of the respondents are found to be selling the products from their homes and it was followed by the sales at local market i.e., 7.57%. 4.55% of respondents had supplied to other shop keepers, while 1.52% found selling their products at their workshop.

Ceremonial Jobs

The data clearly indicates that majority (96.83%) of the respondents in rural areas were able to find ceremonial jobs such as marriages, festivals, special occasions, deaths and births. The remaining 3.17% could not get. Whereas regarding the availability of the ceremonial jobs in urban areas, there was occasional opportunity unlike rural areas. In most of the ceremonies, the potters need to supply pots, lamp posts and other products made with earthen materials and these rituals provide them good amount of money and other gifts.

Government Schemes

Regard to the a ailment the Government schemes by the respondents, majority of the respondents i.e. 96.43% said that they could not get the benefit of any government scheme while only 3.57% said that they could benefit by the Government scheme. It was found that those 14.29% who benefitted seem to have secured some tools under Aadarana Scheme.

It may be noticed that Government has not recognized the need for initiating any policy measures to help these communities to continue in the trade and modernize it so that it will be beneficial to them. So far successive Governments had failed to propose any specific policy towards resolving the problems of these backward class groups of people. Governments seem to have adopted a general welfare policy or an anti-poverty programme to cover these sections also. Some of the schemes like Aadharana schemes did not cover majority members of Kummari community. No other schemes have any role to play to extend any sort of development support to these people and simply they were left to their own fate.

Impact of Government schemes

It is shocking to observe that all the respondents had expressed that Government schemes are shown negative impact on their lives. Even some of the respondents who got benefitted to some extent also had no satisfaction with the Government welfare measures.

Role of the Associations

Out of the total, a large majority of the respondents (96.82%), felt that the role of the associations in general is not positive. 1.59% felt it as positive and remaining 1.59% are did not given response. It is generally expected that Community Association play a positive role in representing the problems of their respective communities and get their things done at the governmental level. But it may be observed that the Community Associations are not playing any positive role to solve the problems of their respective communities as expected of them.

General Occupational Problems

Table 7 reflects the occupational problems of the respondents in rural and urban areas. Out of the total sample, 34.94% of the respondents found facing the problem of non availability of raw material, and it was followed by non availability of capital (46.99%), 8.43% had worried about the non modernization of products, 4.82% found quality problems and 3.62% posed the problem of market competition respectively.

With regard to urban areas 38.46% each of the respondents are found facing problem of non availability of raw material and non availability of capital and it was followed by non modernization of products (10.77%) 6.15% found the problem of quality assurance, while the remaining found a serious problem of growing market competition.

With regards to rural areas a large majority of the respondents are found to be facing the problem non availability of capital (77.77%), while the remaining 22.23% with non availability of raw material.

The data also indicates the general occupational problems faced by the Kummari Community. Some of the problems identified are almost relevant to both rural and urban Kummari community people. The general problems as said by the respondents include non availability of raw material, lack of investment capital, growing family financial problems, lack of market, lack of proper business and competition from private shops etc. As a result of many problems, there was feeling among the Kummari people, that the profession has become a liability for them. Over the years it may be found many a Kummari families leaving the profession and migrating to urban areas for want of work.

Table 13.7

Occupational Problems (Cumulative)

Sl. No	Problems	Urban	Rural	Total
01.	Non Availability of Raw Material	75 (86.20)	12 (13.80)	**87 (100)**
02.	Non Availability of Capital	75 (64.10)	42 (35.90)	**117 (100)**
03.	Market Competition	9 (100)		**9 (100) (3.62)**
04.	Non Modernization of Products	21 (100)		**21 (100) (8.43)**
05.	Quality Problem	12 (100)		**12 (100) (4.82)**
07.	Others	3 (100)		**3 (100) (1.20)**

Solution to the Problems

The respondents also made certain suggestions which are helpful to resolve their problems. Most respondent suggested that Government should

1. Provide loans, subsidies and margin money to set up pot making units.

2. Government should allot specific area for collecting the required raw materials used for preparation of earthen products.
3. Government should allot a place to set up a workshop shed and production area.
4. Government should facilitate marketing of products.
5. Government should help modernization of the trade and provide training facilities for this purpose.
6. Other suggestions include Allotment of weaker section housing, Artisan Credit Cards, Supply of tools and instruments, Provision for Family Health cards, old age pension etc.,

All this above may go a long way to help resolve some of the problems of Kummari community and initiate the process of their development.

Profiles and Case Studies of Select Kummari Respondents

Peddapally Rajaneekar

My name is Peddapally Rajaneekar, aged 27 years. Native Village Gatla Kanaparthy, Mandal Shayampet of Warangal District of Telangana State. I have studied upto 10th class in Gatla Kaniparthy and Intermediate in Shayampet. Due to financial problems I could not study further and started helping my father in his professional work. I could not do any other job although I tried for it. After my marriage, my responsibilities have been increased. Later my father also died then all the family burden and pain fell on me. At present in my family my mother 56 years, wife 24 years and my twin children 4 months old son and daughter staying with me. My mother is an illiterate; my wife has studied upto fifth class. I have learnt our professional work of making pots from my father. I have been in this work to earn my livelihood and my wife help me in my profession. Apart from this, she also does tailoring work. I also do agriculture as I have 30 guntas of agricultural land. We do cultivate our own land and we get around 30,000/- income per annum on this land.

In our village, I also work as a school van driver from 7:30 am to 9:00 pm and in the evening 4:00 pm to 5:00 pm. I get monthly payment of Rs. 3500/- for this.

I built my own RCC house. I have drinking water facility but I don't have sanitation facility. We have a sewing machine. All the neighbours are our caste people as we live in Kummari street. We have good relations with them. We have also good friendship with other caste people.

We bring 'soil' from ponds and small pits available in a nearby place. For this purpose we spend transport charges Rs 500 to 800. Government allotted place to collect the required mud 8 years back in the neighbouring village but not much good material is available there. We prepare pots with the filtered dung. We mix all these material by pressing with legs. We need 'Kummari wheel' and saare to prepare pots. Salpa, Saarekore etc also needed to prepare pots. Kummari wheel costs nearly Rs. 3000/- to 4000/- rupees. For soil and to keep dry pots, we need an open place and a shed also necessary for our profession. We prepare pot in winter and summer. We don't prepare pots in rainy season. All the family members help in my work. Sometimes I take the support of outside workers. We spend nearly Rs. 3000/- for raw material Rs. 3000/- and for firewood, wood cutting waste, dry grass to dry the wet pots and other material. To dry the wet material we put a "Vaamu" a kind of big furnace to dry the wet materials. Each and every house has this facility of "Vaamu".

We prepare pots, pramidas, small pots for marriage purpose, water drums, thulasi and flower pots, stores, small chippas and white water pots. We prepare several other shaped articles in the village. We don't have regular timings of work. We work for more number of hours when needed.

We sell the materials from at home. Earlier in "santas" we used to sell our material once in a week, but there are no such santas in our village now. Customers purchase our material in March, April, May and seasonally during festivals like Deepavali, Sankranthi and Pothamma Talli, Bonas. After this season, now and then customers ask for our material especially to be used for family ceremonies. We do agriculture in the Gap period. I do my caste profession as per the season. In our village there was not much competition to us in our profession. My family gets altogether around Rs. 1.00/- lakh per annum towards all works. Our material have demand in marriage seasons, Deepavali and ugadi festivals. People use the 'pots' for bad and good occasions and various other family ceremonies and festivals and during those we get good profit. I want to give education to my children.

Over the years there has been lot of competition from various factory based products using metal and plastics and due to this the demand for our products has been reduced over the years. I haven't taken any loan from bank or Private Finance. We are adjusting with what we are earning.

Despite all whatever we earn which is not sufficient. Hence, we need government in extending not only financial assistance towards purchase of tools, raw materials, but also need marketing assistance and support. Government should provide free residential education to our children, housing accommodation, shed for workshop and others. As our community people are poor, less or not educated we cannot afford modern jobs. Hence government should evolve suitable policy to look after our welfare.

Chelpuri Laxmi

I am Chelpuri Laxmi, aged 45 years resident of Pochamma Kunta, Hanamkonda, Warangal District of Telangana. I am illiterate, as my parents had not sent me to school. I have been involved in our hereditary occupational work and household work at home from my childhood. At the age of 15, I got married and later on joined my husband in the traditional occupation of pottery. My husband's age now is 50 years. I have two daughters and one son. Eldest daughter 28 years, studied 10th class and married. Younger daughter aged 23 years studied 8th class then married. Youngest only son aged 21 years studying degree final year and also helps us doing our own profession to support the family. My husband is being sick since 6 years and cannot work anymore. I had to lead the family and carry on the profession of making pots and other earthen bowls. My son is assisting me. We had a hut in the Pochamma Kunta area as the caste society had given us 150 square yards plots, but unable to construct a building, satisfied with a hut. We don't have facilities of drinking water, sanitation, etc., as we have been living since thirty years in pochammakunta, neighbourhood has become friendly. In surrounding house people belonging to Padmashali, Rajakas, Besta, Kamsali, SC and STs make a living, we had good relations with them, over the years there has been some friction among the neighbourhood as they work is producing lot of smoke in the surroundings and polluting the atmosphere. For making of earthen bowls we had purchased Wheel, Sulfa, sarakolakatta etc., we had to spend nearly Rs. 10,000/- for these tools. We collect clay from Government allotted land at Pochammakunta, Komatipally and Bhimaram. We bring it on a cart engaged for this purpose. As the clay is collected from longer distance the transportation expenditure is too high. To make the earthen bowls, such as Ranjans and Water Pots, Flower pots, Flower vases and other traditional items we use the clay and for this purpose we need to prepare clay as soft. We had to do the work by ourselves nobody as knows the work. I had taken Rs.15,000/- as loan from DWAKRA group and built a workshop in 50 square yards. I had also applied for bank loan, separately but could not get it because of lack of registration of the firm. I spent about Rs. 4000/- on firewood every year. Because of lack of space in the shed area for storage products are damaged and protecting them from stray animals has become a great problem for us. When the products are placed outside in an open area in the adjacent place of our house. The products die unprotected and gets damaged and we have no other alternative at it has become a regular problem. I had to work harder in summer and winter than rainy season. They supply the mud bowls at both for wholesale and retail sales are done at home. For all the works gets on an average an income of Rs.6000/- per month. Presumably the income I gets is insufficient to meet the minimum needs of the family. As I have been doing the work since a long time I do not know other works this has been made me to depend exclusively upon my own profession which doesn't fetch income all the time and that has become a serious problem. Only alternative left to me is to for outside labour work which is also not guaranteed. I also prepare artistic or decorative articles made of mud and this actually requires recognition from Government or other agencies. I had submitted representatives to government especially for the supply of 'power-run-wheels' and other equipment on subsidy for provision for Bank loans but there was hardly any response. Though I had developed skills in my profession.

All the products, produced by me are sold from the home by myself. But over the years people are not using them plenty. People are using earthen pots only to a limited extent options for factory made plastic, steel, aluminum etc, has been resulted in fall of my income as I have also witnessed lack of sales many a time. I feel that unless recognizes our profession as 'fast disappearing' and come to their rescue it is difficult for us to survive.

Rudraksha Padma

My name is Rudraksha Padma aged 40 years. I learnt pot making from my mother and father. My native place is shivanagar of Warangal District in Telangana State. I studied upto 10th class and married at the age of 16 years. I am living with my family members at Hanamkonda near pegadapalli cross road area since 24 years after marriage.

My husband aged 48 years studied upto 5th class and we have two daughters and one son. My elder daughter aged 17 years studying intermediate 1st year and the youngest daughter aged 16 years studying 10th class. My son is blind admitted in a Blind school at Elkathurthi village and studying. We tried our best to get his eye sight improved but failed in our attempts.

We have one RCC building constructed by us in 150 yards of land and a shed in open place with 50 yards. We have minimum facilities like water, toilet and other including electricity.

We prepare Pots and for that suitable mud is required. For that purpose we need suitable tank bed or water pond. Presently we are collecting the required mud from Pochamma Kunta nearby our house. Government allotted some land especially for this purpose. We need to prepare the mud while making it smooth and then mix it with ash and other material in it. We spend nearly Rs. 5000/- to 6000/- to get the (sare) revolving 'wheel' on which we develop pots.

We need an amount of Rs. 6000 to Rs. 7000/- to get the tools required and we prepare different types of pots, including flower pots and other daily useful materials in the house. We also prepare tiles which are useful for roofing the house.

While preparing the pots and other materials some of them will be spoiled and damaged. We get loss towards it. All our family members will work daily for more than 10 hours for preparation of the material we sell them in the open market. There has been a lot of competition during these days from outside designary materials and plastic products. People prefer them. Now a days most of the public prefer our material only for ceremonial functions and due this we are not able earn much. It is becoming difficult to lead a reasonable life to survive. We did not get any help from the government so far not even from cooperative societies. We earn nearly Rs. 2000/- to Rs. 3000/- per month. My husband works as an Auto trolley driver and his income is also meagre. My son studying 6th class and is in Blind school and we have to perform the marriage of our two daughters and it is becoming very difficult to lead the family.

It may be suggested that Government should provide us bank loan and material on subsidy basis and help us under different schemes. Otherwise we remain the same.

Kanugula Sammaiah

My name is Kanugula Sammaiah aged 65 years. Due to poverty and illiteracy of my parents I had not gone to school. My native place is Shayampet Village in Warangal District. My parents are illiterate and doing the traditional pot making occupation since 50 years.

We are 7 members in my family. My wife aged 61 years is illiterate, doing Beedi work and also provides assistance in my pot making work. My son 31 years, discontinued education after intermediate and doing the same work and also work in agriculture field. My daughter in-law aged 28 years studied upto 7th class assist in our work along with Beedi making work. My four grand children are going to school and stay with me.

I have my own RCC building constructed by me 20 years ago. It has only minimum facilities. There is a problem of scarcity of water. We do not have any pet animals like cow, hen etc. Since my birth I am living at this place and our street is known as Kummariwada. Before constructing our present house we used to live in a small hut, in which we survived.

The tools required for the preparation of pots and other materials costs about 5 thousand rupees and we need mud for the preparation of articles and we get it from village pallipaka. To prepare the mud a lot of hardship we have to face. We prepare pots, flower wases and some other storage pots and all our family members work together. The mud we use is not good. We have to get it far off places. It cost about Rs. 4000/- per tractor and grass we require costs about Rs. 5000/- per tractor and some sand kind of ash it costs about Rs. 1500/-. Every year we take a loan to get all these things and after selling the products we repay the loan. Sometimes all the articles produced are not sold and then the repayment will become difficult. This has been the 'case' for the last ten years.

We work from 8:00 am to 5:00 pm and beyond. It has become compulsory for me to take loan from money lenders at the rate of 3 to 5% interest. We work together daily for 10 hours per day in preparing and selling the material from home and on every saturday. I go to weekly market and put a stall there for sales. We need the assistance from the government to purchase the mud required from a distant place but we are not getting any assistance form government or any other organization. I get an amount of Rs. 4000/- to Rs. 5000/- per month out of pot making which is very megre amount for the labour we invest in the occupation.

I am having one Acre of agriculture land in my village and all the family members are also involved in the agriculture work during the seasonal time. We get an amount of Rs. 20000/- per year from agriculture. My wife and my daughters in law do the Beedi's work through which they get an amount of Rs. 1000/- to Rs. 1500/- per month. In this process all our family members work hard but even then the earnings we get are not sufficient to meet the expenditure. During the festival season of sankranthi and Pochamma Bonalu and Dussehra we get additional income as there will be lot of sales during the days. Now a days people are using our products mostly for ceremonies and family rituals. I need a lot of amount towards the studies of my grandson and granddaughter as I send them to private English medium schools. We want them to get good education and find suitable jobs.

The main issues are:

1. No bank loans are provided to our Community workers and it is suggested to arrange bank loan.
2. It is suggested to provide 'open' land to acquire needed mud.
3. It is suggested to sanction pension to the senior citizen of our caste.
4. Government should provide free medical checkup and medicines
5. Free education to the children's and Hostel facility.
6. Training facilities on the new technologies developed so that we may produce modern mud wear.

Our lives are routine and we have witnessed not much change in our life during the past ten years except facing further deterioration in our conditions. The Government and the civil society do not bother whether we survive or not. Whatever development has taken place over the years in the society, the benefits never reached us. The so called modernization process has only ruined our lives encouraging only the high capital, high technology based production processes. We are not sure to lead a peaceful life in future and now our survival itself has become a big question.

14

Summing Up

The volume presents the reports of empirical based case studies of 12 major BC artisan communities drawn from Telangana and Andhra Pradesh States. They carry their traditional hereditary occupations for their livelihood and had witnessed major changes only during the present generation. They have many common issues, common problems and common contradictions which may need to some extent, common solutions.

The occupational groups within the OBC communities in Telangana as well as Andhra Pradesh are involved in producing goods and services not only as 'individual members' but many a time 'the entire family' as a unit depending on the type of commodity they produce or the kind of service they extend to the society or their clients. Thus, these caste groups continue to produce and serve the society. These castes transmit the skills from one generation to the other. They use simple tools and acquire skills by observation and practice. They usually depend on the locally available raw material to produce the goods that needed and demanded by the local people. Their market is mostly confined to the village or a particular locality in a town in which they live.

Economically, they depend upon their traditional occupations, their physical labour and small and marginal landholdings in case they own any. The living conditions at their respective homes are not healthy as the amenities available do not even cover the basic minimum needs (Annexure).

The 12 case studies of 12 different BC/OBC traditional occupations presented in the preceding pages of the volume present their gross neglect, indicating deteriorating and degrading conditions of all artisans and service castes groups. They live in unhygienic conditions (Annexure). The reasons for such a debacle are almost common, being applicable equally to all artisan communities.

Traditionally, as far as the material or commodity producing communities are concerned, there would be one or two artisan families in each occupation in each village who would meet the demands of the village people, as a whole such as making agricultural implements or repairing them or producing other goods/services needed. These people own simple tools. In most of the cases, they create their own tools with their own innovation and creativity which are used in production. But most part of their work is done by their own hand. They work in their own dwelling areas by converting a part of the house into 'workshop'. They produce implements on the basis of orders they receive from time-to-time. These artisan groups also produce goods which they market in rural or periodic markets. Due to the traditional type of social relations, their income was invariably linked to the agricultural prosperity since early times. The customary mode of payment was not only the cash but also in kind in many a place as the welfare of these families is looked after by guaranteeing a share in the agricultural produce. This provided them with a regular income and sustenance. Thus these families formed an integral part of the village economy and worked as a backbone in making the village a self-sufficient unit.

The inflow of industrial production and emergence of market forces resulted in a new kind of relationship in the village or towns where these castes operate. This phenomenon has disturbed the existing set of communitarian life. Gradually, the services of these families have come to be computed in terms of wage or a piece rate. In this process, the traditional arrangements got eroded and the concept of adequate maintenance of artisan families lost its tenor. This resulted in the disintegration of social structure and the artisan families were forced to migrate to other areas mainly due to lack of work. And once for all they were delinked from the communities they served and also members of the families and are reduced into 'nomadic sellers' selling their products and services, which were once valued and judged on impersonal and competitive basis. In the changed circumstances, people started preferring industrial products rather than artisan products as they see more advantages in the former. This resulted in the fall of their income causing deterioration in their economic conditions Further, due to lack of formal education and other alternative skills required by the modern economy they turned to be 'aliens' to outside occupations and found 'excluded' in market orientation. In these circumstances they had to adopt one of the following courses:

1. Migration to cities or other villages or towns and opting for other jobs had invariably which have no connection with their previous occupation and skill.
2. Staying back in the village or town but adopting a different job in most cases involving physical labour for making a livelihood.
3. Staying back within the village or town and continuing in the same occupation irrespective of the kind of social and productive relations and the suffering they experience.

The above is also true in the case of Service Castes as they also find the same phenomena. The major difference however has been in rural areas the service castes such as Chakali, Mangali, Meru, etc., may not face stiff competition as that of other BCs, but the income they get invariably found to have been marginalized and their position has not witnessed any change over the years. Due to this the present generation in these Communities prefers to move to other occupations and those who can afford to get higher education could move to modern jobs. But the percentage of such people is marginal. Thus over the years most of these communities had witnessed only marginal changes in their lives.

The nature of production activities and services led to cultural diffe-rentiation among them and stratification in the social hierarchy. In the past, there was no freedom for an individual to choose his/her occupation for livelihood accor-ding to his/her talent, choice or interest as there was religious restriction. But after 'independence', there was some freedom 'to choose' their occupations. But paradoxically the changes in the socio-economic and political conditions worked out to be disadvantageous to the artisan community. Artisan communities had lost their significance and value in terms of trade due to mechanization, enhanced technology, market competition and loss of identity and inter community support. For instance, Blacksmiths in general are found clinging to the same profession by joining the workshops in nearby cities as wage labour. Carpenters however, are found more mobile. On the other hand, a large number of Weavers from the state during the last 100-odd years migrated to various cities of Gujarat and Maharashtra States and got absorbed in the textile industry as wage workers. Some moved to bigger villages or took to selling their goods from door-to-door. A few families with a degree of economic viability turned into small businessmen and traders of manufactured goods. A large number of weavers are found selling manufactured cloth on a mobile basis or opening the cloth shops in cities and towns. Only a small %age of artisan families, mostly in their old age, tend to be in their traditional weaving occupation. A large number of the traditional artisan workers are forced to join the ranks of the agricultural labourers. All these developments indicate emerging social relations which eroded the socio-economic base of artisans who have lost their tools, traditional skills and independent life. For a majority of artisans, life is a struggle for existence.

Artisans face a number of problems and due to this, there has been not only shift in their occupations but also unprecedented crisis the families are facing now (annexure).

Despite many problems they face, the social and cultural or political organizations, which used to represent them hardly able to 'organize' them to assert their rights. The Backward Class Movement was also weak in these States. As a result of it, the response of the state was also lukewarm. Except some piece-meal, rehabilitatory measures, no long term development plan or programme seem to have been formulated and backward castes continue to be discriminated or ignored by government. Due to all this the status of caste based traditional artisans is getting further worsened over the years, even after independence.

Annexure

Table 1

Amenities available at Home of the 12 Select Traditional Artisans

S.NO		Medari	Bestha	Dudekula	Padmashali	Meru	Mangali	Kanchari	Kammari	Vadrangi	Chakali	Kamsali	Kummari	Total
1. Bathroom	YES	132 (88) (6.64)	138 (69.70) (6.94)	156 (100) (7.84)	309 (96.26) (15.54)	168 (93.33) (8.45)	198 (91.67) (9.95)	72 (100) (3.62)	129 (100) (6.48)	135 (100) (6.79)	252 (91.30) (12.67)	120 (100) (6.03)	180 (95.23) (9.05)	**1989 (92.86)**
	NO	18 (12) (11.76)	60 (30.30) (39.22)	Nil	12 (3.74) (7.84)	12 (6.67) (7.84)	18 (8.33) (11.77)	Nil	Nil	Nil	24 (8.70) (15.69)	Nil	9 (4.77) (5.88)	**153 (7.14)**
2. LATRINE	YES	126 (84) (7.42)	120 (60.60) (7.07)	126 (80.77) (7.42)	147 (45.80) (8.66)	168 (93.33) (9.90)	150 (69.44) (8.83)	72 (100) (4.24)	129 (100) (7.59)	135 (100) (7.95)	234 (84.78) (13.78)	120 (100) (7.07)	171 (90.48) (10.07)	**1698 (79.27)**
	NO	24 (16) (5.41)	78 (39.40) (17.57)	30 (19.23) (6.75)	174 (54.20) (39.19)	12 (6.67) (2.70)	66 (30.56) (14.87)	Nil	Nil	Nil	42 (15.22) (9.46)	Nil	18 (9.52) (4.05)	**444 (20.73)**
3. ELECTRICITY	YES	141 (94) (6.63)	192 (96.96) (9.03)	156 (100) (7.33)	321 (100) (15.09)	180 (100) (8.46)	216 (100) (10.16)	72 (100) (3.39)	129 (100) (6.06)	135 (100) (6.35)	276 (100) (12.98)	120 (100) (5.64)	189 (100) (8.88)	**2127 (99.30)**
	NO	9 (6) (60)	6 (3.04) (40)	Nil	Nil	Nil	Nil	Nil	Nil	Nil	Nil	Nil	Nil	**15 (0.70)**
4. GAS	YES	123 (82) (7.27)	132 (66.66) (7.80)	150 (96.16) (8.87)	144 (44.86) (8.51)	150 (83.33) (8.86)	186 (86.11) (11)	69 (95.83) (4.08)	129 (100) (7.62)	129 (95.56) (7.62)	204 (73.91) (12.06)	117 (97.5) (6.91)	159 (84.13) (9.40)	**1692 (79)**
	NO	27 (18) (6)	66 (33.34) (14.67)	6 (3.84) (1.33)	177 (55.14) (39.33)	30 (16.67) (6.67)	30 (13.89) (6.67)	3 (4.17) (0.66)	Nil	6 (4.44) (1.33)	72 (26.09) (16)	3 (2.5) (0.67)	30 (15.87) (6.67)	**450 (21)**
5. T.V	YES	120 (80) (7.40)	114 (57.57) (7.04)	120 (76.92) (7.41)	141 (43.93) (8.70)	180 (100) (11.11)	180 (83.33) (11.11)	51 (70.83) (3.15)	102 (79.07) (6.30)	114 (84.45) (7.04)	234 (84.78) (14.44)	114 (95) (7.04)	150 (79.36) (9.26)	**1620 (75.63)**
	NO	30 (20) (5.75)	84 (42.43) (16.09)	36 (23.08) (6.90)	180 (56.07) (34.48)	Nil	36 (16.67) (6.90)	21 (29.17) (4.02)	27 (20.93) (5.17)	21 (15.55) (4.02)	42 (15.22) (8.05)	6 (5) (1.15)	39 (20.64) (7.47)	**522 (24.37)**

6. RADIO	YES	45 (30) (10.71)	144 (72.72) (34.29)	48 (30.77) (11.43)	Nil	24 (13.33) (5.71)	6 (2.78) (1.43)	24 (33.33) (5.71)	39 (30.23) (9.29)	45 (33.33) (10.72)	12 (4.35) (2.86)	24 (20) (5.71)	9 (4.77) (2.14)	**420 (19.60)**
	NO	105 (70) (6.10)	54 (27.28) (3.13)	108 (69.23) (6.27)	321 (100) (18.64)	156 (86.67) (9.06)	210 (97.22) (12.19)	48 (66.67) (2.79)	90 (69.77) (5.23)	90 (66.67) (5.23)	264 (95.65) (15.33)	96 (80) (5.58)	180 (95.23) (10.45)	**1722 (80.40)**
7. SEWING MACHINE	YES	21 (14) (5.93)	30 (15.15) (8.48)	18 (11.54) (5.08)	24 (7.48) (6.78)	180 (100) (50.85)	12 (5.56) (3.39)	6 (8.33) (1.70)	6 (4.65) (1.70)	24 (17.78) (6.78)	12 (4.35) (3.38)	15 (12.5) (4.23)	6 (3.18) (1.70)	**354 (16.53)**
	NO	129 (86) (7.21)	168 (84.85) (9.40)	138 (88.46) (7.71)	297 (92.52) (16.61)	Nil	204 (94.44) (11.41)	66 (91.67) (3.70)	123 (95.35) (6.88)	111 (82.22) (6.20)	264 (95.65) (14.77)	105 (87.5) (5.87)	183 (96.82) (10.24)	**1788 (83.47)**
8. REFRIGERATOR	YES	3 (2) (2.5)	6 (3.04) (5)	24 (15.38) (20)	Nil	6 (3.33) (5)	6 (2.78) (5)	3 (4.17) (2.5)	3 (2.32) (2.5)	Nil	Nil	66 (55) (55)	3 (1.59) (2.5)	**120 (5.60)**
	NO	147 (98) (7.27)	192 (96.96) (9.50)	132 (84.62) (6.53)	321 (100) (15.88)	174 (96.67) (8.60)	210 (97.22) (10.39)	69 (95.83) (3.41)	126 (97.68) (6.23)	135 (100) (6.67)	276 (100) (13.65)	54 (45) (2.67)	186 (98.41) (9.20)	**2022 (94.40)**
9. NEWS PAPER	YES	Nil	Nil	Nil	Nil	6 (3.33) (7.41)	6 (2.78) (7.41)	3 (4.17) (3.70)	12 (9.30) (14.81)	3 (2.22) (3.70)	12 (4.35) (14.81)	33 (27.5) (40.75)	6 (3.18) (7.41)	**81 (3.78)**
	NO	150 (100) (7.28)	198 (100) (9.60)	156 (100) (7.57)	321 (100) (15.58)	174 (96.67) (8.44)	210 (97.22) (10.19)	69 (95.83) (3.35)	117 (90.70) (5.68)	132 (97.78) (6.40)	264 (95.65) (12.81)	87 (72.5) (4.22)	183 (96.82) (8.88)	**2061 (96.22)**
10. VEHICLES	YES	111 (74) (9.23)	144 (72.73) (11.97)	108 (69.23) (8.98)	63 (19.63) (5.23)	120 (66.66) (9.98)	150 (69.44) (12.47)	54 (75) (4.49)	69 (53.49) (5.73)	93 (68.89) (7.73)	144 (52.18) (11.97)	93 (77.5) (7.73)	54 (28.57) (4.49)	**1203 (56.16)**
	NO	39 (26) (4.15)	54 (27.27) (5.75)	48 (30.77) (5.11)	258 (80.37) (27.48)	60 (33.34) (6.39)	66 (30.56) (7.02)	18 (25) (1.92)	60 (46.51) (6.39)	42 (31.11) (4.47)	132 (47.82) (14.06)	27 (22.5) (2.88)	135 (71.43) (14.38)	**939 (43.84)**

Table 2

General Problems of Traditional Artisans as identified by the Respondents

Sl.No	Problems
01.	Caste Discrimination
02.	Negligence by Society
03.	Upper Castes Domination
04.	Double Standards
05.	No Help from Neighbors
06.	General Oppression and Degrading Phenomenon
07.	Lack of Information about Government Schemes
08.	Negative attitude of successive governments
09.	Lack of Outside contacts
10.	Poverty
11.	Illiteracy
12.	Lack of modern implements, tools and technologies
13.	Increasing importance of capital and lack of it
14.	Growing Market Competition
15.	Exploitation by brokers, mediators and agencies
16.	Rapid Growth of Ready Made Products
17.	Quality problems and failure to maintain quality
18.	Lack of minimum support price
19.	Debts
20.	Non Availability of Raw Material
21.	Increasing Corruption Practices among Government Officials
22.	Lack of interest of children towards traditional occupations
23.	Lack of other alternative source
24.	Increasing degradation of traditional occupations
25.	Negative approach of upper castes
26.	Lack of Associations and failure of those exist

27.	Caste associations not finding appropriate solutions to problems
28.	Political parties not taking interest to find out appropriate solutions to problems
29.	Accumulation of problems among BC's due to internal contradictions
30.	Lack of Unity and Failure to represent the problems to Government collectively
31.	No clear cut policy of government towards traditional occupations
32.	Lack of initiative of governing bodies
33.	Lack of consensus about the reason for occupational degradation
34.	Apathy and negative attitude of Bank officials
35.	Functional failure of DRDA and other Corporations
36.	Other Problems

Index

• • •